POND SCUM

A N D

VULTURES

POND SCUM
AND
VULTURES

America's Sportswriters Talk About Their Glamorous Profession

GENE WOJCIECHOWSKI

MACMILLAN PUBLISHING COMPANY • NEW YORK
COLLIER MACMILLAN CANADA • TORONTO
MAXWELL MACMILLIAN INTERNATIONAL
NEW YORK • OXFORD • SINGAPORE • SYDNEY

Macmillan Publishing Company
866 Third Avenue, New York, NY 10022

Collier Macmillan Canada, Inc.
1200 Eglinton Avenue East, Suite 200
Don Mills, Ontario M3C 3N1

Library of Congress Cataloging-in-Publication Data
Wojciechowski, Gene.
 Pond scum and vultures: America's sportswriters talk about their glamorous
profession / by Gene Wojciechowski.
 p. cm.
 ISBN 0-02-630851-7
 1. Sportswriters—United States—Interviews. I. Title.
GV742.4.W65 1990   90-35443 CIP
070.4'49796'0973—dc20

Macmillan books are available at special discounts for bulk purchases for sales
promotions, premiums, fund-raising, or educational use. For details, contact:

Special Sales Director
Macmillan Publishing Company
866 Third Avenue
New York, NY 10022

10 9 8 7 6 5 4 3 2 1

Printed in the United States of America

Designed by Helene Berinsky

To my wife, Dina,
and my parents, Chet and Vera.

Contents

Acknowledgments

About the title. While covering the Denver Broncos in 1983, I heard a player call us (the assembled local media) "pond scum" as we entered the locker room. That sort of insult tends to stick with you.

A few other items I'd like to pass along.

More than 130 sportswriters took time to talk to me about their experiences in the business. I have never enjoyed myself more. To each of them, my heartfelt appreciation. This is their book.

Special thanks go to Macmillan editor Rick Wolff, who took a chance on a first-time author. That requires some nerve. Also, he didn't cringe upon hearing the book's title. I admire a person with an open mind. And of course, he's a former sportswriter.

Shari Wenk, my agent, gets 15 percent, but deserves more. Let's just keep that our little secret.

Editor's Note

What you're about to read in this book is totally true. While it sounds like fiction, believe me, as a former sportswriter, I can readily attest to the veracity of these stories. Indeed, there are literally dozens of these incredible sportswriting mishaps and ironies occurring every day, which, alas, go unreported in the daily sports section you read.

Every sportswriter has his or her own story to tell, and I hope there will be future editions of *Pond Scum* in which those up-close-and-personal tales can be included. In the meantime, these are a start, and as you go through them, remember to take pity on those ink-stained wretches who write about the daily events in the world of sports. Take, for instance, the first-time ice hockey writer who was assigned to cover a game between the Islanders and the Canucks. He pleaded with his boss, "But I've never covered hockey before. What do I write about?"

The wise and weather-beaten sports editor replied, "Relax, kid, hockey's easy. All you gotta do is write about each goal that's scored, and then interview the winning goalie after the game. It's a snap."

So the ready-and-willing sportswriter drove off to the rink and sat behind his typewriter, perfectly attentive to see every goal and write every detail about it. And then he knew exactly how to get downstairs to the locker rooms to interview the victorious goalie after the game.

Except for one thing. The final score was Islanders 0, Canucks 0. That's right. No goals to write about. No victorious goalie to talk to.

That's just one of the reasons I went into book publishing.

—Rick Wolff

1

Welcome to the Exciting World of Lower Plant Life

$\mathbf{T}$his is my theory: No one actually aspires to become a sportswriter. It just happens, much in the same way someone becomes a game show host. One day you want to write the Great American Novel; the next day you find yourself asking a toothless offensive tackle about his groin pull. It is, quite simply, a hell of a way to make a living.

Leigh Montville of *Sports Illustrated* likes to say that sportswriters are positioned at the edge of two glamorous professions: sports and writing. And he's mostly right. Players and coaches regard sportswriters as an occupational hazard, the literary equivalent of jock itch. On the evolutionary scale, sportswriters would rank somewhere between an amoeba and the farm animal of your choice—at least that's how the fellas in the clubhouses of America generally feel about today's intrepid reporters.

Given the choice between a postgame interview and a heaping plate of asparagus and fried smelt, you'd be surprised how many athletes and coaches would opt for the dinner special. Anything, they'd say, but another session with the roving hordes of tape recorder–toting, notepad-packing pencil pushers.

And even in the confines of the Fourth Estate, sportswriters are housed in the servants' quarters. Highbrow city-side reporters who wear bow ties and think a good referendum is better than sex or a tight spiral refer to sportswriters as members of the "Toy Department."

Former sports announcer Howard Cosell, patron saint of toupees and a supposed journalistic brother, treated all sportswriters the same way—with disdain. Cosell, self-appointed judge of all things proper, considered sportswriters intellectual midgets, a dull match for his self-acclaimed masterful mind. During the middle of a rare interview in 1982, Cosell once snapped at Ian Thomsen, then of the *Boston Globe*, after Thomsen had asked a question regarding the broadcaster's working relationship with a Red Sox player.

"Why are you asking me that question?" Cosell said. "You're not equipped."

Thomsen feigned hurt.

"I'm sorry, I'm sorry," Cosell said. "I didn't mean to be hard on you. What else can I tell you?"

The interview resumed, but not before Cosell gestured toward a sportswriter who was standing near the batting cages at Fenway Park that day. The sportswriter happened to be wearing blue jeans. This upset Cosell.

"There's a sportswriter," he said. "Is that any way to look, like a despoiled pig?"

With that, Cosell began an impromptu lecture on the evils of sportswriting. He even questioned Thomsen's choice of career.

"Why would you want to be a sportswriter, young man?" he said.

"But you're a sports journalist," Thomsen said.

"I never meant to be, young man. I never took it seriously."

Howard, we know; we saw your ill-equipped variety show.

Despite what Cosell said, I still think sportswriters are the

foot soldiers of journalism, the sergeants who eat cold
K-rations out of a can. They battle deadlines, travel, fatigue,
editors and ballplayers all at once. And more times than not,
in a perverted sort of way, they love every moment of it.

In essence, sportswriters get paid to antagonize. Not on
purpose, mind you, but it seems to work out that way.
You've heard the phrase, "The truth hurts"? Try second-
guessing some knucklehead move of the exalted Indiana coach
Bobby Knight and see what happens. Russ Brown of the
Louisville Courier-Journal did just that and look what it got
him: Knight told him that if he ever set foot in the Indiana
locker room again he would ram Brown's head through a wall
and stick a typewriter up the obvious orifice.

Try gaining access to the innermost thoughts of Pete Rose
as he dove headfirst into the record books in 1985, the year
he surpassed Ty Cobb in hits. It was also the year that
rumors of Rose's fondness for gambling began to ooze to the
surface.

Rick Reilly of *Sports Illustrated* was one of the many writers who were assigned to follow Rose's quest for baseball
immortality that season. Reilly arrived at Riverfront Stadium
one day, introduced himself to Rose and then tried to sit the
Reds player-manager down for an extended interview. No
luck; Rose was as elusive as a housefly.

At game's end, Reilly was part of the pack of reporters
who journeyed into Rose's office. One by one the crowd
began to thin, until only Reilly was left. Just then, Rose
turned to Reilly and s id, "Rick, you want to come home and
stay the night at my house?"

Reilly couldn't say yes fast enough.

As they drove to Rose's house, Rose turned on the radio to
listen to a local sports talk show. A caller asked: "Why did
Rose take out Esasky for a pinch-hitter in the eighth?"

Rose was livid and began yelling at the radio as it glowed
in the dark.

"I'll tell you why, you jerk!" he said. "If you knew anything about baseball, you'd know Esasky can't hit that guy.''

On it went until they reached the Rose residence, where they were met at the door by Rose's beautiful wife, a former Philadelphia Eagles cheerleader, who was attired in high green pumps, a green miniskirt and a low-cut top. She proceeded to cook Rose and Reilly cheeseburgers at midnight.

Meanwhile, Rose made a dash for the television set and satellite dish controls. Comfortably plopped on a seat, Rose then spent the next three hours talking and watching assorted baseball games.

Rose and Reilly got along just fine until later that week, when Reilly visited Rose in his office. Rick needed to finish his interview, but Rose was showering. But that didn't stop Reilly from asking questions. So Reilly fired away while Pete lathered up—and tried to come clean.

Imagine. Interviewing one of the biggest names in baseball while he's showering. What's the matter? Don't you let people interview you while you're showering?

If that's not enough, try examining the phenomenon that is Brian Bosworth and his alter ego, the Boz. Steve Kelley of the *Seattle Times* did and it angered His Royal Mohawk. Sometimes when Kelley ventured into the Seattle Seahawks locker room Bosworth was waiting for him.

"Pussy," he would occasionally say to Kelley. And then he would walk away.

So much for the Bosworth Rules of Etiquette.

And try venturing into a clubhouse or locker room as a woman sportswriter. Perceptions and prejudices continue to change for the better, but there still exists a pocket of Neanderthal players and coaches who can't stand seeing a woman invade their supposed male domain. To make their point, they yell clever things, such as, "Pecker checker," or worse yet, choose not to cooperate with any women sportswriters. It is insecurity at its finest and professionalism at its worst.

Sportswriting isn't meant for the meek. You have to develop an immune system that battles hypocrisy, egotism and false humility. And that's just in the profession itself. As for the athletes and coaches, good luck. It is one of the few jobs in which you can get sworn at, threatened, spat on, manhandled and, in a barnyard twist, mooed at.

I refer to the events of May 17, 1989. California Angels rookie Jim Abbott had just beaten Roger Clemens and the Boston Red Sox at Anaheim Stadium on a clear, pleasant evening. It was cause for celebration, as well as curiosity. After all, Abbott was a former Olympian, a number-one draft choice and (I use the term loosely) handicapped (he was born without a right hand, though you'd never know it if you watched him pitch).

As had become the custom when Abbott started, a larger-than-usual media following was assembled outside the Angels clubhouse. Suddenly the doors opened and we lurched forward, all headed toward Abbott's roped-off dressing cubicle. That's when I heard the moos. Moos so loud and clear that Elsie the cow would have been proud. Harsh, mocking moos, designed to let us know exactly how little we were welcome.

Understand that baseball players are territorial that way. They don't take well to crowds. That night we were invading their inner sanctum and they responded. To them, we were a herd of pens and pencils grazing on a rookie pitcher.

At first I was indignant; didn't they know that we were simply doing our jobs? Then I started thinking about my Uncle Red in Milwaukee. He made a pretty good living selling trophies in his day. Maybe I could go to engraving school (or wherever trophy people go), start my own business, steal some customers from some of the local bowling leagues and be on my way to a normal life. It sounded nice. Boringly nice.

The problem is, I'm sort of hooked on sportswriting. I like its spontaneity. No two days are ever the same. Every game has its own character and every player has his own story. And what other profession, except for veterinary medicine and farming, offers the sound of moos?

So I half-smiled as a roomful of seminaked grown men serenaded us as we assembled around Abbott's dressing area. It was odd music to the ears, but I can say this much: You'd never hear it in a trophy shop.

Sportswriting is filled with tiny, bizarre moments like this, moments that never see the light of newsprint. Maybe they should, though, because these same moments reveal more about the athletes and players than almost any postgame interview. At the same time, they also reveal a little something about the pencil pushers.

Strange thing about sportswriters: Nobody really knows what they do for a living or how they go about doing it.

For instance, after covering a college basketball game earlier in the evening, Frank Burlison of the *Long Beach Press Telegram* ran into several of the home team's coaches at the hotel bar. Burlison joined the coaches and spent the next several hours talking hoops and knocking down beers. Finally, he stood up and said his good-byes. His hotel bed beckoned.

"Guess I better get upstairs," he said.

"Are you going to write your story now?" asked one of the coaches.

Burlison was too tired to even try to explain.

Meanwhile, the players are convinced that sportswriters are up to no good, that they were born without use of their frontal and temporal lobes, that they shop at Polyester-R-Us and that they wouldn't recognize a brilliant athletic strategy if it introduced itself. In fact, Reggie Jackson was kind enough to scream that very thing to me one day during a California Angels batting practice in 1986.

Turns out Jackson was upset over a story I had done the night before, when, using one of his own lines, I wrote that the only way he'd ever get a Gold Glove was if he painted one himself (he had committed an error on a play). To be honest, I thought it was sort of a funny quip on Jackson's part.

Yes, well, I don't think Reg-E was in the quippy mood the

next day. After a half-dozen glares, followed by a chorus of inspired obscenities, Jackson stepped into the batting cage and began knocking balls high into the evening air, far beyond the outfield fences. With each powerful swing, Jackson's temper grew.

"I've forgotten more about this game than you'll ever know!" he bellowed. "From now on I'm going to treat you the way you treated me in the paper. You hear me! I'm going to treat you the same way you treated me: like shit!"

"So?" I squeaked back.

So outraged was Jackson that members of the opposing Boston Red Sox even inched out of the dugout to listen to the lecture. Fans craned their necks to hear the explosion. Not until Angels manager Gene Mauch approached the batting cage did Jackson's outburst subside.

Of course, it wasn't the first time Jackson, whose ego couldn't be mapped with a tracking satellite, had tried to intimidate a writer with his tantrums. He got a strange pleasure out of ridiculing anyone who asked a question that offended his sensibilities. This was the same Jackson who, several days after the batting cage performance, said to me, "Reggie the person apologizes for what he said. But Reggie the ballplayer can't apologize for it. Do you understand?"

Uh, no. Which Reggie said what?

In Reggie's defense, there are those writers who found him quite agreeable. Lynn Henning, then of the *Detroit News,* says that Jackson once took him aside and sincerely thanked him for a short item he had written in that day's editions. Henning was (and still is) touched by the gesture. And while no reporter can question his ability to fill up a notebook, Jackson usually exacted a price for his cooperation. Too often it wasn't worth the cost.

Your average reader doesn't see this sort of thing in the box scores. Your average reader thinks that sportswriters have the greatest scam going. Free games. Hobnob with the superstars. Good seats at the stadium. Exotic travel. The whole shebang. And in a way, the reader is absolutely correct . . . and absolutely wrong.

For instance, at a 1982 game between the Detroit Lions and the New York Giants, punt returner Leon Bright was viciously (and illegally) hit by an opposing Lions player while waiting for the ball to drop from the Silverdome sky. Bright was scraped from the artificial turf, returned to the sidelines and eventually recovered from the blow.

After the game, Giants coach Ray Perkins stormed past the local writers and into the Lions locker room, presumably to give the Detroit players and coaching staff a piece of his mind. A few minutes later, he stormed back out and returned to the visitors' dressing room, where he conducted his own press conference.

Jack Ebling of the *Lansing State Journal* was one of the reporters Perkins brushed aside. Like everyone else, he guessed what had gone on inside between the opposing coaches. Now he had to confirm it.

After interviewing assorted Lions players and coaches, Ebling dashed over to the Giants locker room. Perkins was still there.

"Coach, you seemed pretty upset," Ebling began. "Can you tell me why you went into the Lions locker room, and what did you say?"

Perkins, respected among the writers for his honesty, blew a fuse this time. He grabbed a handful of Ebling's sweater and angrily said, "Weren't you here when I just talked about that? Are you trying to be a smartass?"

Ebling, as calmly as he could in the circumstances, explained that he had been inside the Lions locker room. Perkins, realizing he had just made a terrible mistake, released his grip, smoothed out Ebling's sweater and answered the question.

Back in 1978, Terry Pluto was a twenty-two-year-old rookie beat reporter covering the Baltimore Orioles for the *Evening Sun.* He was sitting in the Orioles dugout one day, minding his own business, when pitcher Jim Palmer walked by and then suddenly stopped and threw a baseball directly at Pluto's groin area. Pluto barely dodged the ball.

"Next time, wear a cup!" yelled Palmer, before jogging away.

Twelve years later, Pluto still doesn't know why Palmer, usually a decent sort, did what he did.

As for that good-seats theory, well, it's usually true. But there are times, especially at well-attended media events, such as the Super Bowl or baseball playoffs or bowl games, that the seating doesn't exactly provide a proper atmosphere for work.

I once had to warm my feet by the heat from the scoreboard lights that lined the front of County Stadium's auxiliary press box. It was early October in Milwaukee, site of the 1981 divisional playoffs between the Brewers and the New York Yankees, and it was bone-chilling cold. Unfortunately, the auxiliary box wasn't enclosed.

After a while, I rooted openly for three-and-two pitch counts. Why? Because that was the only time all the bulbs located near my toes would light up.

This is how it goes sometimes. For every memorable seventh game of the World Series there are a dozen Reggie-like incidents. For every trip to Wimbledon there are ten trips to Cleveland. For every first-class flight from New York to Los Angeles there are countless adventures on some prop-engine crop-duster of an airline in the Midwest. Vomit Comets is what we call them in the business.

But just when you think you've had enough, when Eric Dickerson, fresh from lunch, is sending bits of tuna in your face, or Jim Rice is ripping the shirt off your chest, or Jack Kent Cooke, owner of the Washington Redskins, is lecturing you in his private stadium suite, something happens to reaffirm your fondness for the profession. You break a big story, perhaps. You witness a remarkable sporting moment. Or better yet, Dickerson wipes his mouth.

Sports needs its chroniclers, and I don't mean some of those thimble-headed TV sports anchors who cute themselves into a frenzy with highlights of pro wrestling. The way I look at it, sportswriters are the single greatest invention since the Model T or the heart-lung machine. Without us, there would be no sports lore, no Seven Horsemen, no blue-gray skies, no House That Ruth Built. If Sports is a language—and it is—then sportswriters are the interpreters.

Of course, some sportswriters can translate the dialect better than others. Jim Murray of the *Los Angeles Times* writes with humility, humor and honesty. The late Red Smith of the *New York Times* was the Joe DiMaggio of sportswriting: elegant, pristine, nearly perfect in substance and style.

But let's not go overboard on this romance thing. Sportswriting has its perks, mainly that you don't have to wear socks to work, but all in all, it's not a job I'd recommend to those interested in financial security, marital bliss, a Body-by-Jake physique and eight-hour days.

Chain-smoking is big in sportswriting. So are drinking and other forms of entertainment. Shelby Strother of the *Detroit News* and Tom Archdeacon, then with the *Miami News,* were at a strip joint one afternoon in Miami, killing time before a 4:00 P.M. game involving the Dolphins. As they sat at the bar nursing their drinks, one of the dancers ground her way toward them. She wore practically nothing except for a tattoo—a worm wearing a top hat—near her belly button. As the routine came to an end, the stripper lay down on her back and then pulled both of her legs over her head, so that her face was nearly between her ankles. It was at that exact moment that she, well, farted.

Strother and Archdeacon recoiled in disbelief. Realizing the indiscretion, the stripper, her head still between her legs, whispered to the two writers, "Sorry, fellas, must have been the won-ton soup."

Good thing she didn't have the Szechwan beef.

Travel also is a must for sportswriters. For instance, baseball writers probably spend about 180 days on the road. Pro basketball writers check in at the 90 mark. If you're married, this is the perfect recipe for divorce.

What happens is that you lose touch with reality, to say nothing of relationships. There are days when you literally have no idea what city you're in. Life becomes an airport, a hotel, a press box and then room service. The following day you repeat the process until each town blends into the next.

You become best friends with Spectravision, the hotel movie channel. On occasion, you get a tiny bit spoiled. One writer I know once complained to the front desk that his phone rang too loud.

Success stories are rare on the road. More times than not the journeys are as relaxing as working in the control room of a nuclear missile silo. Stress levels go off the charts. Nerves become frayed. Business people everywhere know what I mean. And if you don't, you will. Trust me.

Tom Zucco of the *St. Petersburg Times* and several other writers once found themselves the last people left in the Sullivan Stadium press box one freezing day in Foxboro after a New England Patriots–Tampa Bay Buccaneers game. Huddled over their portable computers, the writers soon discovered that the heat had been turned off by a dimwitted maintenance man. Fingers stiffened. Breath could be seen. Something had to be done.

So Zucco, his toes and fingertips nearly numb, collected his notes and computer and found the only warm place to thaw out and finish his story: the bathroom. Soon, two . . . three . . . four writers made their way into the cramped quarters. Stationed among dirty sinks, wet floors and a stopped-up urinal or two, they wrote their stories and tried to ignore the stench.

Even worse was the time Pluto, who later covered the Cleveland Indians for the *Plain Dealer,* ventured into a tiny airplane lavatory during a cross-country flight on the team charter. All air travelers know how small those bathroom compartments are: You can barely find room to zip your pants.

Anyway, when Pluto tried to leave the lavatory, he found the door wouldn't open. Wayne Garland, an Indian pitcher, had jammed it shut.

Pluto pushed and pounded on the door. No luck. He yelled. Nothing. Two hours later, Garland freed him.

"Was that really that funny?" Pluto asked Garland.

Garland just smirked.

Like I said, it is a hell of a way to make a living.

Deadlines are a constant, too. They hover above a sports-writer's keyboard like a curse. Want to see two hours disappear just like that? Try getting an attack of writer's block as deadline appears on the horizon. You look at your watch and the minute hand seems to be doing wind sprints around the dial. The tick, tick, ticks sound frenzied; so does your heartbeat as you realize that now only eleven minutes remain until your story is due. You stare blankly at your computer screen. Nine minutes left and you have seven paragraphs written. They need thirty.

You type furiously. Back in the home office some copy editor sits at his computer terminal waiting anxiously for your story. He has a deadline to meet, to say nothing of wanting to get home in time to watch Letterman's monologue. You can just see him sitting there, agitated, tapping his nails against his desk. He glances at the wall clock, rolls his eyes in exasperation and says to another desk jockey, "Where in the *hell* is the friggin' story?"

Back in the press box you tap out your last words. You're going to make it. You're going to survive.

Then a television worker, removing the cable from that night's telecast, accidently pulls the plug on your portable computer. Your story vanishes into the air. Or someone spills a beer into the circuitry. Or the phone company refuses to accept your calling card number. Deadline is blown. So is your patience. One writer, his spirit broken by the weight of

a deadline and the malfunction of his computer, once heaved
the machine out of the press box window. The terminal
floated gently in the summer air and then died a hero's death
on the stadium cement.

Pressure is a sportswriting staple. It can be self-inflicted
(usually by those disgustingly organized Type-A personalities), prompted by overzealous editors or induced by competing newspapers or magazines. Whatever the cause, it is the
lifeblood of the profession. It provides a nervous edge. It
makes you do things you wouldn't normally do except under
court order.

The *Los Angeles Times*'s Mike Downey, then working in
Chicago, was running late for a Bulls basketball game one
day. He got into his car, turned the key . . . nothing. He
called for a taxi . . . no one would come. He tried the car
again . . . silent. So he took his computer, which weighed
about twelve pounds, and lugged it fifteen miles to Chicago
Stadium. Needless to say, he didn't make it for tipoff.

And pressure may have prompted Rick Telander to offer
the following idea to his *Sports Illustrated* editors not long
ago: How about a story on sports in prisons?

"We love it," said Telander's editors.

Yes, well, the only catch to all of this is that Telander had
to actually visit a correctional institute or two. And he didn't
limit his trips to Club Fed facilities, where they have tennis
courts and low-impact aerobics classes. Telander went to
places where you wouldn't dare drop a bar of soap. There
were people there with more tattoos than the entire Fifth
Fleet. It was a depressing, haunting and unnerving experience.

Witness the time that Telander went to a federal peniten-
tiary outside Minneapolis. He was escorted into the basement
of the prison, where a basketball court and weight room were
located. Nearby was one of those Foosball games (a version
of table soccer), long since destroyed.

"What happened to the table?" Telander asked a guard.

"Some of the inmates pulled out the metal rods, sharpened

the ends and made swords out of them," he said. "Then they tried to kill each other."

"Oh," said Telander.

It was about this time that Telander noticed that the guard didn't have a weapon, only a walkie-talkie. In fact, none of the guards had guns. Telander felt his pulse quicken. He had walked into the damndest thing: an honor system. The thinking was that guards with guns made for better hostages, or something like that. Whatever the case, Telander wanted out.

Then he noticed one of the inmates staring at him. The man had a crazed, manic look on his face.

"Who's he?" asked Telander.

"That one?" said the guard. "Oh, he took three people, bound their hands with wire and then shot each one in the head."

"Could we leave, please?" Telander said.

All this for a story.

For the most part, though, sportswriters confine themselves to more conventional venues, such as stadiums, arenas, coliseums, maybe a hotel on occasion.

For instance, back when Michael Dokes was the newest heavyweight boxing phenom, he invited several writers, including Rick Bozich of the *Louisville Courier-Journal*, up to his Las Vegas hotel suite. The interview was about fifteen minutes old when a statuesque blonde entered the room, glanced at Dokes in an amorous way and then slowly walked toward the master bedroom.

Dokes jumped up so fast you would have thought he had just beaten a ten-count. He caught up with the blonde, grabbed her from behind and walked into the bedroom. Just before closing the door, he turned back to the stunned writers and said, "Gentlemen, this will only take about twenty minutes. If you'd like to stick around, I'll be happy to answer your questions."

Decorum prevented anyone from staying.

And while we're on the subject of decorum, let's get some things straight, beginning with:

- Not all sportswriters wear fedoras with "Press" on the side, wipe their runny noses on their sleeves and drink a fifth of Jack Daniel's every night (though some have tried).

- Oscar Madison, the rumpled sportswriter of *Odd Couple* fame, is not the patron saint of the profession.

- Sportswriters are like cockroaches (and I mean this in a nice way): They can survive most anything. They are a healthy lot, not easily deterred.

- Some of the best (and worst) writing you'll ever see can be found in the Toy Department.

Understand these four things and you can begin to understand this most wacky of jobs.

Of course, we have our moments of imperfection. Lots of them. For starters, almost every sportswriter alive has sat down and typed, "What a difference a year makes," and thought it was the greatest lead ever written.

Almost every sportswriter, flushed with the excitement of witnessing some great athletic achievement, has asked a player, "How do you feel?"

Almost every sportswriter has botched facts, figures and quotations in a story. It happens more than it should.

But unlike movie critics, who rip from afar, sportswriters must (or at least should) return to the scene of the crime. You screw up a story? You better have the nerve to make an appearance in the clubhouse the next day. You better be willing to get yelled at in public. It's the least you can do.

Former major leaguer Cliff Johnson, then with the Indians, was standing on third base with only one out and the score tied late in the game. A long fly ball was hit to the warning track, plenty far for Johnson to tag and score.

Except that Johnson thought there were two outs, not one. He jogged lazily toward home and was easily thrown out. In the next day's edition of the *Plain Dealer,* Pluto pointed out the bonehead play.

"I should crush your bones," said Johnson to Pluto later.

This was typical stuff, thought Pluto as Johnson raved on. But then Johnson's face grew peaceful, as if he had discovered some sort of inner truth.

"You know," Johnson said, "I've been ripped by a lot better than you."

All in all, a great comeback by Johnson.

John Feinstein, then with the *Washington Post,* once was awakened by an early morning phone call a few years ago. Lefty Driesell, who was the University of Maryland basketball coach at the time, was on the line. Driesell, as often was the case, wanted to discuss a story in that day's edition.

"Son," said Driesell in his odd Southern accent, "you sleeping?"

"Yes, I'm sleeping," said Feinstein.

"Why'd you put that story in the paper today?"

"Because it's true, Lefty."

A pause, and then, "I know, but why'd you put it in the paper?"

Sometimes people take sports and sportswriters much too seriously. Jay Mariotti of the *Denver Post* wrote a critical column on Broncos quarterback John Elway midway through the 1989 season. Elway, in an earlier story, had said that he was suffocating in Denver. Mariotti said that perhaps it was Elway's own doing.

The column did not go over well in Denver. Mariotti received hate mail galore, as well as dozens of nasty phone calls. It happened that the week of the Elway controversy, Mariotti was scheduled to do a radio call-in show at a local bar. Early in the program, Mariotti noticed four Denver police officers standing nearby. During a break in the show, Mariotti motioned one of them to the table.

"What are you guys doing here? Is there going to be a fight?" he asked.

Said the cop: "You've had two death threats. They said they're going to blow you away. We advise you to get out of here as soon as the show is over."

At program's end, Mariotti dashed to his car, and with a police escort, too.

There are some other basic things you ought to know about the business. For instance, sportswriters generally aren't fond of anyone in the electronic (television and radio) media. And (generally) vice versa.

Call it jealousy, envy or inherent dislike, but nothing annoys a sportswriter like a radio or television person. They are a writer's worst nightmare, what with their Q-ratings, tailored suits and hefty paychecks. They usually ask the stupidest questions, root openly for the home team and travel with an entourage that includes a sound person, a camera person and maybe even a producer. And all to say, "You pitched a whale of a game, Jim Bob!"

An example: The day before the 1988 NFC Championship Game at Soldier Field, Chicago Bears coach Mike Ditka arrived at a downtown hotel to announce his choice of a starting quarterback: the popular Jim McMahon or the maligned Mike Tomczak. The assembled press waited anxiously as Ditka made his way to the podium, cleared his throat and then warned everyone that he would name the starter, but not answer a single question about the selection. With that done, Ditka said, "Jim McMahon."

And then it happened. A Chicago anchor person sent to file a live report found herself the victim of poor timing. Ditka had made his announcement before her station had been able to switch to her. Undaunted, she asked Ditka, for the convenience of her live television audience, to repeat his choice of quarterbacks.

There are certain things in life you never do; one of them is tell Ditka what to say and when to say it. Ditka grimaced at the request and then smirked. He was about to teach a pushy anchor person a lesson.

"OK, honey," he said sweetly, "the starting quarterback is going to be . . . Sid Luckman."

Luckman last wore a National Football League uniform in 1950.

But the fun wasn't finished. This was a press conference for the ages, thanks partly to the desperate anchor person and to a reporter for a Spanish radio station.

"Coach Deet-ka," asked the radio man, "could you please say a few words for our Spanish listeners?"

To which Ditka said, *"Arriba, arriba."*

In all fairness, sportswriters ask their share of idiotic questions, too, including this one of the aforementiond Jim Abbott: "Uh, Jim, were you born a natural left-hander?"

If I were Abbott, I would have picked up a Louisville Slugger and begun swinging. But I'm the vindictive sort.

Meanwhile, Abbott politely answered yes.

Then there are the interviews for which the reporter should be issued a bat. Take the time Ray Didinger of the *Philadelphia Daily News* traveled to Chicago to talk to Bears running back Walter Payton. Turns out Payton wasn't in the mood to be interviewed, a fact that became apparent as the team's public relations man escorted him to a meeting room.

"You told me I didn't have to do any of these things after Wednesday," Payton whined.

"Yeah, but this guy flew in from Philadelphia to see you," the PR man said.

When they met, Payton's handshake was as firm as a wet fish. And when Didinger tried asking several questions, Payton opened up a magazine and began reading. Whatever answers he did provide were no more than five or six words in length.

Didinger, bless his heart, closed his notebook and gathered his things. "It's obvious that you're not too interested in talking to me," Didinger said. "I know I'm wasting your time and I definitely know you're wasting mine. Maybe we should do this some other time."

"OK," Payton said.

Hey, who said there's no cheering in the press box? I would have clapped had I seen Didinger's performance.

As for standing ovations, *Phoenix Gazette* columnist Joe Gilmartin deserved one after sparring with former Oakland Athletics owner Charles O. Finley.

Every time Gilmartin asked Finley a question, Finley would snap back, "That's none of your damned business." Realizing the hard-hitting approach wasn't working, Gilmartin inquired about a player Finley once knew. It was a throwaway question, one designed to soften Finley's resolve. It didn't work.

"That's none of your damned business," Finley said. "I don't know why I'm talking to you anyhow. Phoenix? What's Phoenix to me? What's the circulation of your paper, anyway?"

Said Gilmartin: "That's none of your damned business."

Sportswriting isn't the noblest of professions, but it has its moments. Come to think of it, it has lots of them, some sweet and precious, others disturbing and crude. But that's how life is on the edge of glamour.

2

Baseball:
Where Men Are Men
and Sportswriters
Are Necessary
Evils

Gene Mauch, the smartest if not the most quotable manager ever to fill out a lineup card, was forced to place muscleman Brian Downing, a designated hitter extraordinaire, in the California Angels leadoff position one season. Asked about Downing's reaction to the move, Mauch stared straight ahead and said slowly, "Brian Downing would rather eat green flies than bat leadoff."

Mauch didn't know it, but he may have stumbled across the perfect description of how most sportswriters generally embrace the idea of covering baseball. In short, they'd rather dine on green flies.

Baseball beat writers deserve combat pay, what with the unending travel, the constant competition for scoops and the inevitable clubhouse confrontations between reporter and player during the course of a season that begins as early as February and, counting playoffs, doesn't end until October. That's 30 or so exhibition games, 162 regular-season games, an All-Star Game, the League Championships and the World Series. And did we mention the countless stories that will be written about contract negotiations, trade rumors, injuries, litigation and other assorted matters of baseball jurisprudence?

Adding to the difficulties are the fans, who think writers should be home team advocates, always accentuating the positive, ignoring the sometimes slimy underside of sports. They don't take kindly to having their heroes' images tarnished.

Witness the time Rick Bozich of the *Louisville Courier-Journal* and several other writers were making their way out of historic Tiger Stadium after the first game of the 1984 World Series between the San Diego Padres and the Tigers. Bozich's group happened to choose the same stadium exit used a half-hour earlier by San Diego players. Thinking Bozich might be a member of the Padres entourage, the usual collection of rabid Tigers fans assembled outside the exit began yelling, "Padres suck! Padres suck!"

"Hey," said Bozich, "we're not the Padres, we're the media."

Undaunted, the crowd began a new chant: "Media sucks! Media sucks!"

Kevin Horrigan, former columnist of the *St. Louis Post-Dispatch,* frequently picked on the revered baseball Cardinals for assorted wrongdoings. And while he would happily take phone calls at the office from irate readers, Horrigan thought it best not to subject his family to these same criticisms at home. So he arranged for an unlisted number.

One day Horrigan checked his office mail and found a letter from—you guessed it—Kevin Horrigan, who, it turns out, was a Benedictine monk living in the St. Louis area. Every time Horrigan number one wrote a controversial column, Horrigan number two's phone would ring off the hook. Imagine the monk's surprise that first time he answered the phone and was greeted with, "You stupid son of a bitch."

The letter was friendly enough. The monk kiddingly thanked Horrigan for the many phone calls. To this day, the monk occasionally still writes Horrigan to tell him of new and even more inventive telephone greetings from angry readers.

Not so cordial was the note and package *Cincinnati Enquirer* columnist Tim Sullivan received from a reader following a series of critical stories directed at Reds manager and local icon Pete Rose. Among other things, Sullivan had called for Rose's resignation in light of the many gambling allegations involving the former Reds great.

The package contained a box of dead roses. The note, unsigned, began, "These roses are dead, you ought to be too . . ." Soon after that, Sullivan, Rose's harshest critic, received a letter suggesting that the writer should be lynched. This note was signed.

Baseball writing is not a popular line of work. Each year the Los Angeles Dodgers sponsor a "Think Blue Week," a fantasy-type contest in which selected fans can become batboys for a day, or sit in the photographers' well, or spend time in the broadcast booth, or, if the mood strikes them, visit the press box for a firsthand look at life behind a portable computer. One season, not one winner selected the trip to the press box. Ouch!

Yes, well, if you cover baseball, it's best not to take such moments personally. It also helps to have a sense of humor.

Scott Ostler, columnist for the *National,* once overheard a conversation involving two baseball writers. One of the reporters had been at the game from the start, the other had stumbled in at about the seventh inning.

Said the first writer: "Where the hell have you been?"

"None of your business," said the second writer. "Now catch me up, will you?"

So the first guy went through his scorebook and provided the second writer with an inning-by-inning account of the game. "And by the way," said the first writer, "you should put a star next to this out: The center fielder made a hell of a play to save a run."

The second writer, who hadn't seen a single moment of the game, frowned and said, "I'll be the judge of that."

In 1981, the Rangers were playing the Boston Red Sox at

Fenway Park when an announcement was made in the press box: "The Indians' Len Barker has just pitched a perfect game in Cleveland," boomed a voice over the speakers.

Without missing a beat, Randy Galloway of the *Dallas Morning News* stood up and yelled back, "There is no such thing as a perfect game in Cleveland." Sadly, he was right.

Baseball writers endure more abuse than you can shake a Louisville Slugger at, including Cleveland. Melanie Hauser of the *Houston Post* had a bottle of champagne poured down her back by then–Astros general manager Dick Wagner after the team clinched the 1986 divisional title. Then an Astros public relations official sprayed her with beer. Hauser, her clothes and hair soaked with booze, borrowed several towels from the clubhouse boys and returned to the press box. Shivering, she wrote the story.

A special breed are baseball hacks, sort of the Marine Corps of sportswriting. Or as Tracy Ringolsby, also of the *Dallas Morning News,* says, "Being a baseball writer requires a demented mind. It requires you to fuck up the rest of your life."

Strange thing is, Ringolsby is addicted to covering the sport. Wouldn't trade it for anything else. He considers baseball a cousin of life itself. He enjoys its *Mayberry R.F.D.* pace, its subtleties and its subplots. Best of all, he likes the day-to-day contact with the people he writes about, so much so that sometimes he goes beyond the call of duty. For example, on road trips, Ringolsby often arrives at the ballpark by 1:00 P.M., a full six and a half hours before the first pitch. But even Ringolsby, early bird that he is, had to do a doubletake when he walked into the Texas Rangers clubhouse one day in 1986 and found reliever Mitch Williams in uniform, sitting alone at his locker.

"Why are you here so early?" Ringolsby said.

"I don't have anything else to do," the young pitcher said sadly.

So Ringolsby and Rangers trainer Bill Zeigler decided to help. Whenever the team arrived at a new city, they would take Williams to the local zoo. Only in baseball.

And only in baseball can a writer have incredible amounts of access before and after a game. Wander into any clubhouse two hours before the first pitch and you'll find the mood remarkably relaxed. You can shoot the bull with the players, conduct an interview with the pitching coach, check on injuries with the trainer. Try the same thing at an NFL contest and some linebacker would crush your thorax.

Of course, access isn't always what it's cracked up to be. If your team is out of the race by July or August, the job becomes absolute misery. You dread walking into the same clubhouse, talking to the same faces, jotting down the same cliché-ridden answers, watching the same mind-numbing losses. Now reverse the dread and that's how ballplayers probably feel about staring at another notepad and tape recorder.

Back in 1987, the Atlanta Braves were having a typical Braves season, which is to say, not much of a season at all. Mired in last place in the National League West, the Braves had just lost to the Houston Astros, 12–0, in the heat of late August. Needless to say, the Braves clubhouse was so quiet you could hear a batting glove drop.

Gerry Fraley, then with the *Atlanta Journal-Constitution,* was the only beat writer to cover the Braves on the road. So at game's end he walked into the stillness of the Braves clubhouse to dig up some postgame comments. Twenty-four heads turned as Fraley, the lone visitor, opened up his notebook.

Seated in front of a dressing stall was catcher Bruce Benedict, who, upon seeing Fraley, wearily rolled his eyes and pleaded, "What could you possibly want to ask us about?"

Fraley thought about it for a moment, closed his notepad and said, "You're right," and left the room.

At the risk of generalizing, ballplayers and managers can

be the most endearing of personalities or the biggest jerks in the world. Then again, so can some sportswriters.

Mauch once found himself cornered at spring training by a little girl who wanted to do a school report on what it was like to be a major league manager. Mauch grimaced—imagine the Little General granting interviews to someone in elementary school. But then he looked carefully about to see if all his players had retired to the clubhouse. With that done, he motioned for the little girl to join him for a chat. It was a touching gesture by a man known for his pointed retorts and self-guardedness.

The legendary Gaylord Perry, master of the doctored ball, was pitching for the Texas Rangers one evening when a foul ball arched high and hard against the Arlington Stadium press box window, leaving a suspicious greasy smudge on the thick glass. At last, empirical, uncontestable evidence that Perry had dipped the ball in the petroleum jelly of your choice.

Perry, a smirk on his face, would have none of the postgame accusations.

"So, Gaylord, just what did you have on that ball you threw?" asked Galloway that night.

"Nothing," Perry said sheepishly. "Must have hit a mosquito on the way up."

Priceless.

Not so poignant was the time Steve Fainaru, then the Boston Red Sox beat reporter for the *Hartford Courant,* walked into the visiting clubhouse at Oakland's Alameda County Stadium after a 1987 game against the Athletics to do what he normally did: talk to the manager, interview a few players, then make his way back to the press box to write his story.

But this time Red Sox CEO Haywood Sullivan was in the clubhouse and he was granting interviews. So Fainaru joined a small pack of reporters, only to hear a voice in the background. It was designated hitter Jim Rice and he was mocking the writers huddled around Sullivan.

Fainaru turned and sneered in Rice's direction. It was a "what-an-idiot" sneer, pure and simple.

Rice stared back. "You got a problem with me?" he said.

"Yeah, I do," Fainaru said.

"What?" said Rice, now face to face with Fainaru.

This was dangerous, thought Fainaru. It was also a tad dramatic. So rather than press the issue, Fainaru walked away, only to reconsider a few moments later. He was tired of dealing with players like Rice. Rice was an ass, he decided, and it was time to tell Rice that very thing. So, as he waited for Rice to emerge from the showers, Fainaru informed a Boston writer of his plans to confront the former all-star. The writer nodded and then, oddly enough, complimented Fainaru on his choice of clothes that night. "I really like that shirt," the writer said.

About that time, Rice began walking back to his dressing stall. Fainaru met him.

"I just want you to know that if you continue to give me shit, I'm going to give it back," Fainaru said calmly. "I'm not going to continue to take it."

Rice didn't say a word. Instead, he grabbed Fainaru by the shirt—his brand-new black shirt—and pulled it hard. There was a ripping sound as the fabric gave way to Rice's mighty tug. Rice began screaming at Fainaru. Fainaru screamed back. There was scuffling and pushing and shoving. The whole thing resembled a rugby scrum.

For Fainaru, it was almost an out-of-body experience as he felt his shirt disappear from his back. Clutching what material was left from the shirt, Fainaru aimed and threw it at Rice. Rice charged, but was stopped by several players. Meanwhile, Red Sox player Mike Greenwell escorted Fainaru out of the clubhouse.

The next day, Rice approached Fainaru near the batting

cage and extended his hand. Fainaru mumbled something, but neither man apologized.

And one other thing: Rice never offered to replace the tattered shirt.

The San Diego Padres had just lost a game, 2–1, against the Montreal Expos when Bill Plaschke, making his debut as a beat reporter for the *Los Angeles Times,* and several other writers were ushered into then–Padres manager Larry Bowa's office. Bowa had a reputation for being cooperative enough with the regular writers, but not so cooperative with out-of-town reporters. On this night, he was a jerk to both, responding to all questions with one-word answers.

Lynn Henning, formerly of the *Detroit News,* was doing a story on Padres all-star Tony Gwynn. As a courtesy to the other writers, he took a stab at getting a monosyllabic answer from Bowa.

"Larry, I haven't seen your team play this year, but is tonight's game kind of indicative of the way things have been going for you?"

Bowa looked up from his salad plate. "That's a stupid fucking question," he said.

Henning didn't back down. "No it wasn't a stupid question."

Bowa's eyes grew wide. He slammed his hand on the desk and began yelling at Henning. "Get this motherfucker out of here!" Bowa yelled. "Get this motherfucker out of here!"

Henning left the room, talked to a player and then decided to try to patch things up with Bowa. As he neared the office, Bowa walked out.

"Get this motherfucker out of here!" Bowa said, his voice echoing through the clubhouse. So much for mutual understanding.

So loud was the tantrum that Gwynn pulled a writer aside and whispered, "What was the question? What was the question?"

At last, a Padres trainer or clubhouse man tugged gently on Henning's arm. "Maybe you better leave," he said.

Afterward, Bowa made a decision: He would do no more interviews with sportswriters.

The next night, the Padres lost in the bottom of the ninth on a two-run homer given up by reliever Goose Gossage. Standing outside the clubhouse after the defeat, Mark Kreidler of the *San Diego Union* turned to Plaschke and said, "I think Larry's going to do it tonight: I think he's going to kill one of us."

Soon the clubhouse doors opened and the writers stepped tentatively into Bowa's office. They expected a tempest.

Instead, Bowa was all smiles.

"We did it, we got him," Bowa beamed.

Did what? the writers wanted to know. Got who?

"We just made a seven-player trade," Bowa said. "Look at this deal: We got Chris Brown, Mark Grant, Keith Comstock and best of all, we got Chili Davis."

Kreidler and Plaschke sprinted to some nearby pay phones. This was a remarkable deal for the Padres: Brown and the highly regarded Chili Davis.

Just then, the Padres public relations man grabbed Plaschke. "Uh, Larry was wrong, it's Mark Davis, not Chili Davis."

The reporters filed back into Bowa's office. Bowa's smile had been replaced by a glum, betrayed look. It was hitting him now: the misunderstood trade, the late-inning loss, the embarrassment of gloating openly about his supposed new acquisitions.

"I guess it's not Chili Davis, huh?" said Bowa.

The writers stared at their shoes. Little did anyone know that this unheralded Mark Davis would win the National League Cy Young Award in 1989.

Bowa was equally intense during his playing career. He lashed out at Mark Heisler, then with the *Philadelphia Bulletin,* when Heisler approached him after a loss against the Cardinals on a hot, steamy night in St. Louis. Bowa was having a brilliant year both offensively and defensively, but alas, the Phillies were not.

"What do you think the problem is?" Heisler asked.

"Ask the captain," Bowa hissed, gesturing toward Phillies third baseman Mike Schmidt's locker.

So Heisler did as he was told. As he waited for Schmidt, Bowa began yelling. "What do you know about being criticized?" he said. "You guys are all alike."

"Hey, how would you like it if I said you guys were all alike?" said Heisler.

This set Bowa off, prompting Manager Danny Ozark to rush out of his office. "Mark, I better ask you to leave."

As Heisler departed, Bowa ran up behind him and slammed a soda bottle into a trash can, scaring the bejabbers out of the writer.

The next night Bowa had another great game, but refused to talk to reporters whenever Heisler joined the group.

The night after that, Bowa nearly fought with a *Camden Courier Post* reporter before the game began. The incident certainly didn't affect his on-field performance: He collected several key hits and made some splendid plays at shortstop. The next night, during the postgame interview with Ozark, veteran beat reporter Bill Conlin asked the only question that mattered.

"Danny, are you prepared to sacrifice a writer a night as long as Bowa keeps playing like this?" Conlin said.

As you might expect, ballplayers and sportswriters endure an odd coexistence. It's sort of like England and France: They need each other, but they're not crazy about the arrangement. For example, you'd be amazed how accommodating a ballplayer can become when he wants his side of pending contract negotiations made public. Or how difficult he can get when second-guessed in print. That's what baseball writers are: chroniclers of games and off-field happenings, professional second-guessers.

Some players take the constant critiques better than others.

For instance, infielder Jim Fregosi was in the twilight of his career when he played for the hapless Rangers in the early-to-mid-1970s. Late in a ballgame one night, a ground ball was hit to Fregosi, who promptly booted it for an error. As fate would have it, the error cost the Rangers the game.

Randy Galloway was there that evening and in his story the next day, Galloway wrote that the difference between a Rangers win and a loss was "Fregosi's inability to field a routine grounder."

Fregosi was steamed when he saw the story. He sent a clubhouse boy to find Galloway and bring him back to the Rangers dugout. The message delivered, Galloway, no shrinking violet himself, marched to the dugout ready for a confrontation. He found Fregosi there, all right, cupping a cigarette in the corner of the dugout, looking primed for an argument.

"Galloway," said Fregosi, "sit down!"

Galloway sat down.

"I just want you to know one goddamned thing," Fregosi said as Galloway braced himself for the tirade. "And that one thing is that no ground ball hit to me is *ever* routine."

And then Fregosi smiled. Galloway had been spared.

It isn't always this easy. Ballplayers and managers love to test the tenuous relationships between themselves and sportswriters. Back down and, in all likelihood, you've lost their respect. To baseball types, it is a rite of passage.

Tom Keegan, then with the *Orange County Register,* learned about the strange code while dealing with temperamental slugger Pedro Guerrero in 1988. Keegan was walking through the Los Angeles clubhouse when he accidentally bumped into Guerrero, an ornery man even on his best day.

"Excuse me, Pete," said Keegan.

"Oh, no, excuse me," said Guerrero and then, at the top of his lungs, *"asshole!"*

Keegan's problems would continue. One time he decided to write a feature story on Guerrero, something few writers did, what with Guerrero's deserved reputation as an egotistical brat. Keegan approached Guerrero with the idea.

"How about if we meet tomorrow before the game?" said Keegan.

Guerrero sighed heavily. "All right," he said.

"Four o'clock."

"Fine. See you then."

Keegan arrived at Guerrero's dressing stall the next day at 3:45. At 4:30, he was still waiting. At 5:00, Guerrero finally walked in.

"So, Pete," said Keegan, "would you like to get started on the interview?"

Guerrero stared at Keegan. "No, you come too late. Fuck you."

"Great," Keegan said, "next time I'll arrange to meet you in the driveway."

And so it went until Guerrero was sent briefly to the Dodgers' Triple-A club in Albuquerque, New Mexico, for an injury rehabilitation stay. One night with the Albuquerque team, Guerrero hit a home run. Keegan, looking for a good note to add to his daily story, called Guerrero's hotel in search of his nemesis. No answer.

So Keegan left a sarcastic message: "Pete, congratulations on your big home run. Signed, Blumpy." (This was Keegan's nickname on the beat.)

Not long after the homer, a healthy Guerrero returned to the Dodgers. One of his first acts was to interrupt an interview between Keegan and second baseman Steve Sax.

"Excuse me, Blumpy," Guerrero said.

Keegan readied himself for the worst, which could be considerable.

"Thank you for the message," Guerrero said. "It was a real classy thing to do."

Keegan was nearly speechless. "You're welcome," he said.

Guerrero's antics are legendary, if not outright lewd. Back before he was traded from the Dodgers to the St. Louis

Cardinals, he liked to walk around the clubhouse with—how shall we put it?—an erect "bat." He aroused himself, apparently, to shock teammates, coaches and even writers.

One time, as Randy Youngman, again of the *Register,* looked on, Guerrero paraded through the Dodgers clubhouse with his "bat" at attention. Utilityman Phil Garner, in the midst of an awful hitting slump, glanced at Guerrero's appendage and without breaking stride said, "Hey, Pete, put some pine tar on it and I'll use it tonight."

Of course, Guerrero hasn't cornered the market on foul humor or outrage. Nor is he the first or last ballplayer or manager to take exception to the printed word. Players play. Managers manage. Reporters sometimes report things that baseball types would rather not read. Simply put, it is not a match for the ages.

Jay Mariotti discovered this very thing shortly after he began writing columns for the *Cincinnati Post* in 1985. Reds pitcher Mario Soto had unleashed one of his legendary temper tantrums after a poor outing and Mariotti, unimpressed, wrote that Soto was hurting the team with his outbursts and that the tantrums were childish and unnecessary.

Under normal circumstances, Mariotti would have visited the Reds clubhouse the next day to allow Soto the chance to argue the point. But this time Mariotti was dispatched to cover a golf tournament and couldn't get back until the following week.

Meanwhile, Soto refused to talk to reporters "until I get a chance to talk to that fucking Mariotti." Early the next week, Mariotti arrived at Riverfront Stadium to see Soto, only to be greeted by players and shouts.

"Whoo, this is going to get good," said Reds manager Pete Rose as Mariotti walked by.

Even a stadium guard cautioned Mariotti as he waited for Soto. "You know what you're getting into?" he asked.

Word soon got to Soto, who immediately confronted the columnist.

"You motherfucker . . . you cocksucker," said Soto, poking Mariotti in the chest with a bat.

"Hey, man, would you relax?" Mariotti said.

"Relax?!" said an enraged Soto, the bat now cocked.

Just then former Reds catching great Johnny Bench enveloped Soto in a bear hug and pulled him away. All the while, Soto was yelling and swinging.

"You better get out of here," Rose said to Mariotti.

"What do you mean? I mean, what good was this?"

"Just get the hell out of here," Rose said.

A postscript: About a month later, Mariotti was in the Reds clubhouse after a game when Dave Parker, then with the team, sidled up to the columnist.

"Hey, man, get down on the floor and leg wrestle," said Parker, pointing to one of the Reds' backup catchers.

"You're kidding," said Mariotti, who knew Parker well. "I'm not going to fall for this crap."

"Yeah, man, do it."

By this time, many of the other Reds had encircled Mariotti and were egging him on. Mariotti relented. "All right, I'll do it, but none of you assholes throw anything on me."

Moments into the leg wrestling, Mariotti felt something slimy smack against his body. It was mayonnaise. Then a glob of Ben-Gay hit him, followed by all sorts of available food items and condiments from that night's postgame meal spread. Mariotti had made a grievous error: He had trusted ballplayers. Now he found himself prisoner to the baseball equivalent of frat hell week.

Sitting in the slop, Mariotti saw Soto appear from the shadows and douse him with a container of warm, greenish liquid. It had the distinctive smell of urine.

It gets more frightening. Ken Picking, then with the *Atlanta Journal-Constitution,* was in Philadelphia to cover the 1977 National League playoffs between the Dodgers and Phillies when he happened across Dodgers catcher Steve Yeager in the hotel bar. The two struck up a conversation in which

Yeager confided—on the record—that if manager Tom Lasorda didn't play him in the first game, he would demand a trade. Picking, who knew the ailing Yeager was questionable for game number one, nodded.

Later, Picking asked Yeager about first baseman Steve Garvey's standing on the team.

"This is off the record," said Yeager, who then detailed the various reasons why Garvey wasn't the most popular fellow in the Dodgers clubhouse.

In one of his stories the next day, Picking included the item about Yeager's possible trade demand. And that was that until several days later, when Yeager spotted Picking near the batting cage.

"Hey, man, I didn't say you could print that," said an agitated Yeager, stabbing at Picking with a forefinger.

"Wait a second," Picking said. "You said the *Garvey* stuff was off the record. In fact, I thought you wanted the trade stuff to be printed."

This didn't satisfy Yeager, who grew angrier by the moment. As the scene began to attract more attention, Yeager leaned toward Picking and, in a hushed voice, said, "I can have you blown away for fifty dollars anytime I want. Don't forget it."

He hasn't. That sort of threat tends to stay with you.

Nor has Phil Hersch forgotten his adventures with Ralph Houk. Hersch, then with the *Baltimore Evening Sun,* was new to the Orioles beat back when he included a note in his story about a Detroit Tigers team meeting one day. It wasn't much of a note, and worse yet, Hersch unknowingly exaggerated the importance of the meeting.

Houk, the Detroit manager at the time, was infuriated. Hersch was told to report to Houk the next day.

"Did you write that?" he said, pointing to an issue of the *Evening Sun.*

"That's my name on it," Hersch said smugly.

Houk, a former military man, grabbed Hersch by the collar

and began slapping him in the face. Then he took the writer into the clubhouse, where he told him to apologize to the Detroit players.

"I've got nothing to apologize for."

Kicked out of the clubhouse, Hersch covered the game that night and then decided to press charges. Houk was forced to appear for a preliminary hearing, where a continuance was granted. Meanwhile, the Tigers asked if an apology from Houk would be appropriate compensation. Hersch said yes, figuring that it would be a public apology. It wasn't.

But Hersch received poetic justice not long after the incident, as the Tigers went on an extended losing streak. What someone should have done was slap Houk back.

Phil Rogers was fresh out of North Texas University when his first employer, the *Shreveport Journal,* assigned him to cover the local minor league team, the Shreveport Captains, managed by Andy Gilbert. Gilbert was in his late sixties at the time and was known for two things: He was the first person ever to hit the Houston Astrodome roof with a ball struck from a fungo bat; he lived in smallish Latrobe, Pennsylvania, and yet never had met the town's most famous resident, Arnold Palmer.

Shortly after Rogers began covering the Captains, he wrote a story that angered Gilbert. Gilbert confronted him.

Now it is one thing to get yelled at by a fully clothed, elderly gentleman in a dugout, but quite another thing to have to face an elderly man in the tiny confines of a minor league manager's office, which was Rogers's fate. Strange thing was, the story wasn't all that critical.

After several minutes of verbal bashing, Gilbert calmed down. Rogers thought the worst was over, until . . .

"You know," said Gilbert, "you remind me a lot of a writer I knew in San Francisco. The guy used to write for one of the San Francisco papers."

Gilbert paused. "Thank God, he's dead."

One of the more difficult jobs for baseball writers, other

than being compared to dead people, is to approach a player after he's been sent down to the minors. It's like clicking the tumblers on a safe; you've got to do it just right.

The Angels' Darrell Miller, a reserve catcher, was packing his bags near the end of the 1988 spring training camp when *Los Angeles Times* writer Mike Penner, figuring that Miller had just been cut, asked him about management's decision. Miller complained that the Angels hadn't give him ample chance to show his talents.

"So, are you going down to the Triple-A team?" Penner said.

Miller, realizing that no official announcement had been made, suddenly became enraged. "I don't want you to print any of this," he said. "None of this is for print."

"What's your problem?" Penner said.

Miller reached for a bat and began waving it under Penner's nose. "You print any of this and I'll kick your ass," he said.

Miller eventually apologized and the issue was considered closed. Or so Penner thought.

Later that season, Miller was back with the Angels and in the midst of a horrible batting slump. To make matters worse, he was the catcher of record on the day the New York Yankees hit five home runs off Angels pitching. Someone had to call the pitches, suggested Penner in his story, and that person was Miller, thus making him an accomplice to the rout.

"Hey, Penner, come here," said Miller after hearing about the story. Penner walked over to Miller's dressing stall.

"Yeah?" Penner said.

"I should have crushed you in spring training," Miller said.

So much for media relations.

Of course, sometimes a writer creates his or her own problems by asking ill-advised questions. One night in 1989, the Milwaukee Brewers were playing the Seattle Mariners when a close call at first prompted Milwaukee manager Tom

Trebelhorn to bolt out of the dugout and argue the decision. The Brewers were in the midst of a 3–7 road trip, which didn't help Trebelhorn's mood, nor did his ejection a few moments later for arguing the call a bit too passionately.

Afterward, *Milwaukee Sentinel* reporter Tom Haudricourt and *Milwaukee Journal* writer Cliff Christl, who was new to the Brewers beat, headed down to the clubhouse, where they found Trebelhorn, still obviously upset over his dismissal from the game.

Asked Christl: "So, what did you think of the call?"

Trebelhorn was flabbergasted. "What did I think of the call? Oh, I thought it was a great call. As a matter of fact, I was thrown out for overcongratulating the umpire."

Trebelhorn now was thoroughly peeved.

"That's an incredible question and I'm not answering any more tonight," he said. "You guys can leave."

Haudricourt couldn't believe it: a one-question press conference. Back he trudged upstairs.

The next night, as they made their way to the Brewers clubhouse, Haudricourt stopped Christl a few steps short of Trebelhorn's office.

"Cliff, can I ask a favor of you?"

"What's that?" Christl said.

"Can I ask the first question tonight?"

The Chicago Cubs were playing the Cardinals at Busch Stadium one day. Pitcher John Denny of the Cardinals wound up, threw and watched in horror as the ball was lined up the middle . . . straight at him. The ball struck Denny flush on the forehead, caromed high in the air and plopped in front of the Cardinals catcher, who alertly whipped the ball to first, almost in time to throw out the stunned runner. To say the least, it was a bizarre, incredible play.

Afterward, reporters, including Brian Hewitt of the *Chicago Sun-Times,* surrounded veteran Cubs manager Herman Franks, a man not given to humor or hyperbole. One of the reporters asked a bit too breathlessly, "Herman, have you ever, in all your years in baseball, seen anything like that play involving Denny?"

Franks spat out a stream of tobacco juice, paused for a moment, as if he actually were considering the question, and said, "Son, I once saw a monkey fucking a camel."

On rare occasions, a baseball writer gets lucky. Bay Area writers sing the praises of Athletics manager Tony LaRussa. Trebelhorn, despite the aforementioned outburst, is considered a friend of the Fourth Estate, St. Louis Cardinals manager Whitey Herzog speaks his mind, as did Davey Johnson of the New York Mets.

But one of the great conversationalists was former Baltimore Orioles manager Earl Weaver, who almost always had something of interest to say. It wasn't always what you wanted to hear, but it was always heartfelt.

On getaway days, the days teams must hurry to catch their charter flights after a game, Weaver would provide Orioles beat writers with "If Quotes." The process went like this: Weaver would meet with the reporters during batting practice and offer comments on the game . . . before it was played.

"OK," Weaver would begin, "whoever gets the game-winning hit, I'll say, 'That's what we pay him to do.' Whoever gets the victory, I'll say, 'That's why we put him on the mound every five days.'" And then he would reverse his comments to cover himself should the Orioles lose. No wonder Baltimore writers were sorry to see Weaver retire.

One of the best Weaver stories involved Michael Janofsky, who was working for the *Baltimore Evening Sun* at the time. Sitting in a restaurant one night, Janofsky noticed Weaver and Weaver's wife eating dinner. Janofsky, who had covered several Orioles games since coming to Baltimore, finished his meal about the same time that Weaver did. After paying his check, Janofsky walked outside and handed the car valet his parking slip. A few moments later, Weaver and his wife walked out of the restaurant.

Figuring this would be a nice time to reintroduce himself to Weaver, Janofsky moved toward the manager and extended his hand. Weaver looked at Janofsky, reached into his pocket, pulled out a ticket stub and said, "It's the white Cadillac."

No word if Janofsky got a hefty tip.

Several of Weaver's players were equally wacky, most notably outfielder John Lowenstein. Approached after a getaway day game by Dan Shaughnessy, then with the *Washington Star,* Lowenstein listened patiently as the writer launched into a complex inquiry about the afternoon's events. Lowenstein, obviously intrigued, began to make his way toward the clubhouse door.

"Look, that's a really good question," he said. "Unfortunately, I don't have an answer for it right now. But if you think of something I might have said, you can quote me."

And then he dashed out the door. Left standing there was Shaughnessy, who never took advantage of the offer, but appreciated the gesture, nonetheless.

There is a knack to covering baseball. Mostly you have to learn the idiosyncrasies of the people you cover. It's a process of trial and error, mostly error. You learn that Mauch hates any questions that feature himself as the subject; that you never ask Bo Jackson about football during baseball season, or vice versa; that Reggie Jackson can turn on you in the blink of an eye; and that it is best not to challenge Cubs manager Don Zimmer to a clash of wills, something Bernie Lincicome of the *Chicago Tribune* will attest to.

Back in 1988, when it became obvious that Frank Lucchesi would not return as the Cubs manager, Lincicome pleaded in a column that under no circumstances should the team hire Zimmer as a replacement. "Don't let Zimmer get his hands on this team," wrote Lincicome.

Naturally this didn't sit well with Zimmer, who, despite Lincicome's advice, was selected as the new Cubs manager. In fact, when Lincicome visited the Cubs clubhouse shortly after the story was published, he was met by the self-appointed

Cubs captain, third baseman Keith Moreland (since traded), a thick-necked, freckle-laden jock who literally grabbed the Chicago columnist by the arm and led him around the room. Moreland, upset that Lincicome had criticized from far, was determined to "introduce" the writer to the various Cubs he had ripped in print.

His voice deep with sarcasm, Moreland shuttled Lincicome from player to player, doing his best to humiliate him in front of the team and media people alike. Lincicome, determined to escape with dignity intact, was friendly enough, saying, "Hello, how are you?" to each player he met. On it went until a puffy, pink, naked man emerged from an adjacent office. It was Zimmer, hand extended, joining in the fun. The ordeal complete, Lincicome was released by Moreland and allowed to leave.

The next spring, Lincicome introduced himself to Zimmer. "You may or may not remember the last time we met," he said. "Maybe we should chat about what I do and what you do."

Zimmer took Lincicome into his office, offered him food and then told him that the thing that bothered him most was a later column that accused him of being thin-skinned.

"I'll show you I have thick skin," said Zimmer, essentially challenging Lincicome to upset him in print.

This was a first: someone giving a columnist license to rip away. On occasion, Lincicome felt it necessary to do just that with the Cubs. But Zimmer, true to his word, never confronted Lincicome again—at least not without the benefit of clothes.

Meanwhile, if you were a Ranger beat writer when Doug Rader managed the team in 1983, you learned that the man could hold a grudge with the best of them. Rader has since adopted a cheerier disposition, but back then he had a temper as hot as a solar panel.

Randy Youngman was covering the team for the *Dallas Times Herald* when the season began to unravel for the

Rangers. Leading the division at the All-Star break, the Rangers slipped badly during the second half of the season.

Rader grew more frustrated with each loss. It showed, too, as he became more difficult to deal with, a fact that Youngman mentioned in the press box one day. Somehow the comment got back to Rader, who confronted Youngman.

"You think I'm inconsistent?" Rader asked.

Youngman said yes and then patiently explained why.

Rader considered the response and then said, "You know, you're right. From now on, I'm going to be more consistent. From now on, I'm going to answer every one of your questions with 'Fuck you.' "

Youngman thought he was kidding until the next postgame press gathering.

"How'd you think your pitcher threw?" asked Youngman.

Rader looked up at Youngman and replied, "Uh, fuck you."

"No, seriously, what'd you think of him?"

"Fuck you."

"No, really."

"Fuck you."

Three days later, after countless Rader expletives, Youngman gave up.

Not long after that incident, Rader revealed another bit of his intense personality. Understand that Rader was raised in baseball's old school, where brushback pitches and the like were considered part of the game. If a pitcher dusted you, you brushed yourself off, got back in the batter's box and did what you could to send the next offering up the middle, preferably hitting the pitcher on its way there.

U. L. Washington was not a member of Rader's graduating class, as evidenced by an incident involving Rader's Rangers and Washington, who played for the Royals. Danny Darwin had just dusted Washington with a fastball high and tight when Washington, rather than return to the batter's box, jumped up and began yelling at the Texas starting pitcher.

Back in the Rangers dugout, Rader was going crazy. He wanted Washington to charge the mound—that way Rader could join the fight and presumably beat the crap out of him. Alas, Washington made no such move.

Afterward, Rader was furious. As Ranger beat writers looked on, Rader crushed a full beer can with his hand. Then he punched a metal door so hard that it quivered on its hinges. His face flushed with anger, Rader wasn't through. He raked his hand through his tiny closet, sending clothes and hangers into the air. A pair of trousers plopped squarely on the head of *Fort Worth Star-Telegram* writer Jim Reeves, who dared not move.

The two-minute tantrum finished, Rader turned to the astonished sportswriters and asked, "Any questions?"

"Yes," said Reeves, "can I take these pants off?"

Of course, Rader isn't the first (or the last) manager to display his temper. Del Crandall occasionally used to pout after losses by his hapless 1984 Seattle Mariners team. One time, after a particularly grating defeat, Crandall stomped into his Kingdome office, stripped off his uniform and stepped into the shower. A few minutes later, Seattle reporters, including then–*Post-Intelligencer* writer Bill Plaschke, entered the office expecting to find Crandall for the usual postgame quotations.

Instead, they found steam. Lots of it. The reporters glanced at each other wondering what to do. They had plenty of time before deadline, so they decided to wait out Crandall.

Five minutes became ten, then fifteen, then twenty, then twenty-five before Crandall turned off the spigot. By then, the tiny room was enveloped in steam. Plaschke looked down at his watch; it was bathed in fog. His shirt was soaked through. His notepad was wilting. And then he heard a voice—it was Crandall.

"Well?" Crandall called out.

Plaschke didn't quite know what to do. He had never interviewed an invisible man before. So he asked a question about the game. Out of the mist came Crandall's reply. Another reporter followed with a question of his own. And so it went until the reporters, clothes wet and hair sopped, walked out of the office and into the clubhouse.

To this day, Plaschke remembers only the faint image of a middle-aged man wrapped in a towel speaking through the fog. Considering the Mariners' plight, it seemed only fitting.

The Mariners have never been a particularly fun team to cover. They play in the country's ugliest domed stadium, they lose lots of games and they're usually out of the pennant race by late June. And even when someone tries to write an optimistic story, the Mariners take it the wrong way. One time they went so far to give *Seattle Times* columnist Steve Kelley the silent treatment.

Kelley had written a story during the 1985 spring training listing all the reasons why people should feel good about the Mariners that year. Included on the list, though, were several negative items, including one about Barry Bonnell, who was earning a remarkable $600,000, or thereabouts. "There should be an investigation," wrote Kelley of Bonnell's playing salary.

Bonnell's wife saw the story and cried her eyes out. Bonnell heard about Kelley's story and, according to the team's public relations man, was thoroughly upset. In fact, the PR man even went so far as to call Kelley and tell him this very thing.

The Mariners concluded their spring training schedule with a game against their Vancouver minor league affiliate. Kelley was there.

Standing near the Mariners as they went through their stretching exercises, Kelley heard then-shortstop Spike Owen say, "There he is," pointing to Kelley, "let's vote."

And so they did, voting not to talk Kelley under any circumstances. Kelley had been blackballed. Worse yet, then-manager Chuck Cottier walked up to Kelley and began screaming at him. "I don't want to have anything to do with somebody who's ripping my players!" said Cottier, nose to nose with Kelley.

"Did you even read the column?" asked Kelley.

"I don't have to read it."

And then he resumed his finger-pointing and posturing. The whole performance resembled something Cottier might have done were he arguing with an umpire over a blown call.

A day or two later, the Mariners played an exhibition game against the University of Washington at the Kingdome. Kelley decided to watch part of the game in a Plexiglas-protected room located not far from home plate. Sitting quietly in the room was Bonnell.

"Hi, Barry," said Kelley.

"Hi," said Bonnell.

Kelley figured Bonnell had cooled down, that time healed all egos. He was wrong. A few weeks later in Oakland, Bonnell, this time surrounded by teammates, saw Kelley on the field and began yelling at him. Strength in numbers and all that.

Kelley's woes continued even after the team returned to Seattle. Kelley and American League umpire Steve Palermo were chatting inside that same Plexiglas-enclosed room when a ball smacked hard against the window. Startled, Kelley and Palermo looked up and saw Owen getting ready to heave another ball.

"I think he's throwing at me," said Palermo.

"Uh, no, they're for me," Kelley said.

This is the same Kelley who wrote that the Mariners, as they were prone to do, botched the free agent draft one year when they didn't take pitcher Ron Darling, one of the more successful pitchers around. A few days after the column appeared, Kelley was in the Mariners clubhouse as the players made their way to a Sunday chapel service. As they filed into the room for this most religious of moments, several Mariners muttered a comment or two to Kelley.

"Asshole."

"Fucker."

"Dick."

Bless you, boys.

As you can see, ballplayers, when they feel betrayed by media types, can develop mean streaks as wide as the power alleys at Yankee Stadium. The Angels' Brian Downing once told me he was tired of seeing his comments misinterpreted in print. He vowed retribution. "And if I can't take care of it verbally," he said, "I'll take care of it physically. I'm not afraid of a lawsuit."

Lots of players say they don't read the sports sections, but I think they do. I think they read every syllable and remember every word. They also take great pleasure, as I suppose is their right, in reminding writers of their supposed mistakes.

For instance, Ray Knight, then with the Cincinnati Reds, took exception to a game story written by Tim Sullivan in 1981. So angry was Knight that he pulled Sullivan into the Reds' equipment room one day. Knight was holding a bat.

Just then, Reds teammate Ken Griffey walked into the room, glanced at the bat and a slightly apprehensive Sullivan and said, "Uh, Ray, you think you need that with him?"

"I don't know," Knight said, breaking into a half-grin, "he might be tougher than that."

Later, Knight lectured Sullivan on the role of baseball writers. "You should be a fan of this team if you're going to cover us," he said. Sullivan explained that it didn't work that way and, to Knight's credit, the third baseman finally acknowledged the difference between boosterism and journalism.

Not everyone is so accommodating. The Minnesota Twins were readying themselves for a season-ending road trip late in 1987 when *Minneapolis Star-Tribune* columnist Dan Barreiro decided to make a point. The Twins were leading the American League West and had a game remaining against the Kansas City Royals at home before leaving for Texas. But they had been playing only so-so baseball, prompting Barreiro to write that Twins fans should be worried about their team entering this final trip. The gist of the column was this: If the Twins were going to blow their chances of a division title, they would do it on the road, where they often struggled.

So, of course, the Twins walloped the Royals. Then they went to Texas where they beat the Rangers to clinch the AL West.

The next day, Barreiro was in the visiting clubhouse at Arlington Stadium talking to the Twins center fielder Kirby Puckett when Dan Gladden, the left fielder, motioned to Barreiro.

"Hey, Barreiro, come over here," Gladden said sweetly, "I've got to talk to you."

Barreiro walked over. "What's up?"

"Well, me and some of the guys got together and wanted to know if you wanted to take BP [batting practice] with us."

"What?"

"Yeah, a little BP . . . shag some balls with us, maybe take some ground balls. We'll get you a uniform, you'll be all set."

Barreiro was suspicious. This wasn't like Gladden—being nice, that is. But perhaps this was a new and improved Gladden. It certainly sounded like it, what with Gladden's soothing tones and ready smile.

Barreiro bit.

"You sure about this?" Barreiro asked.

"Sure, we got a uniform for you. It will be great."

"Nah, I can't," Barreiro said, "it wouldn't be right. Anyway, I don't know how to take BP."

"Oh, really?" said Gladden, his voice growing angry. "From the sound of it, I thought you knew *everything* about this fucking game!"

Other Twins began smirking. This had been planned and played to perfection. Barreiro had been set up.

"Hey, it's everybody's dream to be a big league ballplayer," Gladden said.

"It's not my dream," said Barreiro, trying to laugh the whole thing off.

"You know, Barreiro, you jump off the bandwagon and then you jump back on. Make up your mind."

"What do you want me to do? You guys kicked the hell out of those guys and I said so."

Gladden wasn't appeased and waved Barreiro away.

Still, as predictable as Gladden's prank was, it did have a sense of style to it, meaning that it worked. Gladden is no class clown, but a former teammate of his, Bert Blyleven, has a hard-earned reputation as a master practical joker. One of Blyleven's favorite gags is to tape a fishing line to, say, a ten-dollar bill, place it on the airport terminal floor and then go sit down. When someone reaches down to grab the bill, Blyleven tugs the fishing line. What you are left with is a person, bent over like Groucho Marx, grasping desperately for a bill that never will be his.

Blyleven also became famous for his spring training sandwich gag, in which Angels players found an official-looking list in their Mesa, Arizona, clubhouse asking them to place their steak sandwich orders for the long bus ride to Yuma, Arizona. Of course, Blyleven's name was at the top of the list, requesting two sandwiches—medium well or such—with mayonnaise and mustard.

Soon other players signed up as word spread around the clubhouse that thick, luscious steak sandwiches would be served during the long drive to Yuma.

Halfway to Yuma, players began asking Frank Sims, the Angels traveling secretary, when they might expect their meals. They were hungry and after all, a promise was a promise. Of course, Sims didn't have the foggiest idea what they were talking about.

"The steak sandwiches, Frank," the players said, "where are they?"

"There aren't any damn steak sandwiches."

"But what about the list?"

"What list?"

That's when it hit them: Blyleven.

It was during that same 1989 season, recalled Mike Penner, that Blyleven was waiting to board the Angel's charter bound from Boston to Milwaukee and discovered that his carry-on was gone. Blyleven, no dummy, suspected foul play. He wasn't disappointed as the bag reappeared several minutes later, but this time with a live lobster inside it.

Blyleven named the crustacean "Skippy" and took it with him on the flight. Occasionally, he would take Skippy from a small bucket of water and perch the lobster on his shoulder. Skippy, naturally, wasn't pleased. So during the bus ride from the Milwaukee airport to a downtown hotel, Skippy began snapping away at Blyleven.

Alas, Skippy eventually died a hero's death, causing manager Doug Rader to deliver a heartfelt eulogy the day after the lobster's demise.

"Let's win one for Skippy," he said. "We're going to bury him at sea, I think. First, though, he'll be cremated in drawn butter, then buried at sea."

Oddly enough, the Angels won the game. Then again, Skippy would have wanted it that way.

And Blyleven would have loved to have tormented Rufino Linares, a quirky Dominican who liked to fib about his age while with the Atlanta Braves. One year he said he was thirty-five, the next he said he was thirty-three.

Linares also had different culinary tastes, as evidenced by the time he approached sportswriter Gerry Fraley near the batting cage at Dodger Stadium.

"You should visit me in the Dominican Republic," Linares said. "If you come, I have my mother make my favorite food for you."

"Oh, yeah? What's that?" Fraley said.

"Gato."

"Is that so? What sort of dish is gato?"

"Gato is cat."

Fraley nearly gagged. "Sure, Rufino, I'll make my reservations right now."

After the Los Angeles series was complete, the Braves were taken to the airport, where they waited to board a short flight up the coast to San Francisco. As the players and Fraley milled about, a stewardess arrived carrying a small cage used for transporting animals. Inside it was a cat.

Linares saw the feline and immediately ran over to Fraley.

"You got them to serve me gato!" he said excitedly. "Thank you, thank you."

Fraley, who never told him that the cat was someone's pet, not an in-flight meal, savored Linares's words. Imagine that: a ballplayer telling a writer thank you.

3

That's No Deli,
That's Eric Dickerson

$\mathbf{F}$ive reasons why the National Football League will always occupy a special place in my heart:

1. Chicago Bears coach Mike Ditka.

Ditka was on a 1987 conference call with Los Angeles writers when someone asked if he had heard about the near-tragic restaurant incident involving former Bears assistant/nemesis and now Philadelphia Eagles coach Buddy Ryan. Ryan, it seems, almost had choked to death on a piece of pork chop before someone dislodged the meat with the Heimlich Maneuver.

Said the compassionate Ditka, who owns a successful restaurant in Chicago: "It must not have been a Ditka pork chop. A Ditka pork chop melts in your mouth."

Is it any wonder that when Ditka was sidelined with a heart attack during the 1988 season that Bears beat reporters sent a huge arrangement of balloons to his house?

2. Former Dallas Cowboys coach Tom Landry.

The 1988 Cowboys were a terrible team, as evidenced by

their 3-13 record. With this in mind, my editors sent me to
Dallas in December to chronicle the many troubles of this
once-proud franchise and its legendary coach, Landry.

After several phone calls to the Cowboys public relations
department, a meeting with Landry was arranged. "But try to
be brief," I was told, "Coach Landry is pretty busy these days."

"Of course," I assured them.

Hey, I'm a nice guy. I knew Landry was trying to turn a
team around and also stave off the growing criticism from the
locals. Brief? Ten minutes, tops.

Finally, it was time. As I walked toward his office, I expected to see an exhausted Landry, his eyes bleary from
watching ten straight hours of game film, his stomach churning from who-knows-how-many pots of industrial-strength
coffee. No doubt he would be hunched over diagrams or
scouting reports, his every thought directed at reversing an
embarrassing losing streak.

Here's who greeted me: a perfectly rested and charming
Landry, who seemed as if he didn't have a worry in the
world. And by the way, he wasn't poring over any game
plans, either. Instead, he was busy signing Christmas cards.

The way I figure it, you've got to like a guy who keeps
things in perspective.

3. Rams place-kicker Mike Lansford.

Don Seeholzer of the *Orange County Register* was walking
by a darkened Los Angeles Rams meeting room and noticed
Lansford and assistant coach Artie Gigantino inside. A television monitor was on, so Seeholzer figured that they were
watching videotapes of recent kickoff coverages or field goal
attempts.

Seeholzer cautiously stuck his head in the room. They were
watching *The Three Stooges.*

4. Indianapolis Colts coach Ron Meyer.

On his first day of work as a *Dallas Morning News* reporter, Tim Kurkjian was told to contact Ron Meyer on the phone. "Ron who?" said Kurkjian, who didn't know Ron Meyer from Oscar Mayer.

Meyer was the Southern Methodist University head coach at the time and rumor had it that he had just interviewed for the vacant New England Patriots coaching position. With the regular NFL writer unavailable, Kurkjian was assigned the story.

So Kurkjian called Meyer's house at least thirty times. Busy signal.

"Tim, you've got to go out to his house," said his editors.

Kurkjian could barely remember how to get to his own house, much less Meyer's house.

"I'm leaving right now," he said.

What you need to remember is that Kurkjian isn't an especially tall person, perhaps five-foot-six or so. He also has one of those boyish faces, the kind that never seem to age. But not even Kurkjian could have predicted the series of events that followed.

He rang the bell and after he had waited several moments in the cold winter air, Meyer, attired in a red velvet robe, opened the door.

"Yes?" Meyer said.

"Coach," Kurkjian said nervously. "I'm Tim Kurkjian with the *Dallas Morning News* and . . ."

Meyer stopped him in midsentence. "Son, what are you doing, collecting?"

Kurkjian didn't know if he should laugh or cry. Instead, he bowed his head and said, "No, Coach, I'm a reporter."

Meyer rolled his eyes. "C'mon inside. It's cold out there."

Two other men already were seated in Meyer's living room when he stepped in. Not knowing any better, Kurkjian thought they were Meyer's neighbors. Turns out that they were SMU assistant coaches.

"What do you need?" Meyer said.

"Well, Coach, have you been to New England to interview with the Patriots?"

"No."

And that was that. Kurkjian returned to his car, got lost trying to find his own apartment, called his editor and told him about the brief interview. Twenty minutes later, Kurkjian's phone rang. It was Meyer.

"Tim, I just wanted you to know that a reporter from the *Dallas Times Herald* just came by and I told him that I did interview with the Patriots."

"But you told me you hadn't."

"Well, you asked me if I had gone to New England for the interview. I didn't; I went to New York. I just didn't want you to get in trouble, that's all."

Kurkjian thanked him and as they ended the conversation he said, "It figures. I finally find your house and now you're moving."

5. Former San Diego Chargers quarterback Jim McMahon. A reporter once asked McMahon, "Are you in pain?"

"Only when I look at you," McMahon said.

Ladies and gentlemen, this is the NFL I love: weird, nutty, mesmerizing.

I'll admit it: I'm a child of the NFL, as are many of us who cover the league these days. We grew up watching the Packers' power sweep, Joe Namath's gaudy guarantee of a Super Bowl victory, the Miami Dolphins' undefeated season, Franco Harris's "Immaculate Reception" and Roger Staubach's scrambles. We lived for NFL Films and the Battle of Guadalcanal voice of narrator John Facenda, who could make an offsides penalty sound as foreboding as a visit by the Grim Reaper. He was especially grave during Green Bay Packers highlights.

"Most men would have gone for the field goal," he would begin, "but not LOM-BAR-DI."

Ooooh, I still get goose bumps. God should have such a voice.

In recent years, we've seen Pete Rozelle develop jowls, John Riggins wear combat fatigues, McMahon become the biggest cult hero since Elvira, Bill Walsh be deemed a genius (and not deny it), Bo Jackson flatten a flat top (Brian Bosworth), Eric Dickerson run and run and run, and Joe Montana ensure himself a place in the Hall of Fame. As journeys go, you can't beat it.

But I'm worried about the league. For starters, it doesn't seem as much fun anymore. Can't imagine why. Between strikes, steroids, substance abuse, salary holdouts and legal suits, it's a miracle the game persists. I think I liked it a lot better when Namath was around.

One guy who needs to lighten up is Washington Redskins coach Joe Gibbs, a workaholic who thinks everyone puts in ninety-hour weeks. Gibbs regularly sleeps at his office during the season and, well, sort of loses touch with the rest of Earth.

Back in 1986, after one of his legendary work sessions, Gibbs emerged from his office to meet the press. Among the reporters that day was Vito Stellino of the *Baltimore Morning Sun.*

"So, what's going on in the world?" said Gibbs.

"Well, have you heard of Ollie North? He's been in all the papers," Stellino said.

"Who's that?" Gibbs said.

Gibbs didn't know a contra from a contract. And he certainly didn't know who Oliver North was. The next year, however, after the Redskins won the Super Bowl, Gibbs invited a special guest to the team's practice facilities. That's right, Ollie North.

Gibbs still isn't exactly Mr. World Affairs. Once, after it became apparent that Gibbs and former Redskins backup quarterback Jay Schroeder weren't getting along, a writer compared their difficulties to those of Madonna and Sean

Penn. Again, Gibbs was clueless about Madonna's and Penn's identities.

"Is this another Ollie North?" he asked, laughing.

Gibbs isn't alone. Writers, too, are affected by the somberness that sometimes envelops the league. After all, they have to cover the strikes, steroid controversies, substance abuse updates and so forth. It tends to ruin your perspective.

T. J. Simers, then with the *Rocky Mountain News,* used to arrange to have the Denver Broncos assign him a training camp dorm room directly above or below that of the *Denver Post,* his paper's competition. He did this after discovering that he could hear the *Post*'s reporters discuss their daily story ideas and scoops through the air vents. It was a rotten trick, but it worked.

Bob McGinn, Packers beat reporter for the *Green Bay Press-Gazette,* makes it a habit to attend all team practice sessions, no matter how cold it gets. He figures that one, it lessens his chances of getting beat on a story and two, it shows the players and coaches that he's serious about covering the team.

Let me add another item, three: It increases his chances of contracting frostbite.

McGinn learned quickly that he had better dress warmly for those December practice sessions. He wears three pairs of socks, a pair of long johns, an insulated t-shirt, a football jersey, a sweatshirt (with the hood up), a pair of heavy pants, a parka (with the hood up) and a pair of heavily insulated boots. And still he shivers.

A few other rules of thumb: You can't use a tape recorder in these outdoor interviews because the wind howls too loud. Also, you can't take notes with a pen after the first fifteen minutes or so. Why? Because the ink freezes.

Leigh Montville, then with the *Boston Globe,* probably had the right attitude when he used to cover the New England Patriots. Told by his boss to pick the NFL winners each week, Montville made light of the whole process. Rather than check the pass-conversion ratios or how the guards blocked down, Montville simply went for the laugh.

Each weekend he would pick the Patriots, who had an awful team at the time, to lose by lopsided scores: 55–3, 42–6, 38–0 and so forth. This was fine until he had to board the team's charter flight one day, where it seemed that every Patriots player had been issued a copy of the predictions. Needless to say, no one shared Montville's light-hearted sentiments.

Then it happened. The Patriots somehow staged a brilliant 20–6 upset of the heavily favored Oakland Raiders in the 1971 season opener. Montville, of course, had predicted another embarrassing New England loss.

As he walked into the Patriots locker room that afternoon, Montville expected a rude greeting. A few players would call him names, he figured. Someone probably would throw a jock strap at him. The threat of violence crossed his mind.

Instead, he found about a dozen players huddled around a flame. Standing in the middle of the circle was linebacker Will Foster, who held the burning remnants of Montville's most recent *Boston Globe* predictions in hand. Even Montville had to smile as the ashes settled to the floor.

As you might expect, there occasionally is an Us versus Them mentality in pro football, where coaches and players tend to use the media as convenient psychological tools or scapegoats for anything that goes awry. Just ask Dan Barreiro of the *Minneapolis Star-Tribune,* who had the misfortune of angering the 1987 Minnesota Vikings with a critical column.

Barreiro observed that perhaps the Vikings, losers of three of their last four regular-season games, didn't deserve to be in the playoffs that year. After all, it had taken an unlikely victory by the Dallas Cowboys over the St. Louis Cardinals during the final weekend to assure the Vikings of a postseason position. Then Barreiro predicted that the Vikings' first-round opponent, the New Orleans Saints, would thrash the struggling Minnesota team.

Final score: Saints 10, Vikings 44.

"Where's that Barrio?" yelled linebacker Scott Studwell during the postgame celebration. "Where's Barrio?"

Then he spotted the writer. "Hey, Barrio, take that notebook and shove it up your ass!"

Barreiro, undoubtedly touched by the suggestion, did no such thing. In fact, the following week he picked the San Francisco 49ers to defeat the Vikings. "It won't even be close," he wrote.

Final score: 49ers 24, Vikings 36.

Again Barreiro ventured into the postgame mayhem. This time he approached offensive guard David Huffman, a pleasant sort from Notre Dame. As he did so, Barreiro noticed several of the other offensive linemen encircling him. This was not a good sign.

Suddenly he found himself held by at least three, maybe four behemoths. Huffman had a roll of thick athletic tape and an evil look in his eye. Barreiro, by all indications, was about to become a mummy.

"Dan," said Huffman, "this is a little initiation rite we have for you here. Maybe sooner or later you'll start believing in this team."

Barreiro felt his legs squeezed together, the better for taping. "Now do you believe? Now do you believe?" Huffman kept repeating.

Interestingly enough, not another writer came to Barreiro's aid. It wasn't until Huffman noticed that the tape might ruin Barreiro's new suede jacket that the players let go of the columnist. Later, a colleague claimed that Studwell actually had engineered Barreiro's release. What a joke, considering that Studwell used to own a photograph of someone mooning the camera. Written across one of the cheeks was the word "Barreiro."

By the way, the following week Barreiro picked the Washington Redskins to beat the Vikings.

Final score: Redskins 17, Vikings 10.

At last.

Lynne Snierson, then with the *Boston Herald*, was sitting at her desk one day when the phone rang. On the line was New England Patriots tight end Derrick Ramsey, who was livid about a story done on him by Charles Pierce, who was filling in for Snierson the day before.

"I'm going to fucking sue!" screamed Ramsey. "I called my agent. I'm going to own that paper of yours. Who is this Charles Pierce? Why is he writing those things about me? He doesn't even know me."

Snierson had read the story and found it harmless enough, even complimentary toward Ramsey.

"Derrick, why are you so upset?" she said. "What parts are you objecting to?"

"Uh, I don't know, I didn't read the story," he said sheepishly. "A lot of my teammates are giving me a bunch of shit about it."

"Derrick, would you like me to read the story to you?" Snierson said.

"Yeah."

So she did, paragraph by paragraph. When she had finished, Ramsey said, "Hmmm, that's a pretty nice story, actually. Never mind."

One of the more entertaining players in the league is Eric Dickerson, who was traded to the Indianapolis Colts by the Los Angeles Rams in 1987. Dickerson's talent is unparalleled, his sense of humor is often refreshing, his confidence is staggering and his opinions are almost always straightforward. But like a lot of players, he doesn't fully understand the role of a beat reporter.

Dickerson and the Rams traveled to New Orleans for a game against the Saints in 1986. The Rams lost, 6–0, and Dickerson took a beating. Afterward, he declined to speak (a first) to the assembled writers and instead hightailed it toward the team bus parked on the other side of the Superdome. It was his best run of the day.

In hot pursuit was *Los Angeles Times* reporter Chris Dufresne, who finally caught up to Dickerson in time to ask about the silent treatment.

"I'm exhausted," Dickerson explained.

"That's fine," said Dufresne, backing off.

But then Dufresne saw Dickerson approach three young women near one of the end zones. Dickerson looked anything but tired as he chatted away. So Dufresne tried once more to squeeze a quotation out of the elusive halfback.

"I see you're talking now, Eric," Dufresne said. "Maybe you're more rested now."

"Nah, I'm exhausted," said Dickerson, pleasantly enough.

"But, Eric, you're the one people are interested in. They want to know what you have to say."

"I'm too tired."

"You're tired after every game and you still talk. [Quarterback] Steve Dils has six stitches in his chin and he talked today."

"No, man, I'm too tired to talk."

With that, Dufresne gave up.

Three days later, while walking out of the Rams' lunch room, Dickerson noticed Dufresne standing outside the nearby media work room and rushed toward him. In Dickerson's hand was a plate of food, including a half-eaten tuna fish sandwich. Dufresne hardly had time to ready himself for the confrontation.

"Who the fuck are you?" Dickerson said, his face inches away from Dufresne's. "Who the motherfuck are you? When I tell you I am tired, I'm tired, motherfucker."

It wasn't the profanity that bothered Dufresne so much as the tuna. Little pieces of seafood were flying from Dickerson's mouth onto Dufresne's face and there wasn't much Dufresne could do about it.

"Eric, you're the star of this team," he said. "When you don't talk, it's my job to find out why."

"I was tired, motherfucker," Dickerson said, spraying more mayonnaise and tuna on the writer's face.

By now, the two were almost nose to nose. As Dickerson continued the tirade, one thought swept through Dufresne's mind: "Please, God, let him hit me so I can retire."

Dickerson never raised a fist, but he did boycott Dufresne for a week.

Not long after the tuna incident, Dufresne was told by his editors to call Dickerson about allegations of wrongdoing at Southern Methodist University, Dickerson's former school. The phone rang and Dickerson answered.

"Eric, this is Chris Dufresne from the *Times* and I was wondering—"

"Where'd you get my number?" Dickerson asked.

"I got it from someone on the Rams."

"I'm not going to talk to you until you tell me where you got this number."

"From the Rams, Eric."

"I'm going to have to call those boys down there."

"But, Eric, about SMU . . ."

Dial tone.

Dufresne and Dickerson didn't speak much until a few months later, when Dickerson was served with paternity suit papers. A representative of Dickerson called Dufresne one day at the office and asked if he might have a few moments to speak with Eric. Sure, said Dufresne.

"How are you doing, Chris?" Dickerson said politely.

Dufresne said he was doing fine.

Dickerson then went on to calmly explain the circumstances of the paternity suit and at the end of the conversation he said, "I wish people would call me more often for my side of the story."

Dufresne was dumbfounded. "Eric, every time I call, you get pissed off."

There was a pause and then, "That's right," Dickerson said. "As a matter of fact, I will change my number tomorrow."

Click.

Denver Broncos coach Dan Reeves and T. J. Simers used

to have similar exchanges. The most heated argument came after Simers noticed Reeves's son selling preseason tickets outside Mile High Stadium one evening. Simers immediately contacted the Broncos' public relations man and told him to tell Reeves about his son's blunder.

Reeves responded with a message of his own: He had told his son to try to sell the tickets.

Simers found this incredible and wrote a sarcastic story saying so. The next day, while Simers was talking to linebacker Tom Jackson at the Broncos' practice facilities, Reeves stormed toward him.

"I want to see you."

They walked through a short corridor and outside to the players' parking lot. It was there that Reeves turned and stuck a finger in Simers's face.

"Don't you ever write about my family again!"

"Then don't you be so goddamned stupid as to put your kid out on the streets selling tickets!"

Reeves explained that he was doing the public a favor by offering the tickets. Most games were sellouts; this way someone who might not normally get to see the Broncos would be able to.

"Why don't you just give the tickets back to the team?" Simers said.

"We can't," Reeves said.

Back and forth they went until Simers eventually apologized. This done, Reeves opened the door, only to find a handful of players huddled nearby. They had been listening to the whole thing, but scattered as soon as Reeves entered the corridor.

Simers did exact a small measure of revenge on Reeves. Paired with Reeves in an off-season golf tournament, Simers began to chide Reeves, a likeable but incredibly competitive person, about his swing. Everything was fine until the fourth hole, when Reeves yanked two consecutive shots out of bounds.

"Dan," said Simers, "you play golf like you coach—horseshit."

"OK, let's bet on each hole," said Reeves.

So they did and by the eighteenth hole, Simers was up thirteen dollars. To Reeves, it might as well have been thirteen thousand dollars. Reeves hated to lose. When he played for the Dallas Cowboys, Reeves made a tidy sum beating teammates at darts or Ping Pong or whatever silly tricks he could invent. One of his favorites was to somehow propel a quarter into a glass of water with his mouth. I know it doesn't sound like much, but years later, at an AFC West coaches conference, I saw Reeves get on his knees, place his mouth near the coin and send it into a tall glass of water. It was amazing. It also earned him a few bucks from us doubters.

As Reeves and Simers approached the final hole that day, Reeves started to complain.

The greens were in awful shape, he moaned. The wind was too fierce. The sun was in his eyes. So upset was Reeves that when he completed play he heaved his ball toward another fairway and stormed off the course.

"Hey, wait a minute," said Simers as Reeves disappeared. "You owe me money."

Too late. Reeves was gone.

So Simers went to the club pro. "When you see Dan, please give this note to him."

It read: "Pay up or read about it."

Reeves stopped by Simers's hotel that night to pay up.

Despite their occasional outbursts, Studwell, Dickerson and Reeves are tame compared to some of the other bullies who have taken exception to the written word. Jets quarterback Richard Todd once grabbed *New York Post* reporter Steve Serby by the throat and slammed him into a locker stall. Serby blacked out and was taken to a nearby hospital, but later recovered.

The horrible offense: Serby had written that Todd would never lead the Jets to a Super Bowl.

In the next day's edition of the *Post* was a photograph of the injured Serby and a headline for the ages: "Todd Assaults Our Man."

Two days later, Serby walked out to his car and found one of his tires slashed. Coincidence, or the actions of readers who supported Todd? Not long after that, two thugs threatened to "get" Serby. Serby, like any good New Yorker, went out and bought himself a metal night stick. Such was life on the Jets beat.

And pity *Houston Post* columnist Dale Robertson, who last year celebrated the tenth anniversary of one of the greatest sportswriter-player fights of all time.

Robertson was covering the Oilers in 1979 and noticed that quarterback Dan Pastorini was having difficulty throwing the ball. He asked about it and was told Pastorini merely had a sore arm. Later, when it became obvious that Pastorini wasn't throwing as often, the coaches said they simply wanted to work on the running game.

Robertson knew something was wrong and ventured a guess in print that Pastorini's career was over or that he was suffering from an unspecified injury. Naturally, Pastorini was outraged.

"You're hurting the team, you're hurting me," he told Robertson after an exhibition game. "Why are you doing this?"

Turned out that Pastorini had been playing with a nerve ailment in his throwing shoulder. It showed, too, as he struggled through the early part of the schedule, enough so that tight end Mike Barber complained openly about the lack of offense. Robertson asked Pastorini for a reaction to Barber's remarks.

"I don't care a goddamn what Mike Barber says," said Pastorini.

"Then no comment?" said Robertson.

"That's fucking right," Pastorini said.

Robertson and Pastorini didn't talk again until midseason.

This time Robertson was sitting on the Oilers' charter flight when Pastorini stormed down the aisle with a sports section in his hand. In the section was an analysis by Robertson comparing Pastorini and Miami Dolphins quarterback Bob Griese. Neither quarterback was having a banner year.

"Stick this up your ass sideways," said Pastorini, as he threw the paper at Robertson.

The Oilers managed to advance to the playoffs, where they beat the Denver Broncos in a wild card game, but in doing so, lost the services of Pastorini, who was injured in the contest. The next week they beat the San Diego Chargers to advance to the AFC Championship Game. The question, of course, was whether Pastorini would be able to play by then.

Robertson wrote a story concerning Pastorini's chances and, as had become the custom, Pastorini was miffed.

"I don't ever want to see my name mentioned in your newspaper again," Pastorini demanded. "If you do it again, I'll kick your ass all over the place."

Robertson had had enough. He was sick of Pastorini's threats and decided to tell him so. He followed Pastorini to the interview room and there, in front of television cameras and reporters, began yelling back at the quarterback.

Profanity filled the room. Insults were traded, threats made. Just outside the trailer were coach Bum Phillips and then–*Pittsburgh Press* reporter John Clayton. As fate would have it, Clayton had just asked Phillips about media relations.

"Well," said Phillips in his Texas twang, "we've got the best media right here. We ain't never had a problem with the media . . ."

At that precise moment, Robertson came flying out of the trailer door and landed at Clayton's feet with a thud. Clayton, his eyes the size of saucers, looked at Phillips, who pawed at the ground with his cowboy boots and said, "Except for this."

Pastorini wasn't through. He threatened to kill Robertson if Robertson dared to call him names again. Of course, it was OK if Pastorini called Robertson names.

Nearby was running back Earl Campbell, who sauntered over to the scene and said, "Hey, man, what you and Dan jamming about?"

The whole wild exchange jammed its way onto the nightly newscasts. One of the local sports anchors called for Robertson's dismissal. Another, dressed in a powder-blue Oilers hat, accused Robertson of trying to ruin the Houston team. No boosterism there. The same anchor asked his viewers to call the *Post* "and let them know what you think."

There were two thousand phone calls in the next ninety minutes. About one hundred of them were death or bomb threats. Not surprisingly, Robertson was given a police escort home.

Meanwhile, a gentleman from a nearby town called the *Post*. He was perplexed because his phone kept ringing. "Excuse me," he said. "I'm not really a sports fan. Can somebody tell me what's going on? All these people want to kill me."

His name: Dale Robertson. Another one.

Robertson covered the AFC Championship Game in Pittsburgh that weekend. When he arrived at his hotel, a local television crew was waiting. Even more embarrassing was the moment when the hotel desk clerk asked to shake his hand and pose for a photograph. In short, Robertson was a hero in Steel City.

Things were so nuts that a press conference was scheduled just so other reporters could interview Robertson. And two days later, on game day, fans began chanting, "Robertson, Robertson, Robertson," as he walked through the press gate.

The Oilers lost the game and about three months later Robertson broke a story saying that Pastorini would be traded for Ken Stabler. Told of the report, Phillips said, "People like [Robertson] should be put in jail."

Two days later, the trade was made.

"I should be put in jail, huh?" Robertson asked Phillips at the press conference officially announcing the trade.

Phillips smiled and spit a line of tobacco juice. "Yeah, but how'd you like the way it turned out?"

One last story about those wacky Oilers.

In 1986, while training at San Angelo State, Oilers running back Mike Rozier happened to meet a man who owned a leopard. Don't ask how. Anyway, Rozier convinced the man to bring it to the campus dormitory where the players, coaches and reporters were housed. Reporters were on the fifth floor, rookies and free agents on the fourth floor, veterans on the third and second floors.

Every night, just before dinner was served, the players made their way out to the television lounges located near each floor's elevator. There they would relax before heading down for supper.

On this evening, the elevator door to the fourth floor silently opened, revealing one ferocious-looking leopard. The leopard, named Cowboy, crept out of the metal compartment and toward the unsuspecting rookies. For effect, he then unleashed a little roar.

Screams filled the air as players scrambled over each other to reach the safety of their rooms. It was a mad, horrific rush as they sprinted down the hallways in blind fear. And then Cowboy was gone, magically whisked inside the elevator for a trip to another floor.

Among those covering the Oilers that year was John McClain of the *Houston Chronicle.* McClain was in his room writing a story when his phone rang. It was David Chapin of the *San Antonio Light.*

"John, you've got to come down here," Chapin said excitedly. "There's a leopard in the dorm and he's scaring the shit out of the players."

"A what?"

"A leopard."

"I'll be right there."

McClain and Chapin arrived downstairs only to find the leopard standing calmly next to its owner and a smiling Rozier. The leopard, Rozier happily informed the terrified rookies, had no teeth or claws. It was as tame as a house cat.

This disclosed, McClain and Chapin returned to their rooms, dictated a short story about the leopard's run through the dorm, and then made another trip downstairs. They wanted to pet Cowboy.

I can think of many sportswriters who wouldn't mind having a leopard available for retribution duties. You could sic it on the knucklehead of your choice, including those football types who feel it is their inalienable right to use scare tactics on anybody carrying a notepad. Ol' Cowboy would be busy for months.

My first nominee would be 49ers owner Eddie DeBartolo, Jr., who once confronted *San Francisco Chronicle* writer Ira Miller after Miller correctly chose the Chicago Bears to beat the 49ers. Yelled DeBartolo: "It's my team. If you're going to cover the team, you should pick them." Then, as a pleasant aside, DeBartolo added, "I can kick your ass."

This wasn't the first time little Eddie had tried to power play with a writer. Displeased with Miller's coverage of the 49ers in 1977 (DeBartolo's first year of ownership), little Eddie resorted to dubious tactics.

"Is it your job to keep people from coming to our games?" asked DeBartolo of Miller in the team hotel the morning of a game.

No, said Miller, but it was his job to detail the troubles of a struggling team.

"Well, it's my team," DeBartolo said. "I don't like that and I can keep you away."

Miller is still on the 49ers beat. So take that, Eddie.

Next up would be Cincinnati Bengals coach Sam Wyche, who suffered some sort of stupidity seizure after a 1986 game against the Broncos at Mile High Stadium. Witnesses to the bizarre scene, including then–*Cincinnati Post* columnist Jay Mariotti, still can't believe what they saw.

The Bengals had just lost the game in the closing moments and Wyche, who is well known for his temper, was ready to pop a neck vein. He stormed out of the Bengals locker room by slamming open the door. Along the way to the interview room, he kicked a chair, nearly sending it into Denver columnist Dick Connor. This was a man in a bad mood.

Standing at the back of the room was Mariotti, who was consulting another *Post* reporter about story assignments. As Wyche took his place at a makeshift podium, Mariotti glanced up.

"Hey" barked Wyche, "wipe that smile off your face, asshole!"

Mariotti, who hadn't been smiling in the first place, stared straight ahead. This was a press conference where you needed a chainsaw to cut through the tension.

"Somebody ask a question, damnit!" Wyche said.

So somebody did. A radio reporter, who normally did metro traffic for one of the local stations, offered this inquiry:

"OK, Coach, why did you kick the door?"

Wyche went nuts. He grabbed the reporter by the neck and demanded he be escorted out of the room. Wyche took the small sponge covering atop the reporter's microphone and threw it at the terrified man. And somehow, in the fray, the reporter's face was grazed by a Wyche backhand.

A Denver policeman calmed things down and Wyche retreated to the locker room. Not far away was Bengals owner Paul Brown, who almost keeled over while watching the unsightly exhibition.

Wyche later said he didn't really remember much about the incident. The next day, as a peace offering, he and his wife sent the radio reporter a stuffed teddy bear and a note of apology. The reporter, who declined to sue, said he countered with just one request: He wanted a seat at the Super Bowl . . . in Paul Brown's private box.

No doubt he's still waiting.

And what about former Philadelphia Eagles place-kicker Tony Franklin, who held a grudge against *Delaware County Daily Times* reporter Bill Brown.

Brown was covering the Eagles in 1983 and, for whatever reason, didn't hit it off with Franklin. Eventually, Franklin got so mad at Brown that he announced in front of the entire team that he wanted to slit Brown's neck "and shit down it." Tony was rather graphic that way.

As Franklin said this, Brown took notes, which upset the kicker even more. Frustrated, Franklin walked away. Meanwhile, several Eagles players approached Brown and patted him on the back. Franklin, it seemed, wasn't well loved by many of his 1983 teammates.

What may have started the whole thing was a training camp incident that began as a practical joke and evolved into much more. Jere Longman of the *Philadelphia Inquirer* had kiddingly mentioned to Franklin one day that Brown thought place-kicking was easy. Franklin confronted Brown after that morning's practice.

"All right, wiseguy, if this is so easy, let's see you kick them without anybody in front of you," Franklin said.

Brown didn't bat an eye. "I can kick right- and left-footed from the forty-yard line in," he said.

"You're on," Franklin said.

As Franklin, several trainers and the rest of the Eagles beat writers watched, Brown started kicking. He made every left-footed kick except one. And much to Franklin's surprise, every swing of Brown's right leg produced a field goal over including a final forty-yarder that just squirted, the cross bar.

"We call those leather suppositories," said Franklin, suggesting the kick wouldn't have cleared the center's behind.

Brown called it something else: sweet revenge.

Tiny victories like this are few and far between. More times than not, the sportswriter gets the worst of any exchange involving a player or coach.

Back in 1978, John Clayton reported that the Steelers were practicing in full pads before league rules allowed them to. The infraction later cost the Steelers a third-round draft pick.

Steelers coach Chuck Noll was livid. He called Clayton part of the criminal element in writing, accused him of spying for the Raiders organization and referred to him as part of the new breed of sportswriters. And he didn't mean it in a nice way. Noll didn't acknowledge Clayton's presence for an entire year.

Clayton also managed to upset famed Steelers wide receiver Lynn Swann one season. Swann, who had a reputation of hamming it up for the television cameras, but providing only minimal help to writers, was ripped by quarterback Terry Bradshaw after a game. Bradshaw questioned Swann's commitment to the team. Of course, Clayton printed the remarks.

The next day in the locker room, Swann was all over Clayton.

"I'll never talk to you again, motherfucker," he said. "You had no permission to put that in the paper unless you went through me."

Slightly unnerved, Clayton began to make his way out of the locker room when reserve quarterback Cliff Stoudt stopped him. "Heard you had a problem with Swanny," he said, smiling. And then he patted Clayton on the back.

Receiver John Stallworth came over and started to giggle. Then, in full sight of Swann, tight end Bennie Cunningham motioned to Clayton.

"How you doing?" he said sweetly and loud enough for Swann to hear. "How's your family?"

In their own way, the players were sticking up for Clayton.

Even though I'd rather cover the NFL than baseball any day, there is a certain element of danger. I mean, these are people who usually can do what they threaten. If, for example, a 230-pound linebacker tells me to leave him alone or he'll gnaw my earlobes off, I believe him. If a six-foot-eight defensive end mentions that he served time, I remember such things. And if former bad boy Conrad Dobler, the dirtiest player ever to slip on a uniform and a pair of brass knuckles, tells me not to print something, I do what Tim Rosaforte, then with the *Fort Lauderdale News/Sun-Sentinel,* did: print it.

Rosaforte was covering a Miami Dolphins–Buffalo Bills game in 1981 when Dobler, an offensive lineman, was flagged for a crucial penalty that killed a Bills drive and probably cost them a chance of winning the game. Afterward, Rosaforte and several other reporters asked Dobler about the call.

Dobler snapped. Among other things, he wished the very worst for the official and his immediate family. The reporters jotted away.

Realizing his indiscretion, Dobler grabbed the notepad out of Rosaforte's hands, ripped the sheets out, crumpled them in a ball and threw them down on the wet locker room floor.

"Don't print that," ordered Dobler before retiring to the shower.

Rosaforte looked up in time to see his two competitors leave the room, their notebooks intact. He tried to reconstruct Dobler's statements, but he couldn't: too nervous. He would need those notes.

After walking around the locker room several times, he noticed Dobler safely in the bathroom, shaving. Rosaforte went back to Dobler's locker stall, where he spied the soggy sheets of paper underneath a bench. Just as he leaned down to retrieve them, an equipment man swept them up with a broom. Desperate, Rosaforte grabbed them from the pile, turned to see if Dobler was near and ran. He had made it.

Not quite. Upon reaching his seat in the press box, Rosaforte noticed that his precious notes, written with a felt-tip pen, were totally illegible. And so it goes.

Dave Lagarde, who covered the 1985 New Orleans Saints for the *Times-Picayune*, was gathering quotations in the team's Superdome locker room one Sunday when he heard his name called.

"Psst, Dave!"

Lagarde turned around, but couldn't detect where the voice was coming from.

"Psst, Dave! C'mon here!"

It was defensive lineman Tony Elliott, who was sitting inside his locker stall, shielded by a small curtain.

"Dave, man, go ask somebody what's going to happen to me," Elliott pleaded. "I got fired. They're all mad at me."

Somehow Elliott had angered Saints head coach Bum Phillips and defensive line coach Willie Zapalac with his play during the game. Phillips went so far as to tell Elliott that he was finished, that he would never play for the Saints again.

So Lagarde made some inquiries, beginning with defensive coordinator Wade Phillips. Phillips said not to worry, that Elliott's position was safe.

Fine, said Lagarde, who relayed the information to Elliott and then returned to the press box to write a short story about the situation.

Two days later, as the Saints were walking off the practice field, several players brushed past Lagarde.

"Better watch out for Zap," they said. "Better watch out."

This was followed by the appearance of Zapalac himself, who felt that Lagarde's story about Elliott had undermined his authority with his players. He started yelling and pointing at Lagarde. Lagarde yelled and pointed back.

"You know, after the season, I'm going to find out where you live and beat the shit out of you!"

Meanwhile, Saints players began to encircle the coach and writer. Some of them seconded Zapalac's threat. "Yeah, beat the shit out of him, Zap," they said.

Zapalac was in his sixties at the time, and Lagarde was about half his age. But none of that mattered as Lagarde decided he had been bullied enough.

"OK, let's fight right now," he said.

Lagarde and Zapalac inched forward, but several Saints coaches interceded and ended the confrontation. A few weeks later, Bum Phillips was fired and Zapalac resigned.

Lagarde and Bum Phillips were never best of pals. One year, a hurricane turned New Orleans into a wading pool. Streets were flooded. Road travel was almost out of the question.

As Phillips drove home that day, he came across a stranded motorist. Phillips offered the man a ride and a place to stay that evening. Phillips and the stranger ended up talking football until past midnight. The next day, Phillips helped arrange a way home for the gentleman.

All of this was revealed by Phillips at a press conference. When reporters asked for the stranger's name, Phillips said, "It was Dave something or other. I know it sure wasn't Lagarde."

To this day, Lagarde says Phillips "wouldn't have pissed on me if I was on fire."

Football players are equal-opportunity menaces. They pick on each other as much as they do writers. Sometimes it gets a little rough. Bob McGinn, who covers the Packers for the *Green Bay Press-Gazette,* was standing outside the team's locker room after an embarrassing loss to the Indianapolis Colts in 1985 when he heard a thud against one of the walls. Shouts and screams soon followed, as did more sounds of an apparent brawl.

Then there was silence. About thirty seconds passed before the noises returned, this time louder than ever. Something was going on and McGinn and the rest of writers were dying to find out what it was.

Just as McGinn leaned forward, the double-steel doors flew open, revealing a disordered locker room, players in various stages of undress and team strength coach Virgil Knight. Someone pulled the doors shut and that was that until several minutes later, when the reporters were allowed inside.

"What was all the noise about?" McGinn asked a player.

"That? Oh, that was just Coach [Forrest] Gregg kicking over a garbage can."

Oh no it wasn't. McGinn later discovered that Gregg had openly challenged players after the game. One of the players was linebacker Mike Douglass, who apparently stood up and said he wasn't going to take this sort of abuse. It was at this point that Knight allegedly threw a soda can at Douglass and just missed the linebacker's head. The free-for-all took place shortly thereafter. Incredibly enough, no one was hurt, including those writers who had nerve enough to ask about the melee.

Of course, there are instances when reporters have a difficult time staying out of harm's way. I submit the adventures of former Washington Redskins defensive lineman Dave Butz and his victim, the *Los Angeles Times'* Chris Dufresne.

Dufresne was in Washington to do a story on the playoff-bound 1987 Redskins and their defensive anchor, Butz. Only one problem: Few of the Washington players, including Butz, wanted to do interviews that day.

Out of desperation, Dufresne tried following Butz as the hulking lineman made his way to the Redskins Park parking lot. Too late. Butz climbed into his van and revved the engine.

With this, Dufresne turned around and glumly started back toward the Redskins' office. Just then, he heard a vehicle coming. He looked back in time to see Butz, face contorted, driving right at him.

Dufresne dashed out of the way just in time. No less desperate, Dufresne secured Butz's home phone number and called about an hour later.

"Dave, I don't know if you remember me, but I'm the guy you almost ran down today in the parking lot," Dufresne said.

Butz laughed and later, after Dufresne pleaded his case, invited the writer to his house where he granted him about an hour interview. Go figure.

The Redskins were an entertaining bunch in their prime. There was Riggins, who told a Supreme Court justice to "loosen up." There was Butz, of course, who liked to scare the bejabbers out of writers. And then there was owner Jack Kent Cooke, one of the world's richest and more peculiar men.

Cooke treats every Redskins game as a social occasion. His private box is often filled with dignitaries, senators, congressmen, syndicated political columnists, television personalities and so forth. The Redskins serve as entertainment.

One time he summoned *Washington Post* reporter Christine Brennan to his stadium suite for the sole purpose of yelling at her. It was an odd lecture, one that centered on a trade rumor involving the troubled but gifted defensive end Dexter Manley. At the end of it, Cooke said, "I had a lot of respect for you, but I'm thinking less of you. In fact, never come to any of my parties. And never come by here again."

Cooke is quite a character. He once offered a ride to then– *Washington Post* writer Gary Pomerantz as Pomerantz made his way from one end of the team's Carlisle, Pennsylvania, training facilities to the other. Against his better judgment, he accepted Cooke's invitation.

This was a mistake. As soon as Pomerantz settled into the late-model Jaguar, Cooke slammed his foot on the accelerator. Soon the speedometer was lurching past fifty . . . sixty . . . seventy . . . seventy-five miles per hour. Trees and cows and center divider lines became blurs as Cooke wheeled the mighty car toward its destination.

The ride didn't take long. When it was over, Cooke parked the car but didn't turn the engine off. Instead, he turned to a terrified Pomerantz and said, "Now you give it a whirl, my boy."

Pomerantz got out of the car and ran.

Cooke also inspired fear in his players. In 1983, after a heartbreaking loss to the Dallas Cowboys on *Monday Night Football,* Pomerantz wrote that the game was probably lost when Redskins quarterback Joe Theismann overthrew wide receiver Charlie Brown late in the game. The pass was intercepted, thus sealing the Redskins' fate.

Later, from the postgame statements, Pomerantz learned that Theismann hadn't erred. Actually, Brown had run the wrong pattern.

So Pomerantz inserted a new paragraph and sent the revised edition to his copy desk. Unfortunately, Theismann's paper didn't include the correction, which explains why he cornered Pomerantz the next day and started screaming.

"Joe, can I tell you my side of the story?" Pomerantz said when Theismann settled down.

"Yeah, this ought to be fucking great!"

So he told him and Theismann eventually calmed down. Then he revealed the real reason for his outburst.

"Ah, I really don't care what you write," he said. "All I care about is what the crazy fucker [Cooke] reads. He's going to blame the game on me."

One player who fears little is the aforementioned Dexter Manley. He once accused Pomerantz of keeping him off the Pro Bowl team, which is silly, since Manley's peers are the ones who actually vote. Tired of listening to Manley's whining, Pomerantz decided it was payback time. When he arrived in Honolulu, site of the annual game, Pomerantz purchased a postcard of a scantily clad woman and sent it to Manley. It read: "Dear Dexter, Wish you were here."

Manley loved it. In fact, Manley has demonstrated a keen

sense of humor on more than one occasion. He once told his teammates that the Redskins just had been sold to the Reverend Jesse Jackson. Surprisingly enough, several of his teammates believed him.

Sportswriters appreciate this sort of behavior. How gloomy to have to cover a team where nobody can take a joke or give one.

Consider the time that Jack Sheppard, then working for the San Angelo, Texas, newspaper, showed up at Oilers training camp one day wearing a brand-new pair of cowboy boots. Sheppard had saved for weeks to buy the boots, his first pair ever.

Now you have to understand that then-coach Bum Phillips is a connoisseur of cowboy boots. At the time—and this was in 1979—he had more than 160 pair of boots, all with toes so pointy that you could pick a lock with them. However, Sheppard's sorry pair of boots were square-toed. Very uncool.

After practice that day, Phillips retired to his small office, which was well stocked with hundreds of long-neck bottles of Lone Star beer. It was there that he conducted his daily press conference while sipping on a bottle of brew. It was also there that Sheppard walked in wearing his new set of walking shoes.

"Well, Bum, I got my first pair of boots," Sheppard said proudly.

Phillips stared at the boots and drawled, "Ah see. You got the kind either you or your wife can wear."

Sheppard was devastated. When he got home that night, he put the boots in his closet and never wore them again.

One of the great teams to cover was the Raiders, who weren't always the most hospitable bunch, but were certainly the most interesting collection of characters ever to snap on chinstraps.

Back in 1983, Gary Pomerantz was in the Oakland Raiders locker room interviewing defensive lineman Lyle Alzado when linebacker Ted Hendricks interrupted the conversation. Hendricks, it seemed, didn't like the questions Pomerantz was asking Alzado. To be more specific, he didn't like Pomerantz and told him so. In fact, he threatened to heave Pomerantz out of the locker room.

Alzado, bless his heart, intervened.

"Hey, he's all right," said Alzado, gesturing toward Pomerantz. "He's my cousin."

"Oh," said Hendricks.

Some cousins. Alzado checked in at six-foot-three, 250 pounds. Pomerantz barely reached five-foot-ten and weighed about 160. Alzado looked as if he trimmed his beard with a Bowie knife. Pomerantz was the picture of East Coast cool: well dressed and proper.

Now Hendricks knows the awful truth. He was duped.

Famed cornerback Lester Hayes, perhaps the greatest quotation machine in the history of the league, used to call reporters at home and offer assorted observations. If he thought the quotation was extra special, he would call it a "spine chiller supreme."

Hayes had his own language. He referred to reporters as "scoopmen" or "scoopers." He had pet phrases, too. "This is not my destiny," he would say. Or "It's accy," which was short for academic.

As best anyone can remember, he once said that running through the Raiders defense "was like wearing pork chop underwear and then trying to run through a gauntlet of pit bulls."

Hayes once found a way to link a 1985 victory over the Denver Broncos with the Khmer Rouge of Cambodia. The Raiders have never been the same since he retired.

Then there is Raiders general managing partner Al Davis, the architect of Silver and Black greatness. No one can question his expertise as a football man, though there are those who wonder who picks out his clothes.

Davis isn't fond of sportswriters who criticize his motives

or actions. He once tried to have *Los Angeles Times* reporter Mark Heisler removed from the Raiders beat—and failed. Davis was upset with what he considered negative coverage and did his best to make life difficult for Heisler, as well as any other writer who angered him.

After the 1988 season, Heisler approached Davis for an interview at the league's winter meetings in Palm Springs.

"I'd like to speak with you," Heisler said.

As he said this, Heisler noticed that Davis had balled his fist.

"No, I never would with you," Davis said. "I think you're a prick. You fucked us again."

"Al, it's my obligation to try to talk to you, but I don't have to sit still for this."

"I think you should leave."

If I could talk football with anyone, it would probably be Miami Dolphins coach Don Shula, who is an eminently decent man hidden behind one of the great jutting jaws of all time. He can be difficult (as proven by his occasional treatment of beat reporters), but he also can be sweet and funny without meaning to.

Michael Janofsky, who used to cover the Dolphins before joining the *New York Times* staff, recalls when Shula used part of his off-season to take the family to New England. Shula, whose team had won the Super Bowl that year, wanted to find a remote area where he and his family could go unnoticed.

One night, Shula and his wife decided to see a movie at the town theater. As they walked into the near-empty movie house, a patron turned around and began applauding. Soon, the remaining members of the small audience were clapping as the great Shula walked down the aisle.

Shula couldn't help himself. He beamed proudly.

"Thank you," he said. "It was a great season, a great accomplishment."

The applause stopped and was replaced by looks of wonderment. One gentleman asked Shula, "What are you talking about?"

"Why, the Super Bowl," Shula said. "It was nice of you to recognize me."

"Listen, pal, all I know is that the projectionist said he wouldn't start the movie until we had ten people here. You and your wife make ten."

Shula hurried to his seat.

4

What Better Way to Spend a Saturday Afternoon?

There are plenty of reasons to dislike college football, beginning with the greed, Brent Musburger, Georgia fans, the cheating, the NCAA, Brent Musburger, freshman eligibility, the hypocrisy, the bowl system and, of course, Brent Musburger.

The way I see it, everything can be remedied, except Musburger, who I am afraid is here to stay. If nothing else, though, we now know why the mute button on our television remote controls was invented.

As a sportswriter, you tend to root for turmoil. Let's face it, melodrama provides better reading. This is where college football makes such a strong showing. On the turmoil scale, its cup runneth way over.

Where else can you find former coach Barry Switzer, his Oklahoma University program crumbling around him, pleading his innocence and ignorance at the same time?

Where else can you discover the new and exciting ways (some actually legal) college coaches recruit their players?

Where else can you witness the grand monitoring organization that is the NCAA, protectors of all that is good and right with college athletics? Now if we only had someone to watch over the NCAA.

And where else can you discover the verbal bon mots of Notre Dame's Lou Holtz, Penn State's Joe Paterno, Florida State's Bobby Bowden, Iowa State's Jim Walden or Kentucky's Bill Curry?

Even with its many problems, college football still makes your heart beat a little faster on a Saturday afternoon. Forget about innocence: The college game lost its virginity a long time ago, when television began waving those wads of dollar bills in front of the assorted athletic directors. But at least the game retains most of its considerable charm.

For instance, a college football press box is the only place where sportswriters are asked to stand up and applaud . . . the Pork Farmers of America. It happened—honest. The public address announcer at a Miami–Mississippi State game in Starkville (and believe me, the city name fits the scenery) solemnly requested that we stand and pay homage to the people who supplied our pregame lunch that day. I thought we were standing for the National Anthem.

This was the same press box that wasps the size of sparrows decided to invade one afternoon. Never has a game program been put to such a deadly use. This was the same stadium in which Mississippi State fans clanged their cowbells whenever their beloved Bulldogs did well. At times, you didn't know if you were at a football game or a 4-H Club convention.

But I loved every moment of it.

College football is full of little surprises. Back in 1982, while I was covering the Miami Hurricanes, the sports information director asked if I wanted to meet two of their newest recruits, both of whom were quarterbacks. It was the first day of practice and I didn't have anything better to do, so I said sure, why not?

One of them had the look of an athlete: tall, imposing, a handshake to kill for. The other was equally tall, but thin and frail looking. I decided that moment that the skinny one would probably never see the light of the first-string huddle. Bench material, if I ever saw it.

Which goes to show how smart us sportswriters are. The delicate, gangly-looking quarterback was none other than Bernie Kosar, who would later lead Howard Schnellenberger's Miami team to the 1983 national championship. The other guy was Vinnie Testaverde, who managed to make a name for himself by winning the 1986 Heisman Trophy. So I was only half wrong.

Sportswriting is like that. It's a business of perception and misperception. The trick is to be able to distinguish between fact and first impressions, something not easily done.

For example, Colorado's affable Bill McCartney just about breaks out in hives if he sees anyone, including reporters, show up at his practices wearing red. McCartney can't stand red because it reminds him of Nebraska, a Big Eight Conference rival. He once chided Natalie Meisler, who covers the Buffaloes for the *Denver Post,* for using a red pen.

And take the time Bill Curry, then the coach at Georgia Tech, stormed into a postgame press conference after his team just barely tied little-regarded Furman. Under most circumstances, Curry, hired in 1990 to revive Kentucky's program, is as engaging, personable and pleasant as they come.

This wasn't one of those circumstances.

Thomas Stinson of the *Atlanta Journal-Constitution* was there that day in 1985 when Curry exhibited his formidable temper. Curry began by gritting his teeth and congratulating Furman for a game well played. Then he entertained questions, what few there were, considering his foul mood.

Midway through the interview session, a young radio reporter from one of the local stations came into the room. Stinson had seen the reporter in the press box earlier that afternoon. The reporter was easy to spot: He was the one stuffing the free ham sandwiches into a knapsack normally used for his radio equipment.

As Curry testily answered a question, the radio reporter blindly reached back into his knapsack to pull out a microphone. This done, he placed the instrument directly in front of Curry's face, the better to achieve proper audio quality.

Except that it wasn't a microphone. It was a ham sandwich.

Curry was in midsentence when he noticed the sandwich. He stared at it, as did the rest of the assembled press. No one dared laugh, Curry's postgame mood being what it was. So everyone waited and watched, including the terrified radio reporter, who never pulled the sandwich away from Curry's view.

Of course, you've never known true terror until you've interviewed a true legend. Paul "Bear" Bryant's name comes to mind.

Bryant's remarkable winning record at Alabama assured his place in college football history. It also helped create an aura that not even the best sportswriters could entirely ignore, no matter how hard they tried.

In 1979, Malcolm Moran of the *New York Times* was sent to Tuscaloosa to do a profile on the state's most popular man, Bryant. At the appointed time, Moran was led into Bryant's spacious office, the one with the desk the size of a helicopter launching pad, and directed toward a nearby couch. Moran sat down and immediately began sinking deeper and deeper into the soft, plush cushions. Before long, he only could see the top of Bryant's head—and that was when Moran craned his neck.

The interview began. Moran carefully asked his questions and Bryant, obviously interested in the subject matter, answered. The conversation was lively, animated and . . . completely useless.

Moran couldn't understand a word Bryant had mumbled during the lengthy interview. Buried deep in the couch, he nervously thumbed through his bare notepad. There were words here and there—guesses, really, at what Moran thought

Bryant had said—but nothing more. Here Bryant had gra-
ciously granted him an audience and Moran had nothing to
show for it.

Bryant glanced at his watch and announced that the interview was finished: He was late for practice. Moran, who
struggled to escape the grasp of the couch, asked one more
question.

"Coach, there might be a couple of things I'll need to
check on when I get back to New York," he said. "Can I give
you a call at home."

"Sure," said Bryant.

Moran visited the practice field that day and started talking
to several of the Alabama beat reporters.

"So, how'd it go with the Bear?" said one of the local
sportswriters.

"Not very well. I couldn't figure out what he said. Is
it me?"

"Hell, no. None of us can understand him, either."

A few days later, his story still lacking some key ingredi-
ents, mainly Bryant's words, Moran called back.

"Uh, Coach, I have just a few more questions."

"Fine, what is it?"

Moran couldn't believe his ears. He actually could comprehend Bryant. Turns out that the Bear enunciated his words
better on the phone than in person. A story was saved.

Bryant knew how important the media were to him and his
team. He wasn't always fond of sportswriters, but he understood their role and how they could be used to his advantage.
He was smart that way.

Herschel Nissenson, the longtime national college writer
for the Associated Press, knew Bryant as well as anybody.
Once, in the late 1970s, Nissenson had an appointment to see
Bryant before the Crimson Tide played Mississippi State.
Nissenson got off the plane in Birmingham, rented a car,
turned on the radio and began the forty-five-minute drive to
Tuscaloosa. The first news story was about reported racial

dissension on the Alabama team. Nissenson nearly swerved off the road.

Once in Bryant's office, Nissenson tried to figure out the best way to broach the subject of team dissension. After all, he had come to Alabama to discuss the Mississippi State game. But a potentially huge story was developing and Nissenson owed it to himself and the AP to inquire about it.

"Coach," Nissenson said, "you know I'm not down here as a result of that story."

"Sit down, boy!" ordered Bryant.

Nissenson didn't have to ask where. Waiting for him was that gawdawful saggy couch, the one that left Bryant towering over visitors.

"You know, I'm through pussyfooting around," Bryant said. "Anyone who doesn't like what I'm doing here can go to hell."

Then he paused. "Aw, shit, I don't know what I'm saying."

"Coach, you know what you're saying: You're giving me a hell of a story."

And he did, essentially telling Nissenson that the reports were untrue and that he was going to run his program the way he saw fit, even if it created rumors of racial unrest on the team.

The story appeared on Friday, which didn't make the local newspapers too happy. The next day, one of the local sportswriters approached Nissenson.

"You know, he told me the exact same thing on Monday," said the sportswriter. "But the Bear said if I printed it, he'd kill me."

Nah. All the Bear wanted was a national audience to disprove the reports. He got it with Nissenson and the AP.

Bryant retired after the 1982 season and, as you might expect, Nissenson was the one who broke the story. He got the tip, surprisingly enough, from a source at Auburn, Alabama's archrival. The source said Ray Perkins, then the New York Giants coach and a former Alabama player, was to succeed Bryant.

Nissenson called Bryant's house—busy signal. He called again. And again. And again. Nothing but busy signals.

He called the president of the University of Alabama. He called Bryant's friends and associates. Little by little, Nissenson began to think the rumor might be true.

As deadline approached, Nissenson reached a close friend of Perkins's. Was it true, he asked? The friend said he would call Perkins and find out. Precious minutes ticked by as Nissenson waited. Finally, the phone rang: It was true. Perkins said so.

Meanwhile, another newspaper was reporting that Perkins was leaving the Giants to become Alabama's offensive coordinator, not the head coach. Nissenson heard about the report and tried Bryant's house one more time. He had made up his mind: He was going to file a story saying that Perkins was the next Alabama head coach. Now if he could get just one final confirmation.

"Hello?"

It was Mrs. Bryant.

"Mrs. Bryant, this is Herschel Nissenson," he said. "I have got to talk to Coach."

"Well, he's out recruiting in Mississippi."

"OK, but I just wanted to let you know that in about ten minutes your phone is going to be ringing off the wall. Ray Perkins is going to be the next coach and Coach is going to announce his retirement."

"Oh, I'll believe that when I hear it," she said.

"Well, I just thought I'd give you the courtesy."

Mrs. Bryant paused and then said, not too happily, "You're a good friend of Paul's. Why can't you wait until the press conference in the morning?"

Bingo. Confirmation.

"Well, if you had called and told me and asked me to sit on the story, I would have. But now I can't."

Nissenson thanked Mrs. Bryant and called his editors. "I've got the story," he said.

"It's your career," the editor said.

You know the rest: Perkins became the coach.

The 1982 Liberty Bowl was Bryant's last game as head coach. Nissenson was there. He talked with Bryant for about an hour the day before the game. Because of tight deadlines, he wasn't able to visit the Alabama locker room after the game. But it was in the aftermath of the Alabama victory that Bryant told the assembled writers that if they ever made it to Tuscaloosa, they should look him up—they'd break bread together.

From Memphis, Nissenson was sent to the Sugar Bowl and then the NCAA meetings in San Diego.

The first guy Nissenson saw at the meetings was Tennessee coach Johnny Majors.

"Where have you been? Coach Bryant's been looking for you," he said.

That was nice, thought Nissenson, who promised to write Bryant a note when he got back to New York.

And he did. Nissenson wrote how much he appreciated Bryant's help through the years; how it was a privilege to cover his Alabama teams; how much he would miss him. He even made tentative plans to take Bryant up on his offer of breaking bread.

Nissenson sent the letter on a Monday. On Tuesday, Bryant became gravely ill. On Wednesday, Bryant died.

Not every sportswriter enjoys the same type of relationship with a coach that Nissenson did. The reporters who covered the Perkins Era at Alabama will vouch for that.

Perkins is not known for his charm. Those who know him say it exists, but if it does, he rarely displays it to the media. They are his adversaries, his critics, his enemies, more or less.

After his first season at Alabama, Perkins already was at odds with *Birmingham Post Herald* columnist Paul Finebaum. So strained were relations in the spring of 1984 that a dinner was arranged between Finebaum and Perkins by Perkins's agent. Writer and coach would meet to iron out their differences.

At least, that was the plan.

Finebaum came to Perkins's house for a Sunday dinner. It did not go well.

While sitting at the table, Perkins mentioned to his wife that he was thinking of doing a television show the next season without a cohost. Would that be a good idea? he asked his wife.

Finebaum's ears perked up on this one. He had criticized Perkins for having no flair, no pizzazz.

"I don't think you have the personality for it," said Perkins's wife.

Perkins slammed his fist on the table.

"We're getting a divorce," he said.

Finebaum was stunned. He looked at Perkins and then forced a weak laugh. A few moments later, he excused himself. "I think it's time to go home," he said.

Six months later, a writer from *Sports Illustrated* came to town to do a story on Perkins and his now-troubled Alabama program. For the first time in twenty-five years, the Crimson Tide was about to have a losing season. In those parts, that's almost as catastrophic as the South losing to the North.

Finebaum was interviewed by the *Sports Illustrated* reporter. During the interview, Finebaum told him about the incident at Perkins's dinner table.

As is its practice on all stories, the magazine had a fact-checker call Finebaum shortly before the story was to run. Among the topics was the fist-slamming. Finebaum confirmed the incident—but he added that he was now sure that Perkins merely was joking that night.

The magazine story painted another picture, and it didn't include Finebaum's observation about it all being a joke.

Perkins wouldn't talk to Finebaum after the story came out. Then came the anonymous death threats from assorted sick readers, who had nothing better to do than make a college football team the axis of their lives.

The following Saturday, Penn State played Alabama at Tuscaloosa. Somehow, in Perkins's finest moment that season, the Crimson Tide won. As Finebaum walked from the field to the postgame press conference, he made an extra effort to walk near or behind someone else. He had the distinct and uneasy feeling that perhaps someone was up in the stands with a high-powered rifle aimed at him. Honest.

Finebaum arrived at Perkins's postgame talk a few seconds late. Perkins looked up, saw Finebaum, answered one more question, and walked out.

As the relationship deteriorated further, Perkins used assorted means to make life miserable for Finebaum.

Finebaum had a radio show on the same station that broadcast the Alabama games, as well as the *Ray Perkins Show.* Finebaum's show, usually full of anti-Tide observations, lasted from 5:00 to 7:00 P.M. and was immediately followed by Perkins's show.

Twice during the season, Finebaum would later learn from a station employee, Perkins had called the station manager demanding that the columnist's show be canceled. The station manager declined.

Then Perkins got tough. At season's end, he called the station manager a final time. He said that if Finebaum's show stayed, then the *Ray Perkins Show* would go elsewhere. And so would the Alabama football and basketball games. Perkins, you see, was also the university's athletic director.

Guess who was looking for a new radio station shortly thereafter?

Finebaum eventually was offered a deal (for more money, by the way) at a nearby Auburn station. So there, Ray.

There is a happy ending to all of this. Perkins later left Alabama to become the head coach of the Tampa Bay Buccaneers. Last year, he accepted an invitation to appear on Finebaum's show. And while they're not best pals, they talk. Strange how this all works out.

Karen Rosen of the *Atlanta Journal-Constitution* had her moments with Perkins. One of them came during the 1985 season, after Alabama defeated Cincinnati, 45–10. Perkins, in his postgame conference, was trying to think of what the Crimson Tide had done poorly that day. The best he could come up with was that the defense had encountered several problems.

"But there were reasons for that," he said.

Rosen blurted out the natural question.

"What are the reasons?" she asked.

Perkins glared at her.

"Who are you?"

"I'm Karen Rosen of the *Atlanta Journal-Constitution.*"

"You know who I am, don't you?" Perkins said.

"Yes, sir."

With that, Perkins listed the reasons. It was his best answer of the entire postgame chat.

There are certain coaches you love to see on the podium for a press conference. I'm partial to Bobby Bowden. He's honest, funny and he never talks down to anyone, reporters included. Bowden also returns phone calls, which may not sound like much, but it is. And it doesn't matter if you work for *Sports Illustrated* or the *Podunk Times*—Bowden will return the call regardless of circulation figures. Sportswriters appreciate that sort of thing.

Then there are the coaches who wouldn't know a glib comment if it threw a crossbody block at them. A notepad's nightmare is what they are. They give clichés a bad name.

"They have the best [fill in the blank: offense, defense, special teams, quickness, speed, fabulous babe cheerleaders] we've faced all year."

"I'll have to look at the films before I can comment."

"I'm so damn proud of this football team. These young men grew up today."

And, of course, old reliable: "We just pinned our ears back and went after 'em today. We gave 110 percent."

Sometimes, though, you get a surprise from an unlikely source.

Long-time Georgia coach Vince Dooley was addressing a large gathering of sportswriters at a New Orleans hotel ballroom one year at the Sugar Bowl when someone asked for a medical update on a Bulldog player. The player was recovering from a case of orchitis, which, in professional medical terms, means you have an inflammation of the testes. Very painful.

A few days earlier, the player's condition had been detailed in a story by then–Atlanta sportswriter Dan Barreiro. With the game so close, reporters now wanted to know if the player would be in the starting lineup.

Dooley squirmed at the podium. Truth was, he really didn't want to talk about a player's swollen glands. So he did the next best thing: He passed.

Suddenly Barreiro heard his name being called by Dooley. The coach wanted Barreiro to stand up and describe exactly what orchitis was. Never mind that a couple of hundred reporters were watching.

Surprisingly enough, Barreiro got up and gave a quick—very quick—description of the illness and returned to his seat. Dooley owed him one.

Michigan's great former coach Bo Schembechler isn't what you'd call a wordsmith, but at least he has a sassy, crusty quality to him. Especially entertaining are his inventive excuses for Rose Bowl losses, of which there have been many.

Johnette Howard, now with the *National,* was supposed to follow Schembechler during his stay at Lexington, Kentucky, in 1989. Schembechler, who doubled as Michigan's athletic director, was there to watch the Wolverines play in the NCAA basketball tournament. Bill Frieder had resigned as head coach and was replaced by assistant Steve Fisher on an interim basis. That was until Michigan began making a run at the national championship.

Howard had dealt with Schembechler in the football environment, but never had she witnessed Schembechler as an administrator. A treat it wasn't.

Schembechler stood in the arena tunnel and watched the Wolverines win another game. As he did, Howard introduced herself and asked a question. Schembechler, barely listening, nodded and offered a short, meaningless answer.

Howard tried again, with similar results.

"Uh, yeah, whatever," said Schembechler.

Howard had been ignored long enough. She grabbed Schembechler by the arm and said, "I'm not trying to be an asshole, but I need to ask three questions. Could you please stand still and answer them?"

If there's one thing Schembechler appreciates, it's verve and nerve. He answered the questions.

Years earlier, Schembechler, in association with the American Football Coaches Association, represented the Tea Council of America in some sort of promotional campaign. The Tea Council would spring for air fare and expenses to New York, where a prominent coach (in this case, Schembechler) would explain the many virtues of tea.

Herschel Nissenson interviewed Schembechler. The Wolverines had gone 7-4 the previous season, mainly because of numerous breakdowns in their kicking game. After the interview, Schembechler and Nissenson visited a local pub next door to the AP office building.

As they nursed their drinks (and they weren't tea, either), Schembechler turned to Nissenson.

"You know, you write more horseshit stories than any sportswriter that I've ever known," he said.

"Maybe," said Nissenson, "but at least I've never had a story blocked."

Even big bad Bo had to laugh at that one.

Schembechler's Ohio State nemesis, the late Woody Hayes, was also a bit of a character. Then again, what do you expect out of someone who slugs an opposing player on the sidelines?

Hayes could be gracious or mean-spirited. He could impress you with his knowledge of history or awe you with his passion for football. In the end, it was that blind, blue-flame passion that was his undoing.

Expelled from the football program after the punching incident at the Gator Bowl, Hayes occasionally made cameo appearances at Ohio State games. In 1981, he was invited to Ann Arbor to watch the annual Michigan–Ohio State contest. Rather than give him a sideline pass, officials found a seat in the press box for Hayes.

Big mistake.

Remember, there isn't supposed to be any cheering in the press box. It's a rule occasionally broken, especially in college press boxes. A simple announcement by the school's sports information director usually puts an end to the noise.

But this was different. This was the great Woody Hayes clapping and yelling as the Buckeyes did their best to beat hated Michigan. Every time quarterback Art Schlichter completed a pass against the Wolverines, Hayes would applaud. Every time a Buckeye made a good tackle, disrupted a pass attempt or ran for three yards or more, Woody would clap. And each time he did, an announcement would be made over the public address system.

"The college football writers remind everyone that there is no cheering allowed in the press box. Any outbursts will result in your immediate removal."

Hayes must have been deaf, or perhaps he simply didn't care about the threats of a press box announcer. He applauded louder with each Ohio State success. And with each piece of applause, the press box monitor would warn all those concerned of impending action.

No one ever did a thing to Hayes. And what could they

have done anyway? The worst had happened: He was in a press box rather than on the field, where he belonged.

For sheer entertainment value, nobody could come close to the one, the only, Barry Switzer. He was regarded as one of the best recruiters in the country. His wishbone offense was a delight to watch. His brash statements were music to the ears, especially if you had just spent a week at Nebraska, listening to dry-as-talcum-powder coach Tom Osborne. As for being a social role model, well . . .

Switzer said he didn't give a damn what anybody thought of him, but he did. He read the sports pages. Like Santa he remembered who was naughty and who was nice.

In 1979, Al Carter, then of the *Daily Oklahoman,* was making his first appearance as an Oklahoma University beat reporter. He had never met Switzer, but he knew of his growing reputation as king of the state.

Carter attended a Sooners practice session one afternoon and readied himself for his introduction to Switzer. First impressions were important. He didn't want to appear unsure of himself, but he didn't want to seem cocky, either. Carter settled on just being nervous, and it showed as he met Switzer walking off the field.

"Coach Switzer," he said, "my name's Al Carter of the *Daily Oklahoman* and I'll be covering your games."

Switzer looked the young reporter over and said, "Well, son, just don't screw it up."

And then he walked away.

Carter eventually started writing a column for the paper, which was fine, as long he didn't criticize Switzer or his team. Switzer took that sort of thing personally.

As with any wishbone offense, Oklahoma occasionally fumbled. But during one stretch at OU, no quarterback or running back, it seemed, could hold on to the football. Carter noted the rash of fumbles and blamed the OU coaching staff for not drilling the Sooners players on proper ball-handling technique.

Switzer read the column and was livid. As it happened, Carter visited the OU football offices the day after the game and became embroiled in a spirited argument with Switzer about the criticism.

"It was a bunch of bullshit," Switzer said.

With that, Switzer started gesturing toward the various photos of Sooners players, past and present, on the office walls.

"Look at him," he said, nearly jumping up and down, "he's holding the ball right."

Then Switzer sprinted to the OU trophy case, where a huge Orange Bowl trophy resided. Switzer reached inside the case, pulled out the trophy, which featured a golden football, and tucked the whole thing under his arm. Then he ran up and down the hallway, asking Carter, "Is this the way you want us to carry the football? Do you expect players to run like this? Well?"

Carter was too stunned to speak. His jaws wouldn't open.

By then, several OU assistant coaches had ventured from their offices to watch Switzer. Sensing that he had made his point, Switzer quit running the imaginary off-tackle plays and put the trophy down.

"You see, you've got to hold it away from your body," he told Carter.

Carter nodded. Now came the hard part: He had to request an interview.

Switzer laughed, slapped Carter on the back and invited the columnist inside his office. And the interview went fine, thank you.

Relations between Switzer and the two Dallas newspapers— the *Morning News* and the *Times Herald*—were a bit more strained. The papers, nosy and aggressive, covered OU football as if the Sooners were a local team and, in a sense, they were. The OU roster was filled with players from the Dallas area, the Sooners played Texas every year at the Cotton

Bowl and the OU campus was less than a three-hour drive from downtown Dallas.

Two weeks before the 1988 OU-Texas game, the *Morning News*'s Ivan Maisel called Switzer's office for an interview. Switzer wasn't available, he was told—could he leave a message? So Maisel left a message.

For the next six days, Maisel left messages and never received a phone call back. But why?

Maisel finally decided to confront Switzer. So he drove up to Norman for an OU–Iowa State game and afterward waited outside the dressing room for Switzer to appear. Once and for all, Maisel wanted to know what he had done to anger the OU coach.

"Hey, Ivan," said Switzer, as he walked from the dressing room.

"You pissed off at me?" Maisel asked.

"No."

"Then how come I can't get you on the phone?"

"Ivan, you know I don't talk to anybody south of the Red River."

"Oh, OK, just as long as it's nothing personal."

And it was Switzer who convinced the country's most talented players to come to Oklahoma. Few of them doubled as choirboys.

You know about Brian Bosworth. But how about Buster Rhymes, the electrifying running back Switzer recruited out of Miami? In high school, Rhymes was shot in the back by his father. Rhymes recovered, of course, and was later asked about the incident by Barry Horn, now with the *Dallas Morning News*.

"Why did your father shoot you in the back?" Horn asked.

"You don't understand," Rhymes said. "He was aiming at my mother and I got in the way."

"I see," Horn said.

Oklahoma didn't have a monopoly on craziness. During

Jackie Sherrill's troubled tenure at Texas A&M, several of his players were accused of accepting money from agents while still in school. Rather that simply declare the players ineligible, Sherrill decided he would travel to Atlanta (where the agent was located) and pay the money back, as if that were all it would take to make the problem go away.

Sherrill was—how should we put this?—*different.* You could interview him for an hour and not have any idea what he had said. It wasn't that he mumbled like Bryant. It was just that he rarely made any sense. In midsentence he would begin a new thought, followed by an equally new, but completely unrelated topic. I don't think I've ever talked with anyone quite like him.

Former Houston coach Bill Yeoman was more direct. His image was that of a kind, grandfatherly figure who inspired his players to greatness. Maybe so, but he also could cuss up a blue streak and often preferred to blame the media for his troubles.

In 1983, then–*Houston Post* reporter Kevin Sherrington was covering one of Yeoman's practices. Among the plays that day was a tight end–around using All–Southwest Conference performer Carl Hilton. Sherrington, who was short of material, decided to include the play in his daily notebook. He probably shouldn't have (disclosing practice-field secrets is generally a no-no), but he did. A capital offense it isn't.

When Yeoman read the note in Sherrington's story, he went nuts. For fifteen minutes he yelled at the reporter. Sherrington took the abuse, mainly because he knew he shouldn't have written the item.

On Saturday, Arkansas defeated Houston, 24–3. It was the second consecutive year the Cougars had failed to score a touchdown against the Razorbacks. Even before a reporter could ask a question in the postgame press conference, Yeoman was all over Sherrington.

"Well, Sherrington, since you wrote that, we didn't use the play," Yeoman said.

"I'm sure that cost you the game," Sherrington shot back.

End of conversation.

Some coaches close their practices to reporters. Security reasons, and all that. Now I can sort of understand why Notre Dame might close their workouts a few days before the big game against USC, or why Michigan might ban reporters from viewing its preparations for the Ohio State game. But Rice University? Hapless Rice?

I'm sad to say it used to happen, especially when Al Conover was the coach there in the mid-1970s.

Of course, nobody mentioned this to then–Houston sportswriter Thomas Bonk when he was assigned to fill in for the regular beat reporter one day. Bonk showed up at practice, took a seat high in the stands and casually watched the drills.

A little while later, someone noticed Bonk in the bleachers. Conover was notified.

"Who are you!" yelled Conover to the tiny figure in the stands.

Bonk, who wasn't very familiar with the Rice players or coaching staff, didn't budge. He figured practice was open and, anyway, he couldn't hear a word Conover was saying.

Meanwhile, Conover decided to use scare tactics. He grabbed a starter's gun and aimed it toward Bonk. Bonk, who didn't know it was just a starter's pistol, dove for cover as the gunshot blast echoed through the stadium.

Order was restored and identities revealed a few minutes later.

I'm generalizing again, but most college coaches, it seems, are a bit on the tense side. They never appear to be having much fun. I guess I can see why, what with the constant pressure to win, the time demands, the recruiting, the fickleness of boosters, the inconsistencies of school administrators and the daily dealings with the media.

Look at what it's done to Notre Dame's Lou Holtz. Holtz can't go five minutes without pointing out some supposed weakness in his team or expressing some dire concern about that week's opponent. Holtz somehow found reason to fret about beleagured SMU in 1989. This was the same SMU team that was returning from the NCAA's death penalty.

The old Holtz was much more pleasant. Mark Blaudschun, now with the *Boston Globe,* once traveled to Arkansas to do a profile on Holtz, who was then the Razorbacks' coach. Blaudschun completed his interviews and thanked Holtz for his time.

"When you going back?" asked Holtz.

"I've got a 6:30 flight."

"What airline?"

"Skyways."

"You mean Scareways, don't you? That's the one where you don't buy a ticket, you buy a chance."

"Thanks, Lou."

Blaudschun drove to the airport and boarded the tiny prop plane. It seated eight passengers, but only five people were on the plane as it taxied to the end of the runway. Just then Blaudschun saw the pilot turn to the copilot and say, "Oops."

The plane taxied back to the hangar, where the pilot explained that one of the instrument panel lights was flashing. Some repairs would have to be made.

Oh, great, thought Blaudschun, a delay.

Much to Blaudschun's surprise, a mechanic was never summoned to the plane. Instead, the pilot left the cockpit, walked into an office and returned with a flashlight and a screwdriver. He opened the plane's engine hood and started banging on something. A few minutes later, he climbed back into the cockpit, turned to the passengers and said, "It's all taken care of."

During the entire flight to nearby Dallas, Blaudschun swore he'd never doubt Holtz again.

Notre Dame has made and broken many a coach. And

sometimes, even the press gets caught up in the Irish tradition. After a 1982 game at Notre Dame Stadium, then–*Washington Post* sportswriter Gary Pomerantz found himself in the elevator with several of the Irish coaches who had spent the game in the coaches box high above the field. Somehow, in the mad rush to get to the Notre Dame locker room, Pomerantz was swept into the Irish dressing area before a security guard could notice.

Inside was a jubilant Notre Dame team. They had just won a close game and now it was time to celebrate. Priests were high-fiving one another. Players were hugging one another. Then came time for the postgame prayer. Pomerantz, a Jewish kid from Los Angeles, tried his best to look inconspicuous. He failed. The dead giveaway was when he made the sign of the cross backward.

5

Hoops and Scoops in the NBA

The NBA, for the most part, is the writer-friendly league. The league with a heart. The league that tries harder. Unlike another league I know (hint: starts with an N, ends with an L, has an F in the middle), you can actually interview NBA Commissioner David Stern without having to beg first. With that other league, especially in the days of Pete Rozelle, you needed to be a congressman threatening antitrust legislation before you even got your foot in the door.

Even with the big-money television contracts, the NBA remains refreshingly accessible. Maybe it's because the league remembers when it was starved for publicity, when network television rights fees were $18.5 million in 1980 (compared to $150 million a decade later). Maybe it's because the rosters are smaller, the games shorter, the players more reasonable in their views of the working press. Maybe it's because sportswriters are perceived as being just wonderful people, though I doubt it.

How accommodating are NBA players? Mary Schmitt, then with the *Milwaukee Journal,* once asked Julius Erving, who was making his farewell tour of the league at the time, if she could trace his hand on a piece of paper. She explained that her editor wanted a life-size outline of Erving's hand for a special graphic they were doing.

"OK," said Erving, who promptly placed his huge hand on the paper and let Schmitt trace away.

Sports Illustrated's Steve Wulf, best known for his work on baseball, was once assigned to do a story on then–Houston Rockets center Chuck Nevitt. Nevitt is the seven-foot-five, rail-thin backup who rarely sees any playing time. Anyway, after the Rockets played the Utah Jazz one night, Wulf decided to talk with Jazz forward Thurl Bailey about Nevitt. Bailey had played poorly that night, so Wulf approached him with care.

"Thurl?"

"Yeah?"

"My name's Steve Wulf. I'm with *Sports Illustrated* and I'm doing a piece on Chuck Nevitt."

Bailey's face brightened. "Oh, yeah, Chuck, my man."

Wulf, who was used to the surliness of baseball, was forever impressed. He hasn't given up his allegiance to the national pastime, but he has developed a fondness for pro hoopsters. All thanks to a "Chuck, my man."

I couldn't tell you the first pro football game I ever covered. Or college game. Or baseball game. They all blend into one after a while. But I know where and when I made my debut as an NBA writer. Some moments you never forget.

For the record—1983 . . . the Salt Palace in Salt Lake City . . . Denver Nuggets versus the Jazz. I remember sitting there in utter awe of Nuggets coach Doug Moe. I remember thinking he was a cardiac arrest patient waiting to happen and wondering whether I would be able to administer proper CPR should he suddenly keel over in midtantrum. The guy was amazing. He began yelling at tipoff and didn't stop until the buzzer sounded at game's end. When it was over, I turned to Terry Frei, then the regular beat reporter for the *Denver Post,* and asked if Moe behaved this way every night. "Usually," he said.

That's another great thing about the NBA: You can see everything. Unlike football or baseball, where you sometimes need the Mount Palomar observatory telescope to find the playing field, the NBA usually seats beat reporters at courtside and right next to the teams they cover. That way, if you want to chart the various shades of red on Moe's face during a game, you can.

It's just one man's opinion, but I humbly submit the name of Douglas Moe as the league's most entertaining character. There are those who would nominate Philadelphia's Charles Barkley, Boston's Larry Bird, Detroit's John Salley, Los Angeles's Mychal Thompson, or a handful of others. And all of them would be worthy candidates, especially Barkley, who often works just as hard in an interview as he does on the playing floor (and by the way, Charles, thank you). But how can you ignore a guy who refers to his wife as "Big Jane," or refuses to take himself seriously, or treats everybody—management, players, reporters—with wit and honesty? You can't. He's a lug, that's what he is. By game's end he looks as if the cops took him back to the station and introduced him to the interrogation room: His hair is a mess, his shirt is sweat-stained, his sportcoat is begging to be sent to the cleaners.

Moe will say anything about anybody at any time, even if it means upsetting his peers. Remember, it was Moe who publicly questioned the wisdom of naming Kareem Abdul-Jabbar to the 1988 All-Star Game roster. The comments didn't earn him many brownie points around the league, but that's the charm of Moe—he doesn't care how the world perceives him. With that weight lifted from his shoulders, Moe can go about doing what he loves best, which is coaching basketball and tweaking the establishment in the rear end.

An example:

As part of their home-game promotion package in 1988, the Nuggets helped sponsor a three-point shooting contest for fans at the end of the first half. As usual, *Post* reporters Mike Monroe and Mark Kiszla, who shared the beat, and an arena usher wagered a dollar on the contestant of their choice. If nothing else, the tiny bets were a way to compensate for the monotony of covering game after game.

As luck would have it, Monroe, Kiszla and the usher had begun their nightly wagering at about the same time that Mayor Federico Pena had launched a campaign to curtail the amount of illegal gambling done in Denver. No sooner had the two writers exchanged their dollar bills when they were approached by a stern-looking gentleman who identified himself as an off-duty Denver policeman who moonlighted as a security officer for the arena.

"So?" said Kiszla.

"So, it's against the law to gamble. The mayor's office has received several calls from season ticket holders complaining about your betting and now we're doing something about it. Now, if the three of you will come with me."

"You got to be kidding?"

"Come with me, please."

The third quarter was about to begin as the cop herded the three criminals into a holding room located under the stands. But what could they do? They *had* wagered—a lousy buck, for goodness' sake—and they had been caught. But this was a little ridiculous, wasn't it? In fact, Monroe made this very point, asking if perhaps Denver's finest didn't have something better to do with its time than collar three working stiffs betting a buck.

The cop ignored Monroe.

A few minutes later, Bill Malone, a former FBI agent who now serves as a security contact for the NBA and NFL, walked into the room and began asking Kiszla, Monroe and the usher about their betting.

"Have you been doing this for a long time? . . . Do you wager more than a dollar? . . . There have been reports that your bets have reached the ten-dollar level. Is this true? . . . Are you presently involved with a bookie? . . . Do you feel you need gambling counseling?"

Uh, oh, this was getting serious. Not only were Kiszla and Monroe missing the game, but they were on the verge of being arrested, arrested for putting a dollar down on a forty-two-year-old public accountant from Littleton. How would they explain this to their bosses?

About ten minutes later, Malone decided to let the three offenders return to their posts. "We'll let you off with a warning this time," he said. "But if we ever catch you doing this sort of thing again, it will be cuffs and downtown. Understand?"

"Yeah, sure," said an angry Monroe.

"Understood," said Kiszla and the usher.

As they walked back to their seats, a season ticket holder stopped them.

"What was that about?" he said.

Kiszla told him.

"Huh, that's funny. I heard a guy in my row talking about you guys gambling a few days ago. I think that's the guy who turned you in."

"That SOB," Kiszla said.

So ticked was Monroe that he relayed the whole story to Nuggets trainer Chopper Travaglini, whose seat was located next to press row.

"I can't believe that," said Chopper. "That's terrible. Absolutely terrible."

"Damn right it is," Monroe said.

About this time, Kiszla noticed a reporter from the *Rocky Mountain News,* the competing newspaper, interviewing the head security officer about the entire incident. The reporter was furiously taking notes.

"Oh, shit," Kiszla said.

Imagine the headlines: *Denver Post* Writers Busted in Three-Point Sting . . . Post Fires Two Sportswriters—"They Were Gambling Junkies," Says Editor.

Monroe was visibly upset, enough so that he missed deadline for the first edition. After finally filing his story, he joined

Kiszla inside the Nuggets locker room. Once there, both Moe and an assistant coach asked about the near arrest. Kiszla and Monroe gave the abridged version of the story.

"Well, at least you guys are lucky that you didn't miss the whole game," the assistant said.

"I guess so," said Kiszla, who then made his way into the players' section of the locker room and began interviewing center Wayne Cooper. It was shortly after he started jotting down some notes that he heard Monroe.

"Kiszla, we were frigging framed!" Monroe yelled.

And they had been, beautifully so. Chopper, with the considerable assistance of Moe, the usher and the two security officers, had set the entire thing up. Kiszla and Monroe never had a chance.

It didn't stop there, of course. The next time Kiszla and Monroe took their places on press row, other reporters tossed their credit cards at them. Just a friendly reminder, that's all.

I'm not entirely sure why, but there isn't the same ill will toward sportswriters in your average NBA locker room as there is in, say, a baseball clubhouse. NBA players are, well, cooler. I know it's not the most scientific reason you'll ever hear, but it's the truth. NBA players seem to have a higher tolerance for reporters and, in some cases, an actual understanding of our job. Bless them.

Bird, the supposed hick from French Lick, might be the brightest of them all when it comes to media relations. In another life, he must have been a sportswriter.

Sports Illustrated's Jack McCallum was in Boston to do a story on the Celtics when he stopped by Bird's locker after a game. Also there were several local beat reporters, who were asking specific questions about game strategy, performance and so forth. This wasn't doing McCallum any good. He needed something more general than Bird's comments about that night's contest. Not wanting to disrupt the flow of questions from the local writers, McCallum waited patiently for them to finish. As he did, Bird looked at him, as if to say, "Don't you want to ask anything?"

McCallum spoke up.

"I can't ask you anything in this environment," he said.

"Oh, you want something that isn't quite this timely, right?" Bird said.

"Well, actually, yeah."

"OK, when I'm done here, I'll meet you later."

It wouldn't be the last time Saint Bird did a good deed for a sportswriter. In 1988, McCallum and a reporter for the *Washington Post*, as well as about ten television film crews, were camped outside the Celtics dressing room waiting for Bird to emerge. Bird had been suffering from heel injuries and there was talk that surgery might have to be done, thus ending his season—huge news in Boston.

At last the door opened, but it wasn't Bird who walked out. It was one of the team managers, and he ordered everyone to leave immediately. There were protests, but slowly everyone began to depart. Just then, the manager whispered to McCallum and the *Post* reporter, "As soon as the TV crews are out of here, Larry will talk to you."

Bird used to have a reputation as a sullen, tough interview, but that was mostly a holdover from his days at Indiana State, when his personal life was considerably more complicated and confused. Now he is regarded as one of the best players to deal with in the entire league.

Sam Smith of the *Chicago Tribune* learned of Bird's generosity during the 1987 season, when he arranged an interview (his first ever) with the Celtics forward. The Celtics public relations department was supposed to set the whole thing up. The team would arrive in Chicago, practice and afterward Smith would visit with Bird.

On the appointed day, Smith approached Bird after the team workout, introduced himself and told him about the arrangements.

"Nobody said anything to me," Bird said.

"You're kidding," Smith said.

"Tell you what. Why don't you just give me a ride back to the team hotel. We can talk on the way back there."

"Great," Smith said.

The interview went well. What didn't go so well was Smith's sense of direction. He knew the Celtics' hotel was located near O'Hare Airport, but he couldn't remember exactly where. Of course, he couldn't tell Bird that. Instead, he kept making turn after turn, hoping to somehow run into the Marriott.

After about an hour in the car, Bird decided it was his turn to ask a question.

"Are we lost?" he said.

An embarrassed Smith said yes.

"Well, I don't know about you, but I'm going to have a hard time explaining this to Red [Auerbach]," Bird said.

By now, Bird was supposed to be in his hotel room resting for that evening's game. But rather than get upset about the situation, Bird joked about it. Smith finally stopped at a toll booth and asked for directions. Soon, Bird was in his hotel room safe and sound.

Bird is consumed by basketball. It is his love and because of it, he sometimes loses touch with the rest of the world. Case in point: While in Dallas several years ago, beat reporters Dan Shaughnessy of the *Boston Globe* and Peter May of the *Hartford Courant* bought tickets to see a Bruce Springsteen concert at Reunion Arena. Because of a favorable scheduling quirk, Springsteen, who was in the middle of his celebrated "Born in the U.S.A." tour, was playing the night before the Celtics were to face the Dallas Mavericks.

The day after the concert, Shaughnessy and May ran into Bird. During the course of the conversation, the two reporters mentioned how entertaining the Springsteen show had been.

"Who's Bruce Springsteen?" Bird said.

Shaughnessy and May looked at each other in amazement. Then one of them turned to Bird and said, "He's the you of rock and roll."

Leigh Montville, now with *Sports Illustrated,* was covering the 1980–1981 championship series between the Celtics and the Houston Rockets when he noticed Bird and Celtics backup center Rick Robey in the hotel lobby. Robey had fallen asleep in a chair and his mouth was wide open. From across the room Bird was lobbing cheeseballs into Robey's mouth.

Bird is also a master of the sucker bet. In fact, the general rule of thumb is that if Bird begins a sentence with, "I'll betcha five dollars I can . . ." one should walk quickly away. Oddly enough for someone with Bird's bank account, five dollars means the same thing to him that five dollars means to you and me. And nothing makes him happier than stuffing a few more bills into his wallet.

May was at a Celtics practice one day when Bird offered a wager.

"I'll betcha I can make a shot from here," he said.

May, who should have known better, considered the proposition. Bird was standing on the baseline, well behind the basket. To make the shot, Bird would somehow have to heave the ball through the opening of the basketball support, up over the backboard and through the hoop on the other side. It was a near impossible shot.

"You're on," May said.

Keeping one foot in place, Bird took a giant step toward the front of the basket and then casually flipped the ball into the hoop.

"You can't do that," May said.

"Sure I can. I said I can make it from here."

May shook his head and started to walk away.

"Hey, my five bucks," Bird said, smiling.

May later offered the money, but Bird declined. He had made his point.

No one is immune to Bird's seemingly preposterous bets. In 1985, as the Celtics prepared to play the Philadelphia 76ers in the Eastern Conference finals, Bird arrived at practice one day wearing a wrap on his shooting hand. The official story was that Bird had injured the hand in a game, but truth was, he had hurt it in a fight.

Shaughnessy took one look at the hand and told Bird, "You can't play tomorrow night with your hand taped like that."

"Yeah, I can," Bird said. "In fact, I could tape my whole hand and shoot better than you. We'll shoot one hundred foul shots and I'll betcha five dollars a foul shot."

Shaughnessy was no NBA player, but he figured he could hold his own against an injured Bird. So he agreed.

A Celtics trainer taped the entire hand as if Bird were getting ready to slip on a pair of boxing gloves. Then they took their places on the free-throw line.

Bird struggled mightily the first dozen or so shots. But then he adjusted his shooting motion and began making free throw after free throw. As each shot snapped the bottom of the net, Shaughnessy glumly calculated his losses. When the contest was complete, the sportswriter owed the millionaire superstar $160.

Figuring he could write the story for the *Globe,* thus saving himself a tidy sum of money, Shaughnessy called his editors.

"Look, I've got this cute little story involving Bird," said Shaughnessy, as he explained the scene for his bosses. "The only problem is that it was a little expensive."

"How much did you lose?" asked his editor.

"One-sixty."

"All right, do the story and stick the losses on your expense account."

Shaughnessy did just that and received all sorts of compliments on the adventures with Bird. He also received his expense report back from the accounting department: an unacceptable expense, it said.

So Shaughnessy improvised. He filled out another expense form, but this time it featured eight twenty-dollar lunches with Celtics center Robert Parish. It passed, too.

Michael Jordan of the Chicago Bulls is another player who

gets high marks for civility. Despite the constant demands of the media, Jordan will sit patiently at his locker after a game and answer every question, however silly. Nor does it matter if the question comes from a *Sports Illustrated* writer or from someone who works for a small suburban paper—Jordan plays no favorites.

To understand Jordan's popularity, simply accompany the Bulls on a road trip. Fans fill the hotel lobby just to catch a glimpse of Jordan as he steps off the team bus. The crunch is just as severe at the arenas themselves.

At the Sports Arena in Los Angeles, the postgame crowd waiting for Jordan once was so large that Bulls team officials instructed the bus driver to pull the huge vehicle into the arena basement so Jordan could go directly from the locker room to his seat on the bus.

In 1988, while killing time before a preseason game in St. Louis, Jordan decided he would go shopping at a local mall. He was there ten minutes before he was besieged by autograph seekers.

Jack McCallum once arranged an interview with Jordan in 1987. In essence, Jordan agreed to let McCallum tag along with him for several days, the better to see what celebrity status was really like. One day, after a workout session at the Bulls facility in suburban Chicago, Jordan found himself mobbed by adoring fans as he made his way to his car.

"Let's go, Jack," he yelled to McCallum as they squeezed through the fans. "Let's move, let's go."

No sooner had Jordan started to drive away than a pair of cars cut him off in the parking lot. For a split second, McCallum thought Jordan was going to be assassinated.

"Oh, geez," said Jordan, as he pulled the car to a stop.

Out of the two other cars came a man holding a sweatsuit he had designed especially for Jordan to wear and a guy who had a tape recording of a rap song he had prepared especially for Jordan.

Jordan thanked them for their efforts and then climbed

back into the car. As they pulled out of the parking lot, McCallum said, "You really have a strange life."

"Yeah, I do," Jordan said.

Welcome to stardom, eh?

Jordan is a great player. Magic Johnson has no peer when it comes to controlling a game. Bird eats pressure for brunch. David Robinson is destined for greatness. But my personal favorite is Charles Barkley, the working man's player.

Barkley doesn't look like a star. He isn't sleek like Dominique Wilkens, or smooth like Clyde Drexler, or poetic in style like James Worthy. But he plays with passion and emotion, some of it occasionally misplaced.

For instance, according to Terry Pluto of the *Akron Beacon-Journal,* Barkley once turned to a referee after being called for a foul and simply said, "Suck my dick." The referee, realizing that this was the Barkley way, ignored the remark. If you can believe it, Barkley didn't mean it personally.

Sometimes players are reluctant to agree to one-on-one interviews with out-of-town writers they don't know. Sam Smith set up an interview with Barkley before the 1988 All-Star Game in Chicago only to be stiffed by the Sixers forward. Another session was planned, this one scheduled at a restaurant in Philadelphia. This time Barkley showed.

Wearing a hat, dark glasses and a large, heavy overcoat, Barkley took his place at the table. The interview began slowly but picked up steam by the hour's end. Out of the blue, Barkley turned to Smith and said, "You know, you're not a jerk."

Barkley is a lot like Doug Moe: He'll speak his mind, no matter the consequences. When someone stole the luggage of Sixers point guard Scott Brooks, who measures well under six feet, Barkley observed, "I guess they're going to be looking for a short thief."

When troubled guard Quintin Dailey botched a golden opportunity with the Lakers by arriving late to the team's training camp in Hawaii, Barkley couldn't believe it. "If the

Lakers had signed me, I'd have swum to Honolulu. And I would have been early."

And while we're on the subject of Dailey, how about the time he ordered a meal of popcorn, soft drink and hot dog—at courtside . . . on the bench . . . during a game. It happened near the end of the 1983–1984 season and Smith witnessed the whole thing from press row. Dailey asked an assistant coach for a five-dollar loan and gave the money to a ballboy, who ran to the nearest concession stand and placed the order. A few minutes later, Dailey was stuffing his face.

It remains the most unbelievable thing Smith has seen since he started covering the league.

Of course, Smith wasn't there the time Frank Layden, then the coach of the Jazz, refused to open the locker room door to reporters after a 1987 playoff loss to the Lakers at the Forum. Layden, normally the picture of jocularity, was peeved at the officiating and apparently thought that the presence of reporters might tempt him to say something he would later regret.

Meanwhile, angry sportswriters placed a sign on the door. It read, "Closed 'til Christmas."

As for saying something regrettable, Layden escaped without uttering a word. The silence, though, cost him a substantial fine from the league office. The NBA doesn't look kindly on gag rules, which is just another reason sportswriters love this league.

You want more reasons? How about the dental plan?

In 1981, Rick Reilly, then with the *Boulder Camera,* was sitting on press row at McNichols Arena when the Atlanta Hawks' Tom Burleson crashed to the floor directly in front of him. It was an awful tumble and as he got up, Burleson picked up something from the floor and flicked it in the direction of Reilly. It hit Reilly's sweater and then settled on his lap.

It was a tooth. Burleson's tooth.

And who can beat the travel experiences?

At least one NBA team (I'm sworn to secrecy on the team's identity) will never forget a flight it took in 1988. While taxiing toward the runway, the pilot reportedly clicked on his public address system and politely asked his passengers and flight attendants to buckle up and ready themselves for take-off. Then, forgetting to click the microphone off, he said, "Great, now all I need is a cup of coffee and a blowjob."

Moments later, a horror-stricken stewardess rushed toward the cockpit. Said a player as she sprinted past: "Hey, lady, you forgot the coffee."

One of the hardest-working players in the league is Hawks center Moses Malone. If nothing else, Malone must lead the league in sweat dripped. He is a tireless rebounder and a competent scorer. But a linguist he ain't.

An interview with Malone has to be heard to be appreciated. Malone tends to mumble, which isn't exactly a plus in the verbal age.

Back when Malone still was playing for the Washington Bullets, *Sports Illustrated* asked Jack McCallum to do a story on the center. As usual, McCallum called the public relations people and asked them to alert Moses to his arrival. When he showed up at practice a few days later, a member of the team's PR department assured him that Malone knew he was there.

After the workout, Malone showered and bolted for the door. McCallum caught him outside.

"Uh, Moses, I thought maybe we could talk."

"Youowemeacover," he said.

"I'm sorry, what's that?"

"Youowemeacover."

"I'm sorry, Moses, but could you repeat that."

"You—owe—me—a—cover," he said slowly.

In fact, the magazine had indeed semipromised him a place on the cover about two years earlier. Rolls of film had been used to capture just the right photo, but for whatever reason, the story was scrapped and Malone never made it to the cover.

"I'm real sorry about that, Moses, but there's nothing I can do about that," McCallum said.

Malone thought about it for a moment and decided he could answer a couple of questions. But only a couple. Five minutes into the interview, Malone said it was time to leave. So off he went.

In 1983, Malone was the starting center for the Sixers team that swept the Lakers in the NBA championship series. Even though he wasn't an ideal interview, he was one of the team's stars, and a crowd of reporters almost always surrounded his locker after a game. One night, as Malone sat naked on a stool in front of his locker, a radio reporter tried to slide his tape recorder through the many legs of the assembled writers.

All you could see was this arm pushing the machine toward Malone, who was busy mumbling about himself in the third person.

Unfortunately, the radio reporter shoved the recorder too far under Malone's wooden stool. Realizing his mistake, the reporter began reaching for the machine. As he grasped for the recorder, he came dangerously close to clutching a certain body part of a certain NBA center.

Among the reporters present that day was Bill Brown of the *Delaware County Times.* Brown watched the hand begin to reach between Malone's legs. And then, in the *clearest* voice anyone can ever remember from Malone, the center said to the arm, "I wouldn't do that if I were you!"

The radio reporter instantly pulled his arm back. After all, what's more important: sound quality or life?

Thug/power forward Maurice Lucas and *Seattle Times* columnist Steve Kelley also had problems in communication. Lucas would call Kelley a "fly-by-night writer." And if Lucas was in a particularly bad mood, he would curl his fists when Kelley approached and tell him, "If you don't get off my case, I'll give you one of these."

The relationship was at its worst toward the end of Lucas's stay with the Portland Trail Blazers. More often than not,

Lucas would threaten Kelley with those closed fists. Kelley, tired of the whole thing, finally told Lucas, "If you do hit me, and I survive, I'll be a wealthy man."

Lucas never hit him.

However, Lucas did help make Curry Kirkpatrick's 1978 visit to Portland a memorable one. Kirkpatrick, a senior writer for *Sports Illustrated,* was researching a story on the Trail Blazers when assistant coach Jack McKinney asked if he would appear on the team's television show, which was taped an hour or so before the game and then played on the local closed-circuit network. Kirkpatrick said yes.

The program was done right outside the Trail Blazers locker room. McKinney first interviewed Kirkpatrick about life as an NBA writer. Then it was time for a chalk-talk, complete with detailed strategy on the Trail Blazers' offense. As Kirkpatrick watched McKinney draw Xs and Os on the blackboard, Lucas and center Bill Walton darted onto the makeshift set, wrapped a blanket around the writer's body, threw a huge cream pie in his face and then ran away. And that's not the worst of it. Somehow a Los Angeles television station received a copy of the tape and ran it on their sports broadcast. From there, the incident was picked up by stations nationwide.

As for Kirkpatrick, all he got out of the deal was a mouthful of pie, a ruined leather jacket and a copy of the program. Some parting gift.

On occasion, the writers strike back.

In the early days of the Dallas Mavericks franchise, player representative Jim Spanarkel proudly announced that the beat reporters would have to confine themselves to the first three rows of the team bus. The beat reporters, who included then–*Dallas Morning News* writer Jan Hubbard, didn't like the tone of Spanarkel's order. It struck them as being self-important and, anyway, what had the reporters done to merit such treatment? Nothing, as far as anyone could figure.

On the next stop, which was Cleveland, Hubbard arranged

for a limousine to meet the team outside the airport's baggage claim area. As the Mavericks trudged toward the bus, the reporters walked toward the limo. In the window of the luxury auto was a sign that read, "Press Only."

As the chauffeur opened the door, Hubbard made a special point of looking for Spanarkel, whose surprised reaction made it all worthwhile. From that day on, no Mavericks beat reporter ever rode the team bus again that year. It was their way of telling Spanarkel what they thought of his rules.

One of the great moments in sportswriting was the time David Dupree, now with *USA Today,* beat Washington Bullets reserve Tom Kozelko in a game of one-on-one. Leigh Montville of *Sports Illustrated* saw it happen. Now granted, Kozelko, who played three years in the league (1973–1976) was no star, but he *was* an NBA player and that should count for something.

Another time, Rich Levin, then with the *Los Angeles Herald-Examiner,* was playing in a three-on-three game after a Lakers practice. His assignment was to guard Hall of Famer Jerry West, who was the team's coach at the time.

Levin did the best he could, but West, being West, kept sinking shot after shot. Finally, one of Levin's teammates turned to the beleaguered writer and said, "What's wrong, can't you guard that guy?"

It is one thing to play against an NBA player and quite another to be a player. For one strange night in Philadelphia, Thomas Stinson of the *Atlanta Journal-Constitution* became an NBA star.

It wasn't Stinson's doing, mind you. He was covering the 1980–1981 version of the Atlanta Hawks when he and Steve Hawes, who played for the Hawks, decided to have a beer in the hotel bar. The hotel wasn't one of the city's finest. It was located near the railroad and, many an evening, the barstools would be occupied by railroad engineers rather than hotel guests.

As Hawes and Stinson sipped their beers, one of the engineers, a big, burly guy, approached them.

"You play in the NBA?" he asked Hawes.

"Sure do," Hawes said.

The engineer then started asking what it was like to play in the league. Hawes answered the question and then pointed at Stinson.

"You know, this guy's been playing longer than me," he said. "You should be asking him the questions."

With that, Hawes got up and left, leaving Stinson to entertain the engineer and his buddies. Faced with no alternative, Stinson began to weave an imaginative tale that the Brothers Grimm would have been proud of.

Stinson, who is five-foot-eleven, told them that he had played at Drake University, that he had almost lost his leg in a car accident, that he was just a slow white guy who played his heart out. The engineers loved it.

"Who's the meanest guy in the league?" they asked excitedly. Stinson leaned back and calmly described the players who had intimidated him the most.

As payment for his time, the engineers kept buying Stinson the drinks of his choice. Half-drunk, Stinson staggered off the stool and said it was time for him to return to his room—curfew. As he left the bar, Stinson turned to his new buddies and told them to look him up if they were ever in Atlanta.

They will now—Stinson owes them money for the drinks.

6

An Ode to Bobby and His Basketball Buddies, and to All a Good Knight

Let me begin by saying that Bobby Knight is one of the finest coaches ever to wear an ill-fitting sweater that emphasizes a prodigious beer gut—bar none. And while I've never chosen an Indiana University team to win our office NCAA basketball pool, I can admit a certain fondness for the Hoosiers' man-on-man defense and Knight's insistence on running a pristine program.

As for the numbskull things Knight has had to say about sportswriters, well . . .

Fact is fact: With the exception of Puerto Rican police officers, I can think of nobody whom Knight despises more than someone carrying a press pass and an independent thought.

It was Knight who once said of sports reporters: "All of us learn to write in the second grade. Most of us then go on to greater things."

Like basketball, which we learned to play in third-grade gym class?

And it is Knight who mostly treats sportswriters as if they

were dirty jockstraps. To Knight's way of thinking, you are either for him or against him. And if you choose the latter, God help you.

Is Knight a great coach? Undoubtedly. A humanitarian? Often. A writer's best friend? Are you kidding?

If I had a son who wanted to play college basketball, I'd want him to play for Knight. However, if he wanted to be a sportswriter *and* cover Knight's Indiana team, I'd tell him to consider the wonderful world of aluminum siding.

This is the problem with covering college hoops: The coaches become the stars, not the players. Players come and go. Coaches stay, as do their sometimes dictatorial ways when dealing with the Fourth Estate. Knight is merely president of the club.

Knight's most publicized tirades involved sportswriter John Feinstein, who wrote a bestseller about the 1985–1986 IU basketball team. Knight hated the book and hated Feinstein for writing it. At one point, Knight accused Feinstein, now with the *National,* of being a pimp. Later, Knight accused him of being a whore.

"Well," said Feinstein, "I wish he'd make up his mind so I'd know how to dress."

It wasn't always this way. There was a time when Knight and Feinstein almost were pals.

Back before the book was published, Knight and Feinstein were leaving the University of Illinois basketball arena after an important Hoosiers victory when they were stopped by autograph seekers. Under normal circumstances, Knight might have signed a few scraps of paper and moved on.

But this was different. His Indiana team had won a big game and by doing so had beaten Illinois coach Lou Henson, whom Knight disliked—a lot. Knight was in a buoyant mood and happily signed away. As he did, one of the autograph seekers turned to Feinstein and said, "Hey, Coach, can we get you, too?"

Feinstein, who obviously had been mistaken for an IU assistant, shook his head no.

With that, the autograph seeker turned to a friend and said, "Get this, Knight signs, but this asshole won't."

Knight roared with laughter when he heard that one. As it turns out, it would be about the last time he cracked a smile at anything involving Feinstein.

Knight's peculiar sense of media relations wasn't confined to Feinstein. Other writers felt his wrath and have the scorch marks to prove it. Or in the case of Russ Brown, a *Louisville Courier-Journal* reporter, the powder burns.

Brown had just finished interviewing Illinois' Henson after a game at IU when he saw Knight standing in a hallway talking to another reporter. Brown walked by, but Knight said nothing. There wasn't even a nod of recognition. A few steps later, Brown heard Knight's voice.

"Hey, Russ," said Knight.

Brown turned around in time to see Knight aiming a gun at him. He saw Knight squeeze the trigger and then the blast of what turned out to be a very loud starter's pistol. The sound caromed off the hallway walls and it wasn't until a few moments later that Brown knew he had been a victim of an ill-conceived practical joke.

"You missed," Brown said.

"Wait until you shake your head," said Knight.

Brown's employers wanted to know if he wished to sue; wanton endangerment is a crime in most states. Brown declined.

Once Brown wrote a story that angered Knight more than usual. So displeased was Knight that he phoned Brown at home late one evening, late enough that both Brown and his wife were asleep. Brown's wife answered the call and was greeted by a polite and apologetic Knight.

Could he please speak with Russ? Knight asked sweetly.

Why certainly, said Mrs. Brown.

Knight's disposition changed shortly thereafter. The more Knight talked to Brown, the madder he got. The conversation ended with Knight threatening to shove a typewriter up Brown's you-know-what if Brown ever visited the Indiana locker room again.

The next game was at Notre Dame and, as you might expect, Brown was there, as was a *Courier-Journal* photographer to record all unpleasantries should Knight be so inclined. At game's end, Brown took his seat in the interview room and waited for Knight to arrive.

At last, Knight walked in.

"Anybody got a question?" Knight said.

Brown asked a question.

"Again, anybody got a question?"

Brown repeated his question.

"Does anybody else have a question?"

"Yeah, does that mean you're not going to answer my question?" Brown said.

"Yes."

Brown covered Knight and Indiana basketball for thirteen seasons. And while they disagreed often, Brown probably will have a soft spot, however tiny, for the difficult Knight. One of his favorite memories is the time Knight walked into the postgame press conference grinning from ear to ear. Indiana had beaten Illinois (again) and Knight was in a charitable mood. Better yet, a *60 Minutes* CBS film crew (complete with Dan Rather) was there to do a profile on him for an upcoming show.

"Damn, I feel good today," said Knight, glancing at Brown. "I feel so good I'm going to ask you how you are."

Brown was amazed by the graciousness.

"You feel all right?" Knight said, shaking Brown's hand.

"All I can say," said Brown, "is that you must be feeling *real* good."

Knight was always picking on somebody. If it wasn't Feinstein, it was Brown. If it wasn't Brown, it was *Sports Illustrated*'s Curry Kirkpatrick. Kirkpatrick made the mistake (at least, in Knight's eyes) of appearing on that same *60 Minutes* show and offering a less favorable view of the fabled

Knight. And although the program hadn't been aired when Kirkpatrick attended an IU game on the final day of the season, Knight acted hostile, as if he had been told the content of Kirkpatrick's taped interview with Rather.

This was the year (1980) that IU won the Big Ten championship on the final day of the regular season. Kirkpatrick was on deadline, but decided to attend Knight's postgame press conference and then return to his typewriter at courtside. Bad move.

Kirkpatrick had just settled into his seat when Knight stomped into the room. The coach began to discuss the game and Kirkpatrick, head down, began scribbling notes. A few moments later he heard, "Kirkpatrick, what are you doing here?"

Kirkpatrick looked up and smiled. How nice of Knight to notice him, he thought.

Problem was, Knight wasn't smiling back. In fact, Knight began a profanity-laden speech that was directed entirely at Kirkpatrick.

Knight wanted the writer out of the room. He even threatened to end the press conference if Kirkpatrick didn't leave immediately.

"I want you all to know that I'm not saying one more word until that asshole leaves and you all know who I mean."

Kirkpatrick gathered his things. "In deference to my colleagues, I'll leave," he said. "I'm leaving, but I'm leaving for these people's sake, not yours."

"You're leaving because I told you so, asshole," Knight said.

Kirkpatrick made his way to courtside and started typing his story on a machine borrowed from another *Sports Illustrated* writer. The computer happened to have an *SI* logo on it. As he typed, several Indiana fans noticed the magazine logo and began heckling Kirkpatrick and throwing debris at him.

"Hey, *SI*, what do you think of that?" one of them yelled.

Another IU fan walked by and began slapping Kirkpatrick with a Hoosiers pennant. Tough day at work.

Sports Illustrated wrote a letter of protest to the Indiana University president, but that was about it. Kirkpatrick didn't mention the incident with Knight or the fans in his game story, which explains why Knight hugged him a few weeks later at the Final Four in Philadelphia. Knight, Kirkpatrick was told, apparently respected the writer's restraint, enough so that he later sent Kirkpatrick an autographed copy of a book entitled, *All I Know About Coaching Basketball.*

The pages were blank.

All was well between Kirkpatrick and Knight until the 1984 Olympic Trials. That's when Knight, coach of the United States team, turned the tryout camp into a security stronghold. Guards, wearing suits and packing guns, patrolled the areas during practice. These were not pleasant people.

Somehow, Kirkpatrick lost his media credentials, but still managed to attend one of the workouts. As he stood talking with the other basketball writers, two of the armed guards approached him.

"Can we see your credentials?" asked one of the guards.

"Well, you see . . ."

The guards grabbed Kirkpatrick and tugged him away. They took him to a small room near the courts and kept him there.

"Who the hell are you guys?" said Kirkpatrick.

No response. At last one of them made a phone call, nodded, and led Kirkpatrick out onto the courts and to a tower occupied by, you guessed it, Knight, who used the vantage point to observe the workout.

Basketballs stopped bouncing. Drills ceased. Knight looked down at Kirkpatrick and then tossed him the missing credentials.

"Fucking Kirkpatrick," he said, "you're just lucky I'm a nice guy."

The writers of *Sports Illustrated* always have had mixed

success with Knight. Depending on the day and the most recent story about him or his IU program, Knight could be steamed or gracious. You never knew for sure until the moment he looked into your eyes or opened his mouth. Then the secret was out.

Jack McCallum once was sent to Bloomington by his *SI* editors to do a story on Hoosiers stars Ted Kitchel and Randy Wittman. Of course, any piece on any player at IU meant having to speak with Knight, which is easier said than done.

McCallum, who had never met Knight, began the process of arranging an interview with the famed coach. After about a dozen phone conversations with the school's sports information department, McCallum was told Knight would see him.

And then it hit McCallum: He would actually have to talk to Knight. *The* Bobby Knight. The great and all-powerful Knight. The Knight who had molded young men into whatever he wanted them to be, which takes one hell of a strong mold. That Knight.

The interview took place in the Indiana dressing room. McCallum asked his questions about Kitchel and Wittman, and much to the writer's surprise, Knight answered them. And politely, too.

McCallum let his mind wander ever so briefly. He wondered why he had ever been nervous about speaking with Knight in the first place. This guy was a pussycat, as soft as cashmere. Any more accommodating and he'd have to send Knight a thank-you note.

Knight started to describe each player on the Indiana roster. It was when he reached the name of Jim Thomas, a guard, that Knight's disposition took a turn for the worse.

"If I only could get Jim Thomas to . . ." said Knight, searching desperately for the right word. "To . . ."

Unable to adequately describe "killer instinct," Knight reached over and without warning grabbed McCallum's shirt and, with it, McCallum's necklace and a small handful of chest hairs. McCallum didn't know whether to cry or scream for help.

"You know, I want this from him!" said Knight.

"Hmmm," McCallum said, wincing.

It is hard to retain your dignity when valuable chest hairs are fluttering toward a locker room floor. But McCallum did his best. He had done nothing to offend Knight, yet the coach, in his own unmistakable way, had sent a message. Knight wanted McCallum to know that this was his domain, that McCallum was merely a guest and only marginally welcome, at that.

McCallum understood immediately.

For a number of reasons, the story on Kitchel and Wittman never ran. And for a number of reasons, including the amount of time Knight had given him, McCallum felt compelled to call to apologize.

"Bobby, you're not going to believe this," McCallum said, "but after all the time you gave me, the story isn't running."

McCallum expected a tempest. Instead, he received a gentle breeze.

"I understand your business a lot better than you think I do," Knight said calmly. "I understand this happens all the time."

McCallum hung up the phone that day freshly intimidated and thoroughly confused. To this day, he understands Knight not one bit.

Knight is an Indiana state treasure. They might as well designate his IU office a historical landmark, such is his appeal in Indiana and the surrounding region.

For example, when word leaked that Knight might accept an offer to coach at New Mexico, people went bonkers. They couldn't believe that their beloved Bobby would leave IU for anyplace else.

There were skeptics, including *Louisville Courier-Journal* columnist Rick Bozich, who thought that Knight was simply using the New Mexico offer to secure his standing at IU, to say nothing of having his ego enriched by concerned Hoosiers fans. So convinced was Bozich of Knight's intentions that he told a radio audience that very thing.

They take their basketball seriously in Indiana and Kentucky. Bozich had been threatened in anonymous letters and phone calls before and there was little doubt that his comments about Knight might prompt similar action. And don't think his friends and neighbors didn't know it, either.

As Bozich pulled into his driveway after appearing on the radio show, he noticed a large cardboard sign attached to the utility pole that stood between his house and his neighbor's. "Bozich lives here," read the top of the sign, complete with an arrow that pointed toward the Bozich residence. "Not here," read the bottom half, this time with an arrow pointed toward the neighbor's house.

You expect the unexpected when dealing with Knight. For instance, Rick Reilly of *Sports Illustrated* once was supposed to meet Knight for a 9:00 A.M. interview session. Knight was visiting Denver at the time, so Reilly arranged to be at the coach's hotel a little before nine.

The appointed hour came and went and Reilly, standing in the middle of the hotel lobby, began to worry. What if he had missed him? What if Bobby Knight, one of the country's most recognizable sports figures, had walked right past him? What would Reilly tell his editors?

At 9:45, Reilly raced to the house phones and called Knight's room. No answer. He hopped on an elevator and then knocked on Knight's door. There was the clicking of locks, soon followed by the grand sight of Knight in his birthday suit.

"C'mon in, I'm taking a shower," Knight said "Talk to me now."

So Reilly, his glasses fogging with steam, sat on a toilet bowl and conducted an interview as America's most controversial coach lathered up.

Of course, it could have been worse. Reilly could have tried to track down the human perpetual motion machine,

Georgia Tech's Bobby Cremins. *Atlanta Journal-Constitution* reporter Thomas Stinson was kept waiting three hours for Cremins one day. Then Cremins walked out of his office and said, "I don't have any time for you."

"But I just need to ask you a couple of questions."

"OK, come with me."

Off they went, with Stinson doing his best to keep up with the hyperactive Cremins. They ended up in the coaches' locker room. Well, not exactly the coaches' locker room, but the coaches' bathroom stall.

"OK, go ahead," Cremins said, as he closed the door to the stall.

Fearing that this would be the only time Cremins would talk, Stinson began the session. A fragrant interview it wasn't.

Knight and Cremins aren't the only coaching characters in college basketball, though Knight is probably the most celebrated. Truth be known, there are those who consider Lefty Driesell every bit as entertaining.

Driesell is a piece of work, all right. He once invited John Feinstein, who was doing a magazine story on the then-Maryland coach, to his house for breakfast. Driesell's wife walked into the kitchen and Driesell said lovingly, "Momma, we need some breakfast. Fix us some pancakes."

So she did, about fifty in all. Driesell and Feinstein, both owners of healthy appetites, cleaned the plates until one pancake remained.

"John," said Driesell, "you go ahead and eat that last one."

"No, Lefty, you go ahead."

"I can't. I'm on a diet."

While researching that same magazine story, Feinstein accompanied Driesell on a recruiting trip one evening—Halloween night, to be exact.

As they were walking toward a recruit's apartment building, a small pack of children wearing brown paper bags appeared.

"Trick or treat!" they yelled in unison.

"Trick or treat, what?" Driesell barked back. "I ain't got no treats."

"Trick or treat!" they said again.

Driesell reached into his pocket and pulled out his money clip. It was dark outside and he could barely see as he peeled bill after bill and dropped the cash into each child's goodies bag.

"Here you go," he said. "Here you go, too."

Moments later, the money clip was bare and the children were gone. Driesell looked at the clip and said. "Damn, I hope I didn't have no big bills in there."

Driesell was the king of early morning phone calls. It got to the point where Driesell's secretary would warn writers of the coach's mood (stern, foul or dreadful) before he even called. At least that way the writer knew how to the prepare for Driesell's voice a few moments later.

Michael Wilbon of the *Washington Post* got a call once. Actually, he got lots of calls from Driesell, but this one illustrated the coach's friendly ways.

The night before, Driesell's Maryland team had been beaten by Notre Dame. Afterward, Driesell mentioned that his team had been outhustled and outwitted. Wilbon added that Maryland also had been outcoached.

Wilbon's phone rang at about seven the next morning. It was Driesell. Someone had dropped a copy of the story by his office and highlighted the offending parts in yellow magic marker.

Wilbon then read to him the entire story, which put the remarks in better and more accurate context.

"Oh," said Driesell, "go back to bed."

This is the same Driesell who called Feinstein in Puerto Rico one morning.

"What time is it, Lefty?" Feinstein asked groggily.

"It's eleven o'clock in Puerto Rico."

Feinstein checked his alarm clock. "No, it's not, Lefty. It's 8:00 A.M."

"Oh," said Driesell, who never could quite figure out that whole time zone thing.

Driesell rarely held a grudge. One day he might yell at a reporter, the next day he would invite the same reporter out for pizza. Driesell used to have a file labeled "Negative Reporting." Wilbon learned of the file's existence the first day he ever met Driesell.

"If you're around here long enough, and you're good enough," Driesell said that day, "you'll be in here."

Sally Jenkins, who also used to cover Maryland for the *Washington Post*, once wrote that Driesell's team wouldn't contend for the Atlantic Coast Conference that particular year. Driesell heard about the story and later, on a radio talk show, he criticized Jenkins and her theories about the team's chances for an ACC title.

Jenkins, a tiny bit unnerved by Driesell's radio performance, didn't go near the coach the next day at practice. Instead, she chatted with the assistant coaches. The radio show was mentioned.

Later, Driesell took Jenkins aside. "You think I'm mad at you," he said gently. "I wasn't mad at you. I was just telling you you was wrong."

Partly because of the drug-related death of Len Bias, Driesell was forced out of his coaching position at Maryland. He eventually accepted a job at James Madison University. Jenkins was sent there to do a story on the transition.

In typical Driesell style, they ate lunch at a truck stop restaurant. Jenkins ordered a cheeseburger.

"That's not enough food," Driesell said, and told the waitress to bring the reporter a chili dog, too. Then he ordered her a chocolate milkshake. At meal's end, Jenkins was ready to vomit.

"Will there be anything else?" the waitress asked, clutching the check.

"Yeah," said Driesell, glancing at Jenkins, "bring her some pie, some pie will do."

Driesell wouldn't let Jenkins leave the table until she ate at least four bites.

That's Driesell for you: generous, almost to a fault.

The same has been said for Louisiana State's Dale Brown, a man who had the governor switch removed form his emotions years ago. If nothing else, he treats each moment with a certain zest. Eccentric, full of life, controversial, Brown is a showman who happens to coach basketball. Some say he kills you with insincerity. Supporters contend that he is merely passionate in his beliefs.

Whatever the case—and nobody knows for sure with Brown—he remains one of the more entertaining characters to kneel at courtside. I know this much: The Southeastern Conference (and the writers who cover it) would miss his little quirks.

Mark Bradley, columnist for the *Atlanta Journal-Constitution,* has done his share of stories on Brown. And contrary to popular belief, the LSU coach struck him as a less comic figure and a more perplexing personality than he had first thought.

There is a period of summer when sports reaches a dead spot of sorts. In Atlanta, it comes especially early, what with the Braves out of the pennant race by June or July, the Hawks season complete and the Georgia Bulldogs not yet underway. Who you gonna call?

Brown, of course.

Brown has saved the day for Bradley, and other columnists, with tales of his vacation exploits on, say, the Amazon River. He has waxed poetic about visiting Yugoslavia and the holy place where, legend has it, the Virgin Mary appears in the sky and the sun spins.

You don't interview Brown as much as you grunt in the right places, says Bradley. A single conversation with Brown can disorder the senses. In no time at all—and we're not making this up, either—Brown can stuff the names of assassin Sirhan Sirhan, singer Lou Rawls, Olympian Jesse Owens, Russian pole vaulter Sergei Bubka, Knight (he hates him), the town of Bunky, Louisiana, and "El Sicko" (Adolf

Hitler, to the rest of us) into just one chat. I don't care who you are, that takes some doing.

And word has it that Brown can't make it through an interview without telling at least one story involving the three D's: death, divorce and dismemberment.

Just last summer, Bradley checked his mailbox and discovered a postcard from, of all places, Crete. It was from Dale Brown.

"Here I am, thinking of you," wrote Brown.

To which Bradley wondered, "Why would he think of me in Crete?"

The explanation comes easily. Bradley once asked Brown why he insists on recruiting players whose backgrounds or situations are a bit out of the ordinary.

"Well," said Brown, "the unique attracts me."

Jimmy Hyams, now with the *Knoxville News Sentinel,* once attended an LSU practice during the 1983–1984 season in which Brown was upset with the Tigers' dubious shot selection. They had just played Houston and shot a miserable 41 percent. That next day at practice, Brown made sure to remind everyone of those very numbers.

"You're not taking good shots," he said. "The ones you're taking are out of your range."

Later, Don Redden, who died several years ago, attempted about a sixteen-foot jumper from the corner and missed. Brown halted the workout and called Redden over.

"Just for fun, let's see how many of those shots you can make in five tries," Brown said.

Redden went back to the corner and promptly made four out of five.

Brown forced a smile.

"OK, we're going to put a defender on you."

This time, even with a defender draped over him, Redden still managed to hit four out of five shots.

Brown raised his arms in disgust. "Well, my point is lost," he said, and walked off the court, leaving Redden to exchange high fives with the team managers.

Travel to the other end of the coaching spectrum and you'll find North Carolina's Dean Smith. Smith's program is above reproach. There is an elegance to his teams, which, of course, is directly related to Smith's coaching style.

Despite his many accomplishments, though, Smith remains a modest person, almost exasperatingly so. John Feinstein discovered this while interviewing him for a story.

For months, Feinstein had tried to arrange an extended one-on-one interview with the legendary Smith. And every time, Smith said his schedule prevented him from making such a commitment.

Then one day Smith called and said he was driving to Charlotte: Would Feinstein like to have lunch with him, accompany him to Charlotte and then drive Smith's car back to Chapel Hill? Feinstein was out the door in minutes.

The month was February, which explains why Smith kept the windows rolled up as they drove to Charlotte. It also explains why Feinstein was gagging for air as Smith, a chain smoker, puffed away.

Halfway there, Smith asked, "Would you like to stop and get a soda?"

"*Yes!*" said Feinstein.

As they searched for a gas station, Feinstein continued his interview. Among the questions was, "What's it like to own a state? Everyone in North Carolina thinks you're a god."

To which the coach said, "I'm just a guy named Smith."

It was about then that they found a place to stop. Short of change for the soda machine, Feinstein and Smith walked into the small gas station office to break a couple of dollar bills.

Behind the counter was a good ol' boy, complete with good ol' boy twang and manners. He glanced at Feinstein and nodded. He looked at Smith and then did a doubletake.

"Oh my gawd," he said, staring at an embarrassed Smith, "it's Norman Sloan."

Smith began laughing. He had been mistaken for former

North Carolina State coach Norm Sloan. He turned to Feinstein and said, "I told you so. I'm just a guy named Smith."

Equally respected but often misunderstood is John Thompson of Georgetown. Thompson's image is that of an over-bearing, overprotective and, at times, overly smug head coach. And on occasion, maybe Thompson is a bit too much on the righteous side.

Members of the media criticize Thompson because he shrouds his program in secrecy. Player access is almost non-existent. Nor is Thompson the most open interview in the world, either. Thompson went so far as to introduce his players to the beat reporters covering the team. "So you know not to talk to them," he would say.

But Thompson also has a soft spot as big as the Sta-Puf Marshmallow Man.

Once, Thompson was talking to Michael Wilbon when Wilbon mentioned that he was late for a going-away party.

"For who?" asked Thompson.

"Dave Kindred," said Wilbon (Kindred was then a *Washington Post* columnist).

"Where's Kindred going?"

"Atlanta."

A hard rain doused Washington that night, but still most everyone made it to the party, including Wilbon. A few hours later, after making his farewells, Wilbon decided it was time to leave. As he stepped out into the rain again, a taxi pulled up. Out popped Thompson holding a bottle of champagne for Kindred. It was his going-away present.

Several years later, during the 1986 NCAA tournament, Wilbon was called home to Chicago because of the death of his father. It was obviously a trying and emotional time, but one made slightly easier by an unlikely source: Thompson.

It was Thompson who sent what turned out to be the largest wreath of flowers to the Wilbon family. It was signed on behalf of Thompson and the entire Georgetown team.

To this day, Wilbon still doesn't know how Thompson got the address.

Another nice guy is Villanova's Rollie Massimino, as Ray Didinger of the *Philadelphia Daily News* will tell you.

Some backround: About eight months before Didinger was sent to cover an NCAA tournament game involving Villanova at Northeastern University, he had written a touching column about his grandfather. He wrote about his grandfather's love for sports and his particular affection for the city's pro teams, specifically the Phillies and the Eagles. He wrote about how his grandfather never booed a Philadelphia team and how he passed this same affection for sports to young Ray.

So here he was, almost a year later, at a Villanova postseason game. It was a close affair, with the Wildcats earning an overtime victory in the waning moments of the game. It was a difficult game to cover and obviously an emotional and exhausting game to coach.

Afterward, Massimino was led to the interview room for a brief talk with the assembled reporters. Massimino might look groomed at a game's beginning, but by its conclusion he looks as if he has been in a bar brawl. It was no different that night. His hair was mussed, his tie only in the general vicinity of his collar and his face bathed in perspiration.

Massimino wearily answered whatever questions there were about the thrilling win. That done, he started to make his way toward the door.

Waiting for him was Didinger, who had never met Massimino before. He wanted to ask the Villanova coach one more question about the game.

"Excuse me, Rollie, my name's Ray Didinger of the *Daily News* and . . ."

Massimino's face immediately brightened.

"That was a beautiful column you wrote on your grandfather," the coach said without hesitation.

Can you imagine that? First words out of his mouth to a

writer he had never met were about a column written eight months earlier. Hey, Rollie, you're OK.

Maybe it's just me, but I think college coaches are a wee bit more sensitive to outside criticism than their professional counterparts. And it's easy to see why. Their every move is scrutinized by boosters, peers and media alike. And many times, they're prisoners of sorts in cozy college towns.

Of course, they know that going in.

At Michigan State, where coach Jud Heathcote presides, times can be tough for those writers regularly assigned to cover the team. Heathcote reads and remembers every word written about his Spartans. Negative publicity is not appreciated.

Lansing State Journal sportswriter Jack Ebling would need an abacus to calculate the number of times Heathcote has thrown him out of practice after a particularly harsh story appeared in that day's paper. The ritual rarely changes.

Ebling writes tough story.

Heathcote gets upset.

Ebling attends practice.

Heathcote sends team manager to tell him to leave.

Ebling and Heathcote make up the next day.

Nor is Heathcote against calling a sportswriter at, say, 7:00 A.M. to vent his anger about a story. Heathcote will explain, in no uncertain terms, why the reporter is absolutely wrong and why he is absolutely right. Five minutes later, Heathcote will say, "So, you want to play golf tomorrow, or what?"

Senses of humor are sometimes in short supply in the Big Ten. In 1989, Ebling did a prediction story for a national basketball magazine. Somebody had to finish last, and he picked Iowa.

Iowa wasn't pleased.

Somehow, results of his preseason choices were leaked before the magazine's actual release, which gave Hawkeye fans, players and coaches even more time to become peeved.

The Michigan State football team visited Iowa in early October. The week before the trip, Ebling received an interesting phone call from an angry Iowa farmer who simply couldn't believe that the sportswriter had picked his beloved Hawkeyes basketball team to finish—and he could barely spit out the word—last.

"I want to bet you one thousand dollars that Iowa will finish ahead of your Michigan State," the farmer said.

Ebling tried to explain that it wasn't really his Michigan State. He only covered the team, he didn't own them.

"C'mon," said the farmer. "One thousand dollars."

"I'm not going to bet you, sir. I'm not going to take your money."

The farmer vowed he would see him at the football game the following Saturday.

Meanwhile, Ebling had written a letter requesting credentials for the game. A few days later, a response arrived. In it, the Iowa sports information department informed Ebling that he had been granted a place in the press box. And by the way, he would be seated between Tom Davis, the Iowa basketball coach, and several Iowa players. The letter, which began, "Dear Jerk, I mean Jack," suggested Ebling might want to secure the use of a flak jacket.

The sports information office was kidding. Well, sort of kidding.

Ebling arrive at the Iowa campus that day and was beseiged by colleagues who wanted comments concerning the week's events. Ebling even appeared on a radio talk show with Davis to discuss the story. Ebling told the listeners not to get too upset. A year earlier, he picked Indiana to finish seventh in the conference. The Hoosiers finished first.

Despite being mocked, taunted and demeaned, there are those rare moments when a sportswriter triumphs. Not often, but enough.

Jimmy Hyams provided college basketball writers with one of their finest victories. It came during the 1987 Southeastern

Conference tournament at Atlanta's Omni, where SEC officials had organized a brief free-throw-shooting contest involving fans randomly chosen from the stands and three
sportswriters. Hyams was one of the three.

Each contestant would shoot ten free-throws. The opponent was none other than Ted St. Martin, who held the
world's record for most consecutive free-throws, something
like two thousand in a row.

Hyams shot third and had made seven straight free throws
when the crowd of about fourteen thousand began to take
notice. His eighth shot rattled the rim and then fell through
the net. The crowd yelled "Eight!" And then "Nine!" And
then "Ten!"

Hyams was ecstatic. He high-fived one of the other writers
and then watched as St. Martin made his way to the free-
throw line. On his first attempt, St. Martin missed. Incredibly, Hyams had won.

Earlier, a trip to Jamaica had been awarded to a lucky fan.
Hyams figured maybe the same. A car was a possibility. After
all, he had beaten the world champion.

Instead, he was presented with a certificate and a basketball.

The next year, the SEC tournament was played at LSU's
arena and, again, St. Martin was hired to take on all comers.
SEC officials then asked Hyams to defend his title.

Hyams said no.

"I don't have anything to prove," he said.

"If you shoot against him, I'll buy you a case of beer and a
pair of tennis shoes," said the SEC official.

"OK, I'll do it," Hyams said.

During the warmups, Hyams couldn't make a shot. Every
attempt clanged off the rim or backboard. It was embarrassing, really.

"The next shot I make, let's just start it from there," he
told the announcer.

Hyams made the next attempt. And his second. Third.
Fourth. Fifth. Sixth. Seventh. As he stood on the line for the

eighth try, the announcer bellowed over the public address system, "I wonder if he'll choke?"

Swish.

Number nine didn't go down as easily.

One shot left. Hyams, his knees shaking, pushed the ball toward the hoop. The ball hit and then settled through.

Out came St. Martin, who made his first shot. The second attempt was good, too. Shot number three wasn't as fortunate.

Hyams was champion—again. In two years, he was twenty for twenty; St. Martin was two for four. Some world record holder, eh?

The SEC didn't ask St. Martin back the following year. And the SEC official never paid Hyams the shoes and beer he owed him. That's OK. We know who won the damn thing—a sportswriter.

Strange, but wonderfully true.

7

The Road Warriors

Have I mentioned my good pal Fidel Castro and how I got him to scribble his commie pinko name on a Cuban-made baseball during a midnight visit to his Palace of the Revolution? Have I also mentioned that they don't take American Express in Havana? I know this because I tried to pay a hotel bill with the aforementioned Yankee imperialistic, capitalistic credit card. (I guess this was one case where I could have left home without it.)

Hey, the road is like that: It giveth and it taketh. One day an autographed baseball by a dictator, the next day the threat of washing dishes to pay off a hotel bill.

Sportswriters learn early on that there is nothing quite as exhilarating or exasperating as travel. The road is their life-blood and their curse. It is a fickle airplane, Friday the thirteenth hotel chains, lost luggage, expense account night-mares and language barriers. And that's just in New York City. You should see it when sportswriters—Ugly Americans personified—land on distant shores. International relations find themselves stretched.

141

Take this trip to Cuba a couple of years ago. As part of a Pan American Games delegation that included about a dozen journalists, we were shown the inner workings of the Cuban sports effort. We met athletes, coaches, assorted bureaucrats and the Bearded One who thinks he can pitch. Of course, the bureaucrats were a lot like bureaucrats everywhere, except that they smiled a lot and wore these odd short-sleeve shirts that Ferdinand Marcos used to favor.

It was quite an adventure, this trip, beginning with the flight from Miami to Havana. Waldo Pepper wouldn't have flown this plane, what with the oil spewing from an engine that coughed and wheezed like an old man fighting bronchitis. The pilot wore a "Top Gun" baseball cap and never once told us about safety precautions should we plunge into the Atlantic Ocean. I guess it wasn't worth the trouble.

We landed and took a bus into the capital. Havana still dresses as if it's 1950-something. The cars are all restored '56 Chevys that look like they could squash a Hyundai in the blink of an eye. There is smog to rival Los Angeles and the bars serve the smoothest rum your throat will ever know. And as you might expect, baseball is the preferred sport of this country and its ruling head.

For some reason, the bureaucrats took us to a Havana hospital one day, ushered us into a room and then showed us a film on the many medical advances in Cuba. Some film: thirty minutes of surgeons twirling their scalpels through patients' innards. How do you say "barf bag" in Spanish? Later, we were taken to a huge public park where we were introduced to some of Cuba's finest Olympic athletes. I didn't have the heart to tell them to never get sick in their own country.

The week ended with our meeting with the big guy himself. In fact, I have a picture on my office wall of Fidel and the rest of us. And yes, he wore those stupid army fatigues that night.

I'm still not sure why he agreed to autograph our baseballs, but I will say this: He has a nice signature, very good penmanship. Anyway, when people ask how I got his John Hancock, I tell them that Fidel and my dad pledged Phi Gamma Delta in college, but that Fidel was blackballed because of ideological differences. Later, he left the States and the next thing we knew, he was running a communist satellite country. He sent the baseball as a token of an abbreviated college friendship.

No takers yet on that yarn.

As for paying that hotel bill, I was saved by a loan from another sportswriter, thus sparing me from KP duty or dissident prison. A few hours later, we were back in Miami, reeking of rum. Hunter S. Thompson would have been proud.

American sportswriters will try anything once, even Cuba. I think we feel it is our duty. We also like to flex our American egos on occasion, especially when on foreign soil. It's a macho thing, I guess.

For instance the Brits can be a bit snooty when the mood strikes them. This is to be expected since they've had centuries of practice. Anyway, Mal Florence of the *Los Angeles Times* was at Royal Troon last year to cover the British Open when he met an English journalist from one of the London tabloids. This same journalist had been baiting American golfers during the pretournament press conferences with loaded questions about recent United States losses at Ryder Cup competition. Florence, who could sing the National Anthem backward, couldn't wait to be introduced to His Angloness.

"I say, old boy, you haven't been to England before, have you?" said the journalist in a tone that struck Florence as blatantly condescending.

"Why, yes, I have," Florence said. "In fact, I was stationed twenty miles from here. Our flight group helped perfect the precision daylight bombing that saved your limey asses."

And then he walked away, leaving the Englishman with mouth agape. Thing was, Florence hadn't actually flown any such missions. A B-24? Florence probably thought it was a vitamin shot. But guess what? The tabloid writer quit acting as if the States were still part of the empire. Kind of makes you want to hum "The Battle Hymn of the Republic," doesn't it?

Mark Purdy of the *San Jose Mercury News* was at Wimbledon one year when he decided to become a patriot of sorts. It is customary when the Duke and Duchess of Kent walk into the tennis stadium for everyone to stand. Normally, Purdy would have complied out of politeness. But on this particular day, the Fourth of July, to be exact, Purdy chose to remain seated. He figured that the Duke and Duchess would understand.

No one else did, of course. Purdy's gesture was greeted by nasty stares and lots of "hrrumpffs" and "tsk, tsks." Just to put them in their place, Purdy was tempted to ask them about General Cornwallis's record against the colonists.

One place you definitely want to watch what you do or say is behind the Iron Curtain—even if the Curtain has rusted and fallen down—where senses of humor are in short supply among Uzi-toting types. Maybe their holsters are on too tight.

Jere Longman of the *Philadelphia Inquirer* was pulled over for speeding while on assignment in East Germany in 1988. The patrolwoman sauntered up to Longmans' West German–made rental car and demanded forty marks, or else things could get ugly. Longman reached into his wallet and promptly offered the money.

"No," she said, "West German marks." Turns out that East German money is so useless that not even their own citizens want it.

Longman didn't have enough West German currency, so another sportswriter in the car paid the ticket. But Longman did have to sign for the ticket. So on the dotted line he wrote "Jethro Bodine." Ms. Robocop didn't even notice.

The Soviet Union is another place where local customs are a bit unnerving. Ken Denlinger of the *Washington Post,* Randy Harvey of the *Los Angeles Times* and Diane Shah, then with *Newsweek,* were covering the 1980 Summer Games in Moscow when they decided to stroll across Red Square in search of a store that reportedly sold Red Army belts. Half-way there, they suddenly noticed a man chain himself to a fence and set himself on fire. Before you could say Vladivostok, about three hundred police materialized out of nowhere, smothering the fire and attending to the burned man. That done, the police began confiscating the cameras of all tourists in the area and not so politely disposing of their film.

Shah had a camera and somehow had managed to fire off a few frames before the police appeared. They grabbed her by the arms and took the camera away. That's when Denlinger intervened, only to be restrained by another member of the local police. So Shah did what any American would do: She screamed. Jamie Lee Curtis, cult queen of slice-and-dice flicks, couldn't have done any better. Stunned, the police handed Shah her camera (and film) back. The incident ended when all tourists were herded off Red Square in twos.

Later, Shah called a central number provided by the Soviets in which journalists could inquire about the day's events in the city—sporting or otherwise.

"Yes," began Shah, "I'm calling about the incident in Red Square today."

"What incident?" the voice asked icily. "There was no incident in Red Square today."

Of course there wasn't. It was a marshmallow roast.

Tom Callahan, then with the now-defunct *Washington Star*, was in Moscow in 1979 covering the Spartacade, sort of a dress rehearsal for the Olympics, when he stepped outside of the hotel lobby with a beer bottle in his hand. Moments later he was confronted by a squatty Russian wearing, recalls Callahan, "a Harry Truman suit and looking every bit the part of Ernest Borgnine." Callahan, six-foot-two, didn't know whether to laugh or move along.

He decided to stay put, which enraged the stubby Russian enough that the man knocked Callahan's precious beer out of his hand. A fist fight started shortly thereafter.

By all accounts, the brief exchange of punches was the

best-attended event of the Spartacade. The Russian was led away by police and Callahan was left to ponder his fate. Nothing, of course, happened during the remainder of his stay, except that the hotel maids, who wore these glued-on I-spy expressions, seemed to be rifling through his belongings a bit more frequently.

It wasn't until Callahan attempted to obtain a visa for the 1980 Summer Games that he wondered if perhaps the little disturbance hadn't made him a marked man. Four consecutive days of camping out at the Russian embassy in Washington had produced nothing but stress and repeated "come back tomorrows." The Games were about to begin and Callahan was stuck in the States waiting for Russian approval.

So he bitched, pompously and belligerently enough to attract the attention of an exasperated Soviet bureaucrat, who finally met with Callahan.

"Let me read you this," said the Soviet as he unfolded a San Diego newspaper clipping on the 1979 games.

"Games of sorrow . . . a lot of the world isn't here . . . a somber opening ceremony," recited the official.

Done, he put away the clipping and said, "I don't care what the *Washington Star* says about us. There has never been a nice word about us."

And that was that. Callahan's visa request was denied. But several years later when he requested one to cover the Goodwill Games for *Time* magazine the Russians said yes. Glasnost.

Perhaps the most adventuresome trip involving an American sportswriter behind the Iron Curtain features John Feinstein, then with the *Washington Post*. On hand to cover the 1986 Goodwill Games in Moscow, Feinstein witnessed the amazing record-breaking performance of Russian pole vaulter Sergei Bubka. Afterward, Feinstein and Dave Kindred, also with the *Post* at the time, made their way down to the track and spoke with two American vaulters, Mike Tully and Earl Bell.

"So, what makes this guy so great?" said Feinstein.

"The doctor," Tully said.

Tully went on to suggest that a wonder drug had been developed by Soviet scientists that enhanced the performance of their athletes. "I'm telling you," Tully said, "there's no way the guy can be that good."

Bell said little, but pressed his thumb down in the air, as if pushing a hypodermic needle.

The next day the *Post* headline read something like, "Bubka Breaks Record: Vaulters Accuse Bubka of Drug Use." The Soviets, of course, were steaming. At a press conference, the minister of Soviet sports said that the reporter responsible for the story was of "low character." Asked to comment, Feinstein said, "I resent it, but I don't deny it."

Later, a representative from Tass, the official Soviet news agency, stuck his finger in Feinstein's face and said, "Are you a professional journalist?" Feinstein, diplomatic as always, accused the guy of being a tool of the state. As you might imagine, that went over real big.

Soon, Feinstein found himself followed everywhere by a Soviet policeman of some sort. And *Pravda,* the Soviet newspaper, mentioned Feinstein in an extensive story it did on the successes of the Goodwill Games. "Who is this dull, unoriginal, roundish American reporter who weaves the long-lost breath of the Cold War?" wrote *Pravda.* Retorted Feinstein: "Dull and unoriginal, maybe, but roundish is hitting above the belt."

It doesn't end there. From Russia, Feinstein was supposed to travel to Czechoslovakia and cover Martina Navratilova's return to her homeland for a tennis match. Then Feinstein's office called: One of Czechoslovakia's brightest young hockey players had just defected to the United States to play for the Washington Capitals—could he do the story?

Somehow Feinstein tracked down the player's coach, and later the player's family. The whole thing was all very hush-hush.

They met at the family's apartment and had chatted for about an hour when there was a knock on the door. Two men entered the apartment brandishing official-looking badges.

"Who are they?" whispered Feinstein.

"Czech secret police," came the reply.

"Oy vei," said Feinstein.

The police wanted to know how Feinstein had found the family and who had given him permission to do so. Feinstein said the country's ice hockey federation had given him approval (a half-lie). After an hour's worth of discussion, the police returned Feinstein's passport papers and told him not to talk to anyone else while in Czechoslovakia. Of course, said Feinstein, who returned to his hotel and sent his story to Washington. Shortly thereafter, Feinstein's sports editor got on the phone and said, "Go see our friends [the American embassy]. If they tell you to come home, come home."

"Fine," Feinstein said. "What about the Tour de France? It ends this weekend."

"John," said his boss, "we still have diplomatic relations with France. Don't go there."

Not all Eastern Europeans lack a funny bone. The *Denver Post*'s Woody Paige was in Sarajevo, Yugoslavia, for the 1984 Winter Olympics when he discovered that an armed guard had been posted at the door of the sportswriter's living quarters. Each day Paige tried to talk to the stone-faced, machine-gun–toting guard, but with absolutely no success.

Monday: "How about some cigarettes?" said Paige. "We snuck some in."

Nothing.

Tuesday: "Hey, I've got a condo in Aspen. Would you like to use it if you're ever in the States?"

Nothing.

Wednesday: "How 'bout a blonde with a great body? She's yours if you talk."

Thursday: "How do you feel about drugs?"

Friday: "M&M's?"

Saturday: "Ever hear of the television show *The Price Is Right?* I can get you on that show."

Sunday: "How would you like an evening with the Gabor sister of your choice?"

On it went until the final day of Paige's stay in Sarajevo. By now, he gave little thought to his daily lines to the stoic guard. "Does a cameo appearance in a Hollywood movie interest you?" he asked.

Nothing. Paige shrugged and had begun to walk away when he felt a stinging sensation near his face. The son of a bitch commie had shot him! Paige fully expected to see blood—his blood!—any moment. Instead, he felt icy slush. He had been hit with one hell of a snowball.

Paige looked up in shock. Standing there, smile as wide as Paige's Aspen condo, was the guard.

"Have a nice day, Mr. Paige," said the guard.

Sarajevo, of course, was the same place where some of the nation's sports editors decided to cut costs and take advantage of a package deal that, according to the travel agents, would send reporters on a cheap flight from New York to Frankfurt, followed by another flight to Zagreb, Yugoslavia, followed by a restful train ride to their final destination. It sounded perfectly charming and, better yet, argued the travel agents, it eliminated any chance of being fogged out of the Sarajevo airport.

Of course, the train was three hours late. Then engineers discovered that the heaters were broken, causing further delay. Once everything was fixed, the assembled sportswriters (more than one hundred, in all) found themselves crammed into the slowest-moving train in the country. It chugged away at a top speed of thirty miles an hour. The writers nicknamed it the Tito Express.

The train ride alone took about eight hours. To kill time, a drinking contest was held among representatives of the various newspapers. The last paper with a writer standing would be declared the winner.

Not surprisingly, the *Boston Globe* won. Leigh Montville, then with the *Globe,* later calculated that the writers had tipped the waitress, at the very least, three months' worth of salary to bring them drinks.

Perhaps I've been too hard on our friends overseas. After all, as frustrating as traveling in Europe can be, the United States is no piece of cake, either. For instance, the Great Continent had Sarajevo, but America had Lake Placid, perhaps the single worst-organized Winter Games in Olympic annals.

The press headquarters were located at a high-school gym. The home economics room had been converted into a bar, prompting Red Smith to track down the school's home ec teacher and show her what the 1980 Olympics had done to her teaching venue. It made for great reading.

Buses failed to run on time. And because Lake Placid was basically a one-stoplight town, no cars were allowed within the city limits, making travel even more difficult. As Olympics went, this one was a logistical nightmare.

Nor did it help sagging American morale that the United States team, except for speedskater Eric Heiden, was having a miserable time. Nothing was going right for the embarrassed host country. And things weren't expected to improve as a little-regarded United States hockey team prepared to begin play in the Olympic tournament.

Housed ten miles outside the town in a makeshift motel was then–*Fort Lauderdale News/Sun-Sentinel* columnist Bernie Lincicome. The motel was really a summer hunting lodge that had been opened for Olympic guests. As you might expect, the conditions were bleak. Lincicome found the room equipped with a bed, a single space heater and a shower that almost always ran cold.

Each morning, Lincicome, who was ill-equipped for the freezing weather, would stand shivering at a nearby bus stop, waiting for the appropriate vehicle to take him into town. Lincicome wore two windbreakers and an orlon sweater. And each morning, Lincicome would find a Russian journalist, attired in a lush, warm fur coat, also standing at the bus stop. The two men would nod politely at each other and then stare into the winter sky.

A few days later, while standing at the same bus stop, Lincicome nodded at the Russian, only to see the man grinning. "Three golds," said the Russian, holding up three fingers for each Soviet gold medal won the day before.

Lincicome smiled back bravely.

The next day, same thing. "Seven golds," said the Russian, again holding up the proper number of fingers to make sure nothing had been lost in the translation.

"Two golds," said the Russian the day after that.

With more to come, thought Lincicome, as he considered the schedule. The powerful Red Army hockey team would play the surprisingly game United States team that night. And, oh, wouldn't the Russian journalist gloat over that victory? Hadn't this same Soviet team defeated the United States, 10–1, in a pre-Olympic game? One could only imagine the next score.

Then the unthinkable happened: A group of amateurs beat the Big Red Machine. America rejoiced and "Do you believe in miracles?" became a catch phrase.

The next day, Lincicome trudged out into the cold and snow for a meeting with his Russian acquaintance. Their eyes met and Lincicome held up one finger—his middle one. He hoped it meant the same thing in Russian as it did here.

A couple of other things about that hockey game. Mark Purdy was there and later asked a Russian journalist about the remarkable upset.

"What are you going to write?" asked Purdy.

"That I think [President Jimmy] Carter told them to win," he said.

"Seriously?"

"Well, I have to check with my editors."

Then the Russian looked both ways, just in case anyone

was watching, pushed the tip of his nose in the air and pretended he was skating. He was clearly imitating the Red Army team.

"Are you going to write that?" said Purdy.

The Russian shrugged. "I don't know, I'll have to check with my editors."

One final note: Hubert Mizell of the *St. Petersburg Times* spoke with United States hockey coach Herb Brooks about five months after the momentous game. Brooks told him that among the many pieces of mail he had received was a letter written by a United States naval officer assigned to an aircraft carrier in the Mediterranean. Throughout the entire game, wrote the officer, messages were exchanged with a nearby Russian warship. When the final score was announced, the United States ship sent one final sentence: "We whipped your ass."

Still, in the end, Lake Placid managed to take a bit of the joy out of the Olympic experience. On the last day of the Winter Games, officials relented and finally let cars into the city limits. Larry Felser, long-time columnist for the *Buffalo News,* invited Mizell to ride along as they visited the press headquarters one last time. The ride, compared to the always-late buses, seemed almost luxurious.

Hours later, their work done, the two sportswriters packed up their belongings and made their way to the parking lot where they found . . . no car. It had been towed. Happy Olympics, fellas.

Of course, had it been a rental car, no one would have cared. Sportswriters are historically uninterested in the fate of cars someone else is paying for.

For instance, Gary Pomerantz, then with the *Washington Post,* was in the middle of a six-day, six-city road trip when he arrived in Cleveland to cover a Browns game at sold-out Cleveland Stadium. Afterward, Pomerantz couldn't remember what kind of car he had rented as he scanned the parking lot, which featured, literally, thousands of vehicles. Worse yet, the key chain failed to include the usual information about make, model and license plate number. So he took a cab to the airport, handed the key back to the rental car people and said, "Here, you find it."

In 1985, Tom Zucco of the *St. Petersburg Times* was sent to Green Bay to chronicle a game between the Packers and the Tampa Bay Buccaneers. Zucco rented a car and as he walked away from the counter the lady said, "Don't forget this, Mr. Zapco. You'll need it."

It was an ice scraper.

There are better places to be than Green Bay in the dead of winter. That night it snowed so hard that it looked as if God had a really bad dandruff problem. Zucco awoke on Sunday morning to find everything buried in snow, including his car.

At first, he thought it had been stolen. Looking out his hotel window at the parking lot, Zucco didn't see a single vehicle. Then he noticed the suggestion of a hump in the snow. And then another one, and another. Zucco didn't know which mound was his car and he certainly wasn't going to try to find out. So he caught the team bus to Lambeau Field and tried to cover one of the most bizarre of games.

League historians will remember this as the contest that Packers defensive lineman Alphonso Carreker hurled Bucs quarterback Steve Young to the ground, only to have Young pop back up, frantically trying to clear the packed snow from his facemask; he couldn't breathe.

Up in the press box the windows were a steamy mess. You couldn't see a thing. That's when the writers took up a collection and hired someone from the stands to wipe the windows clear. The gentleman dabbed at the glass for a minute, gestured to the writers that he would be right back, and never returned.

Seven more inches of snow had fallen by game's end, meaning Zucco's car was a faint memory. But somehow he found it and extracted it from its snowy grave, then babied it to the airport . . . only to find that all flights had been canceled until the next day.

Zucco's troubles were nothing compared to those of *Houston Post* writer Ray Buck and his wife, Mary, who made the mistake of accidentally driving their rental car into the Overtown riots at Super Bowl XXIII in Miami. Rather than fly from Houston to Miami, the Bucks chose to take a leisurely drive down the coast, scheduling their arrival almost a full day before Ray was supposed to write a story.

The Bucks checked into their downtown hotel at 5:00 P.M. and then decided to spend part of the evening at the nearby Biscayne Dog Track. They received directions and were on their way when Ray, who was on the passenger's side, realized that they had taken a very wrong turn somewhere. Lots of people were in the streets. At first, Ray thought they had stumbled onto a parade. But then he saw their faces, angry and wild with hate.

A car stopped in front of them and instantly five people converged on it.

"Isn't this area the same place we saw on the news?" asked Mary.

"Yeah, so let's get the hell away from that car."

Mary hit the gas and as she did, two rocks hit the passenger side of the car. The first one hit with a solid thud; the next one shattered the window, raining shards of glass on Ray. They heard gunshots, but didn't look back as Mary ran stop signs and stoplights in an effort to escape the budding riot.

As they neared their hotel, Mary pulled over and hailed a policeman. Said the cop: "All hell is breaking loose. You're lucky, usually they grab you and pull you through the window."

Interviewed later by the *Miami Herald,* Buck vowed to eat room service the rest of the week. He couldn't afford to go out anyway, what with a bill from the rental car company bound to arrive soon (the Bucks had waived the collision and damage insurance, not to mention riot coverage).

That was before the Greater Miami Convention Bureau, ultrasensitive about the negative publicity caused by the riots, intervened. It told the Bucks not to worry about the damages. Sure enough, when the bill came, the bureau picked up the tab.

Perhaps not as understanding was the car company that rented *San Diego Union* writer Phil Collier a vehicle in Phoenix years ago. Collier was in Arizona to cover the Cactus League and his itinerary called for him to drive from Tucson to Phoenix after a game one afternoon. With him were two other writers.

These were the days when no freeway linked the two cities, so Collier was forced to drive through small town after small town. Halfway there, Collier and his cohorts decided to stop at a bar and quench their considerable thirst. Then they got back into the car, drove a bit and decided to stop again for more refreshment. A little woozy from all the drinking, one of the writers lit a cigarette, rolled down the back window and stretched out in the rear seat. Up front, Collier concentrated on keeping his foot light on the gas pedal. These tiny Arizona towns were famous for their speed traps.

About a half hour later, Collier heard a police siren, glanced at his sideview mirror and saw the flashing light of a patrol car. This can't be, thought Collier. He couldn't have been going over fifteen miles per hour. Maybe he was getting ticketed for going too slow.

The patrolman approached the car.

"Have you fellas been drinking?" he said.

"Why would you ask that, sir?" Collier said.

"Well, because the guy in the backseat is on fire."

Collier jerked his head around to find his backseat passenger asleep and smoldering. That cigarette had apparently fallen from his fingers, ignited the material covering the seat and started a small blaze that was never noticed because of the open windows. Except for some charred clothing, the passenger was fine.

Collier prepared for the worst: a monumental fine, incarceration, his insurance and license permanently revoked. Instead, the officer couldn't keep a smile off his face.

"Have a safe trip back," he said, shaking his head. And with that, he waved the burn-scarred rental car away.

David Casstevens of the *Dallas Morning News* rented a car while in Pittsburgh to cover a playoff game involving the Steelers in January of 1979. This was the infamous Ice Bowl, where the field, showered with sleet and snow, froze in the second half of the game. Not surprisingly, so did all the area roads and highways.

This wasn't good news for Casstevens and the several other Texas writers with him. After they finished their stories that day, the writers tiptoed gingerly on the slippery parking lot, where they found their rental car enveloped in about a two-inch sheet of ice and snow. For some reason, one of the writers had a small screwdriver in his work bag, and he began chipping away at the coat of ice. That done, they started the car and began the drive to the airport and a late-evening flight home.

The freeway was a deserted four-lane ice rink. Nobody was silly enough to drive in these conditions, except an out-of-towner in a rental car trying to catch a flight.

Then it happened. The car hydroplaned on the ice, spinning and caroming off guardrails until it came to a stop at the side of the road. Casstevens's first words?

"It's OK, I've got collision," he said.

Casstevens turned the car around and made it to the airport in time to discover that all flights had been canceled.

On my list of travel terrorizers, rental car companies aren't even in the top ten. Other than charge you $3.50 a gallon to refill the tank, there are only so many things they can do to make your travel life a living hell. Hotels and airlines, however, are experts in the fine art of ticking you off. I think their employees attend special classes to perfect certain annoying phrases and actions.

My personal favorite is the phrase the flight attendant uses when she parks her drink cart near your aisle seat, pulls out a can of soda and opens it up near your head, sending a spray of sugary liquid into the inner reaches of your ear canal.

"Oh, did we get you a little bit there?" she'll say sweetly.

"What? I can't hear you. I have fluids draining."

Or how about the chatty pilot who feels compelled to spend half of the flight detailing insignificant landmarks below?

"And on the left side of the aircraft is Laremy Falls, known as the penny nail capital of the Tri-City area," he'll say in one of those smooth, country-spun captain voices. "Daggummit, folks, I know it's awfully dark out there, but if you squint your eyes just so, you might be able to see the outline of Lake Parkatana, which is where my brother Larry and I almost caught a real nice pike two summers ago. Boy, are the mosquitoes big down there, the size of canned hams. Now back on your left . . ."

The airlines are not your friends. Friends don't expect a bag of peanuts to keep you happy for a three-hour flight. Friends don't serve omelettes with the approximate density of lead. Friends don't overbook. Friends don't scare the living bejabbers out of you.

But airlines do.

Plane travel doesn't have to be so grim. Just make sure you have Bob Uecker along for the ride.

On one occasion, the Brewers were supposed to leave on a charter flight for Anaheim, but the flight crew didn't show up because of a miscommunication. So the team's traveling secretary arranged another charter, this one featuring a smaller plane with a limited fuel capacity. This done, the team boarded the aircraft for its long journey westward.

Somewhere over Nebraska the pilot determined that it was time to land for refueling. Seatbelt lights flashed on, weary ballplayers struggled to buckle up. It was 3:00 A.M. At last the plane touched down on a tiny country landing strip. As fuel was fed into the tanks, Uecker, who does the play-by-play announcing for the Brewers, rose from his seat and walked toward the open door near the front of the plane. Once there, he began waving and yelling into the darkness.

"Hey, how you doin'?" he said. "Good to see you. Thanks for coming."

As Uecker waved, Tom Haudricourt of the *Milwaukee Sentinel* made his way down the aisle to see who Uecker was talking to.

"Ueck, what are you doing?" Haudricourt said.

"Oh, I've always been real big here," he said. "I'm just waving to all my fans."

Haudricourt stuck his head out the door. There was nobody there. Haudricourt walked back to his seat and tried to go to sleep.

Back when the football Cardinals still played in St. Louis, columnist Kevin Horrigan was confronted by NFL Hall of Fame player and club executive Larry Wilson as they boarded the team charter one day after a game. Would Horrigan, who weighed close to 300 pounds at the time (he has since lost 85 pounds), mind sitting in an assigned seat? asked Wilson. No problem, said Horrigan.

Horrigan sat down in an aisle seat. Across the way was All Pro offensive lineman Dan Dierdorf, another large humanoid, who had with him a large trash bag full of ice and beer. Turns out that the Cardinals had a two-beer limit for players on charter flights, but Dierdorf somehow had arranged to have additional brewed beverages placed in the ice for him and his fellow linemen after takeoff.

Still, Horrigan couldn't understand why he had been seated near the players, especially Dierdorf. Then someone told him: Among his various executive duties, Wilson was in charge of making sure that all weight was evenly distributed on the DC-9. Since Horrigan and Dierdorf weighed about the same, well . . .

Horrigan didn't mind. At least he got a couple of free beers out of the deal.

The list of potential road trip problems doesn't stop once

you touch down. You need a place to sleep, don't you? That, of course, means staying at . . . *a hotel.*

No sportswriter's journey is complete without a proper hotel horror story. There are your common difficulties that everyone encounters on the road: misplaced reservations, lost keys, price gouging, outrageous service charges for making a phone call, cold room service food, housekeeping maids who enter the room with their passkeys a millisecond after knocking, pranksters who steal your "Do Not Disturb" signs and so forth.

But how about the terror of learning that your hotel bill is $450 . . . per night—and you don't have enough money to pay it? This happened to a close personal friend of mine: me.

I had been dispatched to Monte Carlo to cover the 1985 Monaco Grand Prix. Naturally, my newspaper's travel agent arranged for me to stay about ninety minutes away in Frejus, France, where I found a clean but tiny hotel room waiting for me. Each day I would commute to Monte Carlo, only to be screamed at by French toll booth attendants (I didn't quite understand their currency system) and Monte Carlo shopkeepers. "Amer-ee-kan, Amer-ee-kan," hissed one Monte Carlo cashier when I tried buying a warm Coke, a comb and a small container of shampoo with a hundred-franc bill.

I didn't eat for two days. Finally, I summoned enough courage to enter the hotel dining room in Frejus. I was handed a menu I couldn't read and a wine list that contained not a single bottle of Mad Dog. So I pointed at a couple of items and waited.

Soon a wonderful bottle of red wine arrived. I drank glass after glass, letting the alcohol dull what was left of my senses. Then I heard something bark. I looked to my left and there, one table over, was a poodle seated at a dinner table eating a meal off a plate.

Check, please.

The next morning the phone rang. It was legendary race car driver Carroll Shelby, whom I had met in Dallas.

"Where the hell are you, son?" he said. "I've been trying to reach you. I've got a room reserved for you here at the Loew's Monte Carlo. You can see the track and the Mediterranean from here."

I'm sure I violated at least a dozen major traffic laws on the way to Monte Carlo. At last, a real room with real people who maybe spoke real English. Could it be?

The room was nice, but not opulent. Imagine my surprise when the hotel clerk informed me that my four-night bill was 19,000 francs, or something like that.

"What is that in dollars, about $300 or so?" I asked casually.

"No, monsieur," she said, tapping her fingers on a nearby calculator, "your converted total comes to . . . $1,800."

Men, have you ever slipped off your bicycle seat onto that bar that runs across the top of the frame? Then you know how I felt. I didn't have $1,800. Worse yet, I also was supposed to go to London to do a story.

As has become my custom, I groveled, borrowing money from one of the Dallas Grand Prix promoters. Off I went to London, where I ate crackers and soup for three days. No wonder I lost seventeen pounds on that trip.

Mine is only one story. Equally exasperating was the time Tom Zucco was sent to cover the 1987 U.S. Open at Flushing Meadows, New York. The tennis tournament was supposed to end Sunday, but then the rains came, postponing the final matches until the next day. Zucco's hotel reservations didn't extend through Monday, so he was kicked out of his Manhattan room and sent looking elsewhere for lodging. At last he found a vacancy near LaGuardia Airport.

What a place this was. A knife fight broke out in the hallway the night Zucco stayed there. The television took forty-five minutes to warm up. There wasn't even a hint of a bar of soap in the room, forcing Zucco to venture down the dangerous hallway to a vending machine where he could buy toiletries. And for all this comfort, Zucco was charged seventy dollars for the night's stay.

In 1988, the Los Angeles Rams front office geniuses decided to bump the team's beat writers out of the club hotel in New Orleans so they could make room for some car dealers who were making the trip with the Rams that week. "But we've arranged other lodging for you," the Rams told the writers.

One writer checked into his room and found bullet holes in the window. Another writer found someone already in his room. Another writer walked into a room where the bed had recently been used for extracurricular activities. You don't want to know what was in the toilet. The day after the writers checked out of the hellhole, the hotel was closed down by local authorities.

Hotels love to overcharge. Room service meals can be unbelievably expensive. And those cute little minibars available in some rooms? Death. Don't touch them. Minibar beers cost about four dollars apiece, maybe more in New York City, ripoff capital of the world.

The smart ones know this. Tim Cowlishaw, then with the *San Jose Mercury News,* was on a road trip in Montreal last year covering a series between the Expos and the San Francisco Giants. After a Friday night game, Cowlishaw invited the other Giants beat writers up to his room for a couple of brews. By the time they finished drinking, all twelve minibar beers were gone. A hefty bill to say the least.

The next morning, before the minibar attendant came to restock the refrigerator, Cowlishaw got dressed and headed for the elevator. When the doors opened, Giants pitcher Mike Krukow was already inside. As the elevator descended, Cowlishaw made small talk.

"Where you going, Mike?" he said.

"Get a little lunch. How about yourself?"

"I'm going to the store to buy some beers before they refill my minibar."

Krukow nodded. "Veteran move," he said.

As for rookie moves, look no further than Tim Kurkjian, who now labors for *Sports Illustrated,* and who made expense-account history with his 1982 New York hotel bill.

Kurkjian arrived in Manhattan with six weeks' worth of stale clothes, the result of an all-work, no-wash spring training with the Texas Rangers. When the season opener was postponed because of a snowstorm, Kurkjian stuffed his belongings in his suitcase and trudged through the slushy streets in search of a laundromat. There were none.

Back to the hotel Kurkjian came. Frustrated by the failed search, Kurkjian decided to try the valet.

"Just wash them, nothing else," he told the man. "Don't worry about folding them or anything like that. I'll do that."

"Yes, sir," said the valet.

Kurkjian then went to a Rangers workout. When he came back, there was a message that his clothes were ready for delivery. Kurkjian told them to bring them up.

Kurkjian should have known he was in trouble when he saw his socks on little hangers, his underwear folded neatly in nifty boxes, his pants and shirts arranged just so. Mouth open in amazement, Kurkjian mumbled, "How much?"

"One-eighty-six, sir," said the valet.

Kurkjian opened his wallet, took out a five-dollar bill and told the man to keep the change. The valet looked at it as if it had been dipped in sewage.

"Sir, it's 186 *dollars!"*

"I don't have $186," Kurkjian said. "Keep the clothes."

Calamity has a knack of following sportswriters around on the road.

This is the reason famed *Los Angeles Times* columnist Jim Murray accidentally got locked in a restroom at old Metropolitan Stadium after a Vikings-Rams playoff game years ago. Murray finally escaped (he jimmied open the door), but not before screaming into the freezing afternoon air and pounding on the metal door so hard that his hand hurt. This same Murray was once trapped in a Philadelphia hotel elevator with a dozen or so other sportswriters. A tad claustrophobic, Murray eventually climbed through the elevator roof hatch to safety and, by doing so, scraped a few layers of skin off his shin. Very ugly.

This is why *Sports Illustrated*'s Rick Reilly got pulled over for speeding while on assignment in Mexico. The cop threatened Reilly with a trip to jail unless the writer was willing to fork over a little donation to the officer's private police benevolent association. Two hundred dollars later, Reilly drove off.

This is why *Detroit News* writer Shelby Strother was left with no clothes to wear while covering the 1987 NBA finals in Boston. Strother had brought his wife on the trip for a few days, but when she had to return home early, she accidentally took the matching suitcase belonging to her husband. That left Strother with a cute wraparound sun dress to wear, but not much else.

Strother improvised. He still had a pair of jogging shoes and gym shorts, but no underwear, socks or shirt. Making matters worse was an unexpected winter storm that had moved in, lowering temperatures by the minute. Strother got dressed (if you can call it that) and walked with as much dignity as possible across the lobby of his plush hotel. He then sprinted to a nearby men's clothing store. When a clerk approached him, Strother cut him off and said, "You're about to make the easiest sale you've ever made."

By the way, the Strothers no longer own matching luggage.

Combine the very worst of all these trips and you have the adventures of *Washington Post* sportswriter Michael Wilbon during a 1987 winter tour of Pittsburgh and Denver.

Wilbon was assigned a season-ending Cleveland Browns–Steelers game at Three Rivers Stadium the day after Christmas. He left that morning with not a minute's worth of sleep, thanks to an all-night Christmas party. It would be his undoing.

After the game, Wilbon returned to the Pittsburgh airport

and boarded a flight for Denver, where the Broncos were playing the Chargers the next day. He would land at Stapleton Airport, catch a cab to his hotel, order room service and then get some much-needed sleep. Or so he thought.

Meanwhile, in Denver, snow was blanketing the city to the tune of three inches every hour. By the time Wilbon's plane neared the city, nine inches of snow was on the ground. Worse yet, the weather forced air traffic controllers to put Wilbon's plane in a holding pattern . . . for two hours.

His plane landed at 1:00 A.M. He got his luggage at 2:00 A.M. He hailed a taxi at, well . . . there were no taxis. A foot of snow on the roads saw to that. Wilbon knows this because he tried getting a cab until 5:00 A.M.

Wilbon called a limousine service and said he would pay someone fifty dollars to drive him three miles to his hotel. By 6:00 A.M., Wilbon was in his room.

But wait, more problems. The snowstorm had knocked out the hotel's electricity, which meant there was no heat. So rather than catch a few hours' sleep before he had to go to Mile High Stadium, Wilbon sat and shivered in his room.

Somehow he arranged for a ride to the stadium, where he found about forty thousand empty seats. Wilbon covered the game, returned to his hotel and discovered that the electricity still was out. At the brink of exhaustion, Wilbon took bold steps.

First, he checked out. Then he called around to find a lodging, preferably with room service, heat and cable television. He found it, but the place was located thirty miles outside Denver. Fine, said Wilbon, who hired another limo.

The limo got stuck in the snow a mile from the hotel. Rather than sit there, Wilbon grabbed his two bags and walked the rest of the way. When you need sleep, you'll do almost anything.

Wilbon checked in, picked up his phone for room service and learned that because of the storm, almost none of the hotel employees could get to work. You guessed it: no food.

Wilbon decided to sleep, his first real chance to do so in three nights. Two hours into his slumber, the hotel's sprinkler system came on. Reason? A gas leak.

Guests were given two choices: They could evacuate the premises and stand outside in what was now twenty-four inches of snow, or they could chance gas fumes and electrocution by waiting in the lobby. Wilbon waited in the lobby.

The next day, Wilbon paid another person fifty dollars to take him to the airport. People were sleeping in the terminals. There was a three-hour wait for ticket agents. When it came Wilbon's turn he asked but one question: "What is the first flight going anywhere that doesn't have any snow?"

These are the unavoidable nightmare journeys. But there also is something about the road that turns some sportswriters into thrill seekers. The select few take more chances when they travel. Their spirit is untethered. More important, they're on an expense account.

I still don't know whom to attribute it to, but a sportswriter once said, "At home we're Ozzie Nelson, on the road we're Ozzy Osbourne." I believe it. Hell, I've seen it.

Of course, you'd go crazy sometimes, too, if you spent more nights in Hyatts than at home, more days in the air than in an easy chair. Not that I'm complaining—I'm not—it's just that travel tends to promote fits of wackiness.

The aforementioned Shelby Strother covered a football game in Atlanta one afternoon, wrote his story, returned to the hotel for some postgame beverages and then joined a group of writers at a late-night bar. Rather than return to the hotel for a couple of hours' sleep, Strother decided he would go straight to the airport from the bar. Bad move.

Strother arrived at his gate in plenty of time. In fact, he decided he would just close his eyes for a few moments before boarding began.

He woke up six hours later, his mouth wide open. Seven flights had come and gone when Strother finally stirred from his seat. He eventually caught a flight to Detroit later that night.

And it was Strother who joined then–*Atlanta Journal-Constitution* writer John McGrath for some cocktails at a hotel bar one afternoon in San Diego, where a college bowl game was scheduled the following evening.

Strother and McGrath consumed their fair share of drinks that afternoon and into the night. At one point, a fashion show was held in the bar, with models parading around wearing the latest styles. The unmarried McGrath was fascinated by the entire concept and excitedly purchased two dresses. Upon their delivery, he stuffed them in the back of his pants, much like a football center does with a hand towel. McGrath and Strother then went to another bar and finally stumbled back to their hotel at 3:00 A.M. Later that morning, Strother's phone rang; it was McGrath.

"Shelby, I've got a question to ask you," McGrath said.

"Yeah?" asked Strother.

"Did we get laid last night?"

"I don't think so. Why?"

"Because I've got all this women's clothing and I don't know where it came from."

McGrath eventually gave one of the dresses to his sister and another to one of the housekeeping maids. What a guy.

It could have been worse. McGrath was guilty only of picking up a few dresses. That's nothing compared to the pair of sportswriters (who will forever go unnamed) who picked up men who actually wore dresses.

I've got to be careful here, what with all your various slander and libel laws, but a certain sportswriter (and you know who you are) unknowingly escorted a he-she to the writer's hotel room during the Super Bowl festivities in Tampa a few years back. There was a full house in the hotel bar that night and everyone, it seemed, knew the she was a he, except, of course, our poor sportswriter. I'm sure he discovered the important anatomical differences in no time at all.

Even more embarrassing was the sportswriter who convinced a young woman (or so he thought) to come look at his etchings in his Daytona Beach hotel room (he was there to cover the famed 500). The writer was later found bound and gagged, his belongings stolen.

Said the cop assigned to the case: "Sir, I have two things to tell you. First, this person has been working the Space Coast for years. Second, she wasn't a she. She was a he."

Hey, it could happen to anyone, right?

More typical are the ridiculous one-liners some sportswriters (single or otherwise) use on members of the opposite sex.

For example, Frank Finch of the *Los Angeles Times* and a fellow writer were in a bar one night when they spotted a shapely blonde across the way. They engaged in some small talk, during which the striking woman mentioned a price for her considerable sexual services. Finch turned to the other writer and said, "You hold her here and I'll go sell the car."

8

Press Box Bimbos and Other Myths

Hide the men and children. Run for cover. Some of those new-fangled women sportswriters are on the loose and you know what that means: trouble. After all, you don't want any of them taking a little looksee at the private parts of your favorite American sports hero or, worse yet, asking a question.

And what do women know about sports anyway? Shouldn't they be home picking out new linoleum for the kitchen floor? Don't they have anything better to do than impose themselves on the last male bastion, the locker room? I mean what's this world coming to?

How about the twenty-first century?

No longer a curiosity, but a staple in postgame press hordes everywhere, women sportswriters are here to stay. This isn't to say they always enjoy total acceptance—they don't—but at least now they enjoy total legitimacy.

Rare is the newspaper or magazine sports staff these days that doesn't include a woman journalist. Or two. Or three. Or four. Or whatever. But it's been a struggle, both in and out of the locker room.

There was a time when sports editors didn't want women on their staffs and players didn't want them in their clubhouses. Women sportswriters were as welcome as the Hell's Angels at the company picnic.

"They'll embarrass us," whined some sports editors.

"They don't belong here," announced the athletes.

Of course, these were the same people who once wore lime leisure suits, considered Erich Segal America's foremost novelist and thought the *Christian Science Monitor* was a medical device.

Things have changed, though it's only taken a few decades or so. But, hey, who's counting?

True, women sportswriters sometimes ask dumb questions. And guess what? So do their male counterparts. Stupidity, it turns out, is an equal opportunity employer. And sure, women sportswriters don't always understand the difference between, say, a hockey crease and a pants crease, but I'm here to tell you that an appreciable number of male sportswriters don't either.

Sports editors now understand this, but a stubborn and formidable number of America's athletes and coaches do not. In short, they'd rather have a case of jock itch than deal with a notepad-toting member of the opposite sex.

The basic problem is this: Many athletes and coaches simply don't understand that a woman sportswriter has the same job as the male sportswriter, which is to gather and report the news. Nothing more, nothing less. In fact, I bet if you asked most women sportswriters, they'd tell you they could do without the postgame trips downstairs. But it doesn't work that way. The locker rooms and clubhouses remain the primary source for quotations and notes and access to players and staff. So off they go, and not always merrily.

Christine Brennan of the *Washington Post* was the first woman sportswriter to cover the Redskins. Needless to say, then–general manager Bobby Beathard didn't appreciate the historical significance.

"It messes up everything that they're sending you here," he told Brennan in 1985. "I know you're a nice girl and I know you don't really want to go in there."

That wasn't the point, Brennan said. And truth be told, she *did* want to be there. After all, it was the most important sports beat in town. What journalist wouldn't want to be part of that?

Head coach Joe Gibbs didn't like the arrangement either. But to Gibbs's credit, he dealt with it a lot better than Beathard and some of the Redskins players did.

Once, while standing in line at the training camp cafeteria, Brennan turned around to find defensive tackle Dave Butz, now retired, looming over her.

"Yes?" said Brennan.

"You covering us this year?" said Butz.

"Yes."

"Well, I'm not going to speak to you in the locker room."

"Well, Dave, maybe I'll have to interview the other forty-four players. I'll work that out."

A few days later, Butz stopped Brennan again.

"You going to be in the locker room?"

"Yes, Dave, I am."

"Well, if you're going to be in the locker room when I'm standing there naked, then you're going to have to be naked."

Brennan laughed. "No, Dave, that's not the way it's done."

True to his word, Butz ignored Brennan in the locker room.

Midway through the season, Brennan was conducting an interview with another player when defensive end Dexter Manley, partially clothed at the time, motioned to Brennan.

"C'mon over here," he said, "I've got something to show you."

What Manley wanted to show her had nothing to do with football, but with anatomy class. Brennan rolled her eyes and kept walking.

Not long after the incident, Brennan found herself in the locker room again. As she prepared to leave, she heard someone calling her name. It was Butz, the same Butz who hadn't talked to her since training camp.

"Hey, is anyone giving you trouble in this locker room?" he said.

"No."

"You sure?"

"I'm sure, Dave."

"Well, OK. But if anyone ever gives you trouble in here, you let me know and I'll take care of him."

Brennan couldn't believe what she was hearing. Butz obviously had been told about the Manley incident and was coming to the reporter's aid.

A year later, Brennan had to call Butz at home for a story. Near the end of the conversation, Brennan mentioned the kind gesture of 1985.

"Hey, I don't like the fact that you're in the locker room," he said. "But if they're going to allow you in there, then you've got to be treated right."

Butz turned out to be nothing more than a soft-hearted lug. Near the end of the 1988 season, Brennan, who no longer covered the team as the beat reporter, was assigned to do a story on the Redskins–Dallas Cowboys game at Texas Stadium. After interviewing assorted Cowboys players, Brennan ventured into the Redskins locker room and walked directly to Butz's locker. Butz, who was half-dressed, had his back to Brennan.

"Mr. Butz, I know you don't speak to women in the locker room, but I just wanted to say hello," Brennan said.

Butz turned around. He was smiling.

"Sit down," he said, "we're going to talk."

Like Brennan, Julie Cart of the *Los Angeles Times* found herself faced with the classic gruff-athlete-hates-women-in-the-locker-room situation. She had just been named the new Kings hockey beat reporter, a position that seemed to change about every couple of years at the *Times*. And don't think the Kings didn't notice.

The most vocal of the 1986–1987 Kings was Dave "Tiger" Williams, a player known best not for his skating, but for his punching. He was, in the vernacular, a goon, an enforcer. It wasn't uncommon for Williams to lead the National Hockey League in penalty minutes. And had there been a category for Most Women Sportswriters Despised, Williams probably would have challenged for that crown, too.

It didn't take long for word to spread that a woman reporter would be covering the team. In fact, when Cart entered the locker room after the Kings' first practice, there was a noticeable hush.

Cart interviewed two players and then made a beeline for the famed Williams, who was lifting weights in another part of the room. As she moved toward him, so too did a small crowd of players.

"Hi, I'm Julie Cart from the *L.A. Times*," she said. "I'll be covering the team this season."

"Jeeeeezus Christ," Williams snarled.

"Well, it's nice to meet you, too. Should I call you Dave, David or Tiger?"

"Don't call me nothing," he said. Williams then went on to explain that he was going to draw a semicircle in front of his locker. If Cart stepped over that line, he said, he was going to deck her. Under no circumstances would he talk to her.

Cart didn't know quite what to say to that.

"Do you know anything about hockey?" said Williams.

"No, I don't."

"Jeeeeezus Christ," he said. "We go from a black to a broad. What is this, the fucking United Nations?"

Despite his lack of playing skills, Williams was an accomplished postgame quotation machine. Reporters flocked to his locker because he didn't resort to clichés when describing the game. Naturally, Cart was among those writers who stopped by.

Problem was, whenever Williams saw Cart stationed in the group of reporters, he would stop talking. Rather than ruin it for the other writers, Cart quit visiting his locker.

Halfway through the season, Cart and the Kings flew to Minneapolis for the beginning of a long road trip. On the very first day of the trip, Cart, while rushing to answer her hotel room phone, stubbed her toe. The toe swelled up immediately, so much so that Cart couldn't fit a shoe over it. So she did the next-best thing: She wore a sock and reported to the Kings trainer.

"You broke your toe," he said. "Talk to me after the game."

Afterward, Cart limped down to the Kings locker room. While she waited for the trainer, Williams gruffly asked, "What happened to you?"

"Well, Tiger, I broke my toe."

"Hmmph," he said. "You wait right here."

A few moments later he returned with several pair of fresh socks. "Here," he said, tossing the socks at Cart. "Take these. Those socks you're wearing will never last the trip."

And everyone lived happily ever after. Well, not really. It would take an act of Congress for that to happen, and I don't recall anyone introducing such a bill. The simple truth is that not every athlete and coach is crazy about locker room equality. Some never have been and never will be.

Some jock types use conventional methods when dealing with women reporters in the locker room (like the Butz silence). Others feel it is their obligation to skip civility and go straight to intimidation.

Dave Kingman, a hitter of some renown, once presented Susan Fornoff of the *Sacramento Bee* with her very own gift-wrapped vermin. Reggie Jackson once asked Lisa Saxon, then with the *Los Angeles Daily News,* if she could please go outside and slide under the California Angels team bus "so we can drive it over you."

Cart and then–*Los Angeles Times* reproter Rick Reilly

were the centerpieces of an ugly confrontation several years ago at the Fiesta Bowl in Tempe, Arizona. Cart and Reilly were there to cover the game, which involved the University of Miami and UCLA.

The Wednesday before the game, Reilly and Cart had to visit the Miami locker room. Reilly was supposed to interview quarterback Bernie Kosar, while Cart was supposed to find wide receiver Eddie Brown for a story. The two reporters had checked with the Miami sports information director for locker room policy and were told that they could go right in after practice was completed.

"Women, too?" asked Cart.

"Sure," said the Miami SID.

Soon thereafter, the players returned from their workout and made their way into the locker room. Reilly and Cart followed them inside.

The two reporters hadn't been in the room for more than a few minutes when Miami assistant coach Gary Stevens walked up to Cart.

"What the fuck are you doing in here?" he asked.

"I'm waiting for Eddie Brown," she said. "I'm doing a story on him."

"Women can't be in here."

"Well, I did check with the SID and he said it was fine that I come in here."

"You can't be in here. Do you know what my wife would do to me if she knew you were in this locker room with me?"

"Look, I'm just trying to do my job."

"Well, you can't be in here. I don't ever want to see you in here again."

Reilly intervened. "Julie, we don't need to mess with this asshole," he said.

"Who are you?" Stevens asked Reilly. "Who the fuck are you?"

"I'm Rick Reilly with the *Los Angeles Times.*"

"Yeah, well, who said you could talk to me like that?"

"Who said you could talk to her like that?"

"Well, get the fuck out of here."

So Reilly and Cart left, but as they did, they noticed Brown nearby. They offered Brown a ride back to the team hotel and Brown accepted.

"Who is that son of a bitch?" said Reilly, referring to Stevens.

"Him?" said Brown. "We call him the Mad Scientist. He always has that look in his eye."

Just then, Reilly noticed a car directly behind theirs. It was Stevens and he was honking the horn. And when they arrived at the hotel, Stevens jumped out of his car and began yelling at Reilly.

"I don't want my players riding with that son of a bitch," he said. "I don't want my players anywhere near that son of a bitch."

The more Stevens yelled, the madder he got.

"I'll stick it up your ass," Stevens yelled.

"Yeah, I bet you're good at that," Reilly said.

All things considered, that probably wasn't the best thing to say. Stevens started to chase them through the hotel lobby area. Guests were checking in at this swank hotel and meanwhile an assistant football coach was running after two reporters. It was quite a scene.

Just as Stevens was about to catch Reilly and Cart, two Miami assistants stepped between their colleague and the reporters. That's when Reilly and Stevens, who was carrying a leather satchel, started screaming at each other. Blocked by the assistants, Stevens decided to hurl his satchel at Reilly. He missed, which wasn't so bad, except that someone kept handing it back to Stevens, who promptly threw it again at Reilly.

Finally, the Miami assistants escorted the still-enraged Stevens away. This done, Reilly returned to his hotel room. Several hours later, his phone rang. It was Miami athletic director Sam Jankovich; he wanted to apologize for Stevens's actions. Not long after that, Miami president Thad Foote called to say the same thing. So did Miami head coach Jimmy Johnson.

"This is Jimmy Johnson," he said. "[Stevens] just gets a little riled up sometimes. He just needs to let off a little steam sometimes."

"Well, he didn't need to let off steam at my head," Reilly said. "I don't care what you say, Coach, it doesn't mean anything unless I hear an apology from him."

"Don't worry, you'll get one. You'll get one before the night is out."

Neither Reilly nor Cart ever heard from Stevens. But several days later, when Reilly returned home, he found a bouquet of flowers. Read the attached note: "Chivalry is not dead." Signed, "the women of *USA Today.*"

Apparently, the women of *USA Today* weren't with the *Denver Post*'s Natalie Meisler when she used to cover the Cincinnati Reds' Triple-A minor league team at Mile High Stadium. This was a team that included, at various times, Kal Daniels, Eric Davis and Rob Murphy. It was also a team that often didn't take kindly to Meisler's presence in the clubhouse.

If it were a doubleheader and Meisler stopped by to get statements for the first-game story, a cry would almost always go out; "Hey, she's here, everybody get your dicks out!"

That sort of clever stuff.

The following year, Meisler was treated with slightly more respect. Players began to accept her and their answers and antics (or lack of them) reflected it. One day, after an incident-free postgame interview session with various players, Meisler began to leave the clubhouse. Just as she reached the door, Meisler turned toward the dressing room and yelled, "Hey, guys, I'm not taking any of your shit this year!"

And she didn't.

In the Southwest Conference, they still talk about the Melanie Hauser Memorial Door at the University of Texas football stadium. Hauser, who works for the *Houston Post,* wasn't exactly a welcome sight when she appeared at the Longhorns locker room door after a 1977 game. Back then, player access still was determined by each school or, more correctly, each head coach. In this case, Texas coach Fred Akers didn't want Hauser walking through the locker area.

So determined were Longhorn officials to abide by Akers's decree that an additional door was constructed later to allow reporters to go directly into an interview room without having to actually walk past the half-dressed players. This done, Texas officials could bring players and coaches into the room without risk of an incident.

I've never understood this sort of paranoia. What did they think Hauser was going to do, faint?

Meanwhile, in the Southeastern Conference, there exists the so-called Karen Rosen Rule, named after the *Atlanta Journal-Constitution* reporter. Rosen was covering a Vanderbilt-Georgia football game in 1988 at Athens when she was barred from entering the Commodores locker room.

"We'll have a student go in and bring out everyone you need," she was assured by the sports information director.

In went all the male reporters and out stayed Rosen, stationed near the front of the locker room door. Eventually, the student helper convinced the Vanderbilt place-kicker to talk with Rosen, which was nice, except that she also needed to speak with the Vandy quarterback and one of the wide receivers.

Rosen peered inside the door and saw the wide receiver conducting an interview. It was then that an older gentleman moved toward the door.

"You don't need to be in there," he said, as he started to close the door.

Rosen stuck her foot in the opening. "Who are you?" she said.

"I'm the Vanderbilt athletic director."

It was Roy Kramer, and he was pushing at the door again.

Rosen pulled her foot from the door and moments later heard the distinctive click of a lock.

Rosen hurried to the back door, where players were leaving to board the team bus. After a while, she saw one of the players she needed to talk to. Unfortunately, Kramer was hurrying them along to the bus. Somehow, Rosen managed a thirty-second interview.

When it was over, Kramer turned to Rosen and said, "We don't let girls in our locker room. We never have, we never will."

A Nashville columnist wrote a story about the confrontation and the Vanderbilt chancellor wrote a letter of apology to Rosen. And within two weeks of the incident, the SEC had an equal access rule for reporters, male and female: They would all wait outside.

Poor Rosen. Poor anybody who has to wait outside a locker room or clubhouse while everyone else is allowed inside. I've seen it happen. Before the New York Giants were ordered to comply with NFL rules in 1985, women reporters were forced to wait outside the door, entirely at the mercy of a team public relations official whose job it was to arrange postgame player interviews. It was a ridiculous situation.

Once, Lesley Visser, then with the *Boston Globe*, and Christine Brennan had to cover a 1984 Giants game at the Meadowlands. Of course, they were stopped at the locker room and escorted to a nearby weight room by a team PR man, who told them not to worry, that he would see to their interview needs.

"You won't forget about us, will you?" Brennan asked.

"No, I won't forget," he said.

He forgot.

After a long wait, a Giants player was led into the room. Visser and Brennan didn't recognize him.

"This is Casey Merrill," they were told.

Brennan glanced at a Giants team roster for Merrill's name. Truth was, she didn't remember him in the game.

No matter. Visser and Brennan conducted a somewhat

lengthy interview and then said their farewells to Merrill. Then Visser looked at Brennan.

"I don't think that guy even played," Visser said.

Brennan found Merrill's name on the team depth chart. He was a third-string lineman who, indeed, hadn't played more than a down or two.

Eventually, quarterback Phil Simms and several other Giants players of note agreed to interviews. Maybe they were embarrassed by their employer's antiquated postgame policy.

As a male reporter, you don't know what to do about the inequities. You know it isn't right or fair when a woman sportswriter is denied access. But what's the alternative, to stand outside, too? I still don't know the answer. When it did happen, I would funnel whatever quotations I had to the writer if she needed them. It wasn't much, but maybe it helped a little.

More meaningful are the gestures extended by the athletes or coaches themselves. And I don't mean the ones they sometimes make with the aid of their middle fingers.

Robyn Norwood, then an intern with the *Washington Post*, was sent to cover a 1985 game involving the Baltimore Orioles. Earl Weaver was the manager.

Norwood told Weaver before the game began that a postgame trip to the Orioles clubhouse was needed for her to do her job. In short, she was providing the necessary warning, which was thoughtful.

Sure enough, at game's end, Norwood was among the reporters trying to inch their way into Weaver's office. She couldn't see him very well, what with all the other writers bunched in the doorway, but Weaver apparently could see her.

"Is that a lady back there?" Weaver asked.

No answer.

"Step out of here for a minute," he said.

Norwood, summoning her courage, didn't budge.

"I have every right to be here," she announced.

"C'mon, step out of here for a minute."

Norwood still couldn't see Weaver, but decided to stay put.

Weaver, in a calm but exasperated tone, said, "Lady, I just want to put my drawers on."

"Oh," said Norwood.

Jack Nicklaus earned my respect (as if he needed it) at the 1985 British Open at Royal St. George's in Sandwich, England. He had played poorly and missed the cut for the first time in years. Whipped by the weather and the course that day, Nicklaus had little reason to be gracious when a pack of reporters, including myself, encircled him in the men's locker room.

Oh, by the way, there was a woman sportswriter in the group, too.

As the interview began, several of the club's members, all of them dressed in these silly blazers, started muttering about the presence of the woman sportswriter. And they howled in protest when she actually asked a question of the great Nicklaus.

Nicklaus, bless his Golden Bear heart, politely but firmly told them to leave her alone, that she had as much right to be there as they did. After a few indignant "Here, heres" the Brits left the locker room, presumably to go polish their brass buttons.

Of course, you'd expect golf to be a bit on the stuffy side. Melanie Hauser was covering a Seniors Tour event at Onion Creek Country Club in Austin, Texas, one year, when she encountered some classic fifteenth-century thinking on women's rights.

Heavy rains had turned parts of the course into a muddy mess. Still, Hauser trudged around the course, doing what she could to cover the tournament.

After regulation play, a six-hole playoff was needed to determine the winner. Tired of sinking ankle deep in the muck, Hauser decided that the best way to keep track of the final few holes was by watching on television.

As luck would have it, there was only one place to view the show—the men's locker room. Good sports that they were, they wouldn't allow Hauser inside.

Hauser had no alternative but to start walking the course again. A few holes into the playoff, Hauser pulled off her mud-caked shoes and threw them into the trash. She spent the last three holes walking barefoot, the mud oozing between her toes. When it came time for interviews, Hauser was there, shoeless. And all because of a men-only rule.

This wouldn't be the last of Hauser's problems at golf tournaments. At the 1985 Masters, no waiter would serve her in the men's grill. As best as Hauser could tell, it was because she wasn't a he. At last the headwaiter took her order.

Apparently, word of Hauser's presence at the prestigious tournament made the rounds. An elderly gentleman, obviously a long-time member of the club, approached Hauser on the first day of play. "I just want to shake your hand," said the man. "He would have wanted it this way."

"He" was the legendary Bobby Jones.

Buoyed by the kind words, Hauser ventured into the men's grill the next day. And wouldn't you know it, no one would wait on her.

The discrimination doesn't stop with restaurant workers. At the 1988 Summer Olympics in Seoul, South Korea, Sharon Robb of the *Fort Lauderdale News/Sun-Sentinel* was part of a minor incident that didn't include much international goodwill.

Put yourself in Robb's place:

You're covering the swimming competition and you're on deadline. You need to write, so you go to the press room, where you find conditions cramped, smoky and noisy, thanks to your South Korean hosts, who have switched the television channel from swimming to sumo wrestling. You're trying to concentrate, but the television volume is unbearable, as are your hosts, who cheer wildly with each wrestling match.

You say enough is enough.

On behalf of the entire American press corps assembled inside the work room, Robb got up and turned the volume down on the offending television set.

"These are for swimming, not wrestling," she said.

The Koreans didn't take kindly to Robb's actions. In fact, says Robb, the Koreans didn't take kindly to her being issued press credentials in the first place.

These were the same Olympics that saw Robb get ignored while covering the boxing competition. Korean media assistants would never issue her bout sheets or results.

And these were the Olympics that saw Robb stranded at various venues as taxi drivers refused to pick her up. The reason? They thought all unescorted American women were hookers. Didn't matter that Robb had a portable computer case in one hand, a workbag in the other. Eventually, she had to enlist the help of males to help get her a cab back to her hotel.

But that was nothing compared to what faced her that day at the swimming venue. After turning the sound down, Robb felt a tap on her shoulder. It was a small Korean man, and he was steaming like a bowl of hot rice.

The man shoved Robb, who shoved him back into several of the television sets. Several American writers came to Robb's aid, which caused even more problems. Before long, it was a press room divided. The Koreans were upset with Robb. The Americans were upset with the Koreans. The European writers were upset with the Americans for causing a louder commotion than the one the Koreans had created with their sumo wrestling telecast.

Anyway, when the Olympics ended, Robb didn't shed a tear.

I think there are two basic reasons, however flawed, that some athletes and coaches (and waiters and South Koreans) don't want women sportswriters around: (1) They don't think they belong near a locker room. (2) They don't think they know diddly about sports.

Fortunately, the question of equal access has begun to diminish as the various professional leagues and college conferences institute and enforce easy-to-follow guidelines. Still, getting into the locker room doesn't necessarily mean you're home free.

Sally Jenkins, then with the *San Francisco Examiner,* was sent to help cover an Oakland Athletics–New York Yankees game at the Oakland Alameda County Stadium in 1982. During the game, the Athletics' Fred Stanley purposely got himself thrown out on the basepaths so Rickey Henderson could try for another steal. Jenkins's job was to interview Stanley about the incident.

This was Jenkins's first baseball game as a reporter and her very first time in a baseball clubhouse. She had been issued all the warnings (keep your eyes above belt level and so forth), but still she was a bit nervous.

Jenkins walked into the clubhouse and went directly to Stanley's locker. He was standing there in what amounted to a pair of longjohns. As she started to ask a question, several of Stanley's teammates began making noises.

"Hey, Chicken [Stanley's nickname]," yelled a player, "show her your machine."

"Yeah," said another, "show her your machine, Chicken."

Stanley tried to be nice about it as Jenkins struggled along. But finally, a grin crossed his face. Shortly thereafter, Jenkins burst out in laughter, too. If nothing else, she had survived.

You learn to adapt if you're a woman sportswriter. You also learn to pretend you're not a tiny bit scared when those locker room doors open.

Johnette Howard, now with the *National,* was fresh out of college in 1982 when she was hired by the *Beaver County* (Pennsylvania) *Times.* One of her first assignments was to help cover a Pittsburgh Pirates game.

At game's end, the *Times'* beat reporter casually asked if Howard had ever been inside the Pirates clubhouse.

"Oh, yeah, it's no big deal," she lied.

Before Howard knew it, she was inside the clubhouse. Not knowing exactly what to do, she went to Chuck Tanner's office, where the manager was holding court. Then she visited Harvey Haddix, the team's pitching coach. Haddix still had his pants on.

One of the first lessons you learn as a woman sportswriter is how to strategically position your notepad while interviewing someone. Howard did just that, holding her notebook in a way that prevented any unnecessary viewing.

Still, she wasn't entirely prepared when Haddix unceremoniously dropped his drawers in midinterview. Her ballpoint pen shot off the page, the ink line resembling something from a Richter Scale reading.

"What's wrong?" Haddix said.

"Uh, nothing," Howard said.

So much for calm and collected.

Howard learned. While covering Michigan's march to an NCAA basketball championship in 1989, she found herself stopped at the Wolverines locker room door by a concerned security guard.

"Do you know there are naked guys in there?" he asked.

"Well," she said kindly, "you better tell them to put towels on."

And then she went in and did her job, this time without pen ever leaving pad. If only it were always that easy.

Melanie Hauser once walked into the Houston Oilers locker room and was confronted by an angry Keith Bostic, who played strong safety for the team. Bostic, in so many words, said he wanted to wash his private parts in, well, private, so could she please get the hell out of the locker room.

Several years later, Bostic again yelled at Hauser as she entered the room. "What do you want to do, the defense?" he said.

Oilers players came to Hauser's aid.

"Hey, man, she's cool," said one of the players. Later, several of the players apologized on behalf of Bostic. "Hey, man, that's Keith," they said.

Players, more than coaches, seem to comprehend that a woman sportswriter isn't there to take notes on their genitals but on the events of the day.

Hauser was walking into the Cincinnati Bengals locker room one time when a security guard grabbed her by the arm and said she couldn't go inside. That was when running back Stanley Wilson looked up and said, "Hey, ain't nothing here she ain't seen before."

Lynne Snierson, a sportswriter for fifteen years, used to cover the New England Patriots for the *Boston Herald*. Just to be on the safe side, she would always have herself announced as she entered the locker room.

"Lady in the locker room!" the security guard would yell.

Once, after a similar cry, Snierson walked into the Patriots dressing area and found several players hurriedly wrapping towels around their midsections. Then one of the players looked up.

"Aw, shit, it's only you," he said.

Off came the towels.

Christine Brennan once walked into the Redskins locker room before a practice to find then-place-kicker Mark Moseley pulling up his football pants.

"Sorry, Mark," Brennan said.

"We're going to have to put a cowbell around your neck," he said.

Players become accustomed to a familiar face, even if they're not crazy about seeing it in their locker room. Witness the time in 1987 when Patriots wide receivers Stanley Morgan and Stephen Starring were giving a female television reporter a hard time for being in the locker room. Tired of the badgering, the reporter pointed toward Snierson, who was at the other end of the room, and said, "What about her?"

"Oh, that's just Lynne," said one of the players.

After a while, a strange trust sometimes develops between team members and reporters. For instance, a Patriot once paid Snierson a compliment of sorts.

"You know," he said, "you're OK. The rest of them all be motherfuckers, but you be nice."

How sweet.

If you're looking for a patron saint of women sportswriters, Mary Garber of the *Winston-Salem Journal* might be an appropriate nominee. Garber joined the *Twin Cities Journal* (now the Winston-Salem paper) in 1944 and, despite a so-called retirement in 1986, still manages a forty-hour work week with no trouble at all.

When Garber began covering sports, equal access wasn't a problem. In fact, it wasn't even considered. Women sportswriters (what few there were) weren't allowed in locker rooms or clubhouses—and that was that. Worse yet, they weren't even granted entrance to press boxes.

Garber recalled the time she was assigned to cover an Atlantic Coast Conference football game in the early 1950s. Credentials in hand, she approached the door of the stadium press box (she won't say which one) and was told firmly that no women, children or pets were allowed inside the hallowed confines.

"But I have credentials," she said.

"Sorry," the security guard replied.

Officials eventually found a seat for Garber inside the viewing box reserved for the wives and children of the school's coaches. So there she sat that day, next to screaming kids and loud-mouthed wives. She might as well have been seated in the percussion section of the band, what with the noise in the cramped box.

Angered by the treatment, Garber complained to her editor, who told her to be quiet, mind her own business and let him take care of it.

And he did. A cleverly worded letter sent to the various

conference schools made it clear that to offend Garber also was to offend the *Journal,* whose circulation was considerable enough to merit attention. Soon thereafter, the newspaper received its replies: Garber would have a press box seat with her name on it.

As for forays into the various locker rooms, forget it. It would have taken a Supreme Court ruling and then some to convince ACC athletic directors and coaches to allow a woman sportswriter inside a dressing room. Realizing this, Garber relied on her ability to adapt.

Rather than wait for a player or coach to shower, dress and then answer the questions of her male counterparts before speaking to her, Garber enlisted the help of several high-school coaching friends. What she would do was give her press pass to a high-school coach, hand him a pen and pad and send him inside the locker room. And while he probably didn't know how to take notes as fast as Garber, the high-school coach did have two advantages.

First, he was a he, which meant he had immediate access to the teams.

Second, he knew a heck of a lot more about football than Garber did. Because of this (and much to the surprise of her newspaper competition), Garber's stories sometimes explained the subtleties and technical aspects of the game better than any of the other writers'. Then again, they didn't have experts working for them.

As for the idea that women sportswriters lack sports knowledge, I beg to differ. Preparedness has nothing to do with whether a sportswriter is wearing a skirt or not. You either know your stuff or you don't.

Melanie Hauser knew her stuff when she walked into the Astrodome interview room after the Oilers had beaten the Seattle Seahawks, 23–20, in the 1987 AFC first-round playoff game. Like everyone else, she wanted to know why wide receiver Steve Largent, who finished with seven receptions for 132 yards and two touchdowns, had been ignored during long stretches.

So she asked, which didn't sit well with Seahawks coach Chuck Knox.

"Coach, did they do something defensively to take Largent out of the game?" she asked.

Fair question. There was always the possibility that the Seahawks wanted to concentrate on their running game or even use Largent as a decoy.

Knox wasn't much in the mood for possibilities that day.

"What do you think, honey? What do you think, sweetheart?" he asked.

"I don't know, darlin'," Hauser shot back.

Knox's voice became stern.

"What is your name?"

"Melanie Hauser."

"Is that Miss or Mrs.?"

"Miss."

"Miss Hauser, is that what I should call you?"

"That's fine."

Back when Dana Kirk was still the basketball coach of Memphis State, Sally Jenkins did a profile of the program for the *Washington Post*. The story was basically a positive one, except for a brief reference deep in the story to Kirk's supposed weakness in the strategy department.

Later that year, as Memphis State advanced to the Final Four, Kirk and Jenkins accidentally met.

"I remember you," said Kirk. "You're the little girl who wrote that I was suspect in the *X*s and *O*s department. You writing about *X*s and *O*s is like me writing a beauty column."

Equally condescending was the famous college football coach, now retired, who would meet with the press after each afternoon's practice. One day, a young woman reporter was among those waiting.

As he made his way toward the sportswriters, the woman stepped forward and tried to introduce herself. But before she could finish, the coach took her notepad and pen from her hands, signed his autograph, smiled and walked toward the other reporters.

And then there is Reggie Jackson, who once chastised Lisa Saxon for a week after she asked a question about an injury to Angels third baseman Doug DeCinces.

"Reggie, is DeCinces the last person the Angels can afford to lose?"

Jackson immediately accused her of being negative. For the next week, Jackson would interrupt her interviews with other players by saying, "She's negative," or, "She's terrible," or, "She shouldn't be here."

Oddly enough, Jackson would apologize for cursing in front of a woman sportswriter, but he would never apologize for yelling at one. His belief was that those who stepped into a major league clubhouse willingly opened themselves up for such treatment.

Jackson has a tiny point: You enter an athlete's domain, you enter at your own risk. Understood.

But what to do when an athlete or coach makes a pass at a woman reporter? Hey, it happens.

In 1983, her first year on the Angels beat, Saxon said she received propositions from players. Some asked sex-related questions. One player even sent a note to her inquiring about her availability.

Try fending off the fellas and doing your job at the same time. The combination nearly caused Saxon to request a change in beats.

Had it not been for then–Angels manager John McNamara, Saxon said, she probably would have left the business. But in one of your more touching pep talks, McNamara sat Saxon down and told her that there had been times when he wanted to quit himself. He said he loved managing and he wasn't going to let other people ruin what he loved. He said that if Saxon really wanted to be a baseball writer, she should try to rise above the distasteful moments and that eventually the positives of the job would outweigh the negatives.

Saxon has lasted five more seasons and, no, it's still a push on positives and negatives.

Meanwhile, Christine Brennan once discovered that a married Redskins player had been using her as an alibi for his illicit love affair. She found this out when one of the player's teammates pulled her aside one day.

"Uh, if [the player's] wife ever happens to ask, tell her you called their house for an interview."

"I don't get it," Brennan said.

She did a few seconds later, when the teammate explained that the woman having the affair called the player's house once. When the player's wife asked who had called, the player said it was Brennan.

"Oh, great," said Brennan, when told this bit of news.

By Brennan's count, about a dozen Redskins players—some married, some not—requested dates. To each, Brennan politely said no.

One married member of the Redskins organization (Brennan won't specify if it was a player, coach or management type) was particularly persistent. In fact, he found it necessary to make his silly attempt at romance while Brennan was busily finishing a story one evening at Redskins Park, the team's training facility. Brennan happened to look up from her computer to find the man staring at her, a stupid grin on his face.

As his opener, he asked, "Do you stay at the same hotel as the team?"

"Yes," said Brennan, hesitantly.

"Would you like to get together this weekend?"

"No thanks," she said.

Having failed at small talk, the man started to leave and then suddenly turned around.

"Would it be OK if I kissed you?" he asked.

"No!"

The man left, leaving Brennan a bit shaken by the experience. That's when an editor from the *Post* called.

"What's taking so long?" he asked.

"If you only knew."

Lynne Snierson, too, was occasionally a center of attention for Patriots players. One player called her up one night and wanted to know if a date was in order. Snierson told him it most certainly was not.

"I won't tell anyone," he said.

"Sure you won't," she said.

Snierson follows two rules when covering a team: First, never go out with a member of the organization (for obvious reasons, beginning with, it totally compromises your ability to do your job), and second, always remember that players are gossips.

Still, Snierson is slightly amused by the countless attempts by players or coaches to earn a date. When she first started covering the Patriots, the rookies used to call her "baby." Eventually, the veterans started calling her "ma'am."

Other times, Snierson has been asked by fans who see her in, say, the team hotel (which is usually the same hotel the media stays in), "Hi, are you one of the cheerleaders?"

Or, "Hi, are you one of the players' wives?"

Or, as the years go by, "Hi, are you a coach's wife?"

Until they ask if she's the owner's wife, Snierson says, she can live with the questions.

On a much more innocent note, Christine Brennan was once the recipient of an unexpected smooch from then–University of Miami coach Howard Schnellenberger. Brennan was covering the Hurricanes for the *Miami Herald* at the time and, as you might expect, had had her share of disagreements with the headstrong Schnellenberger.

But all was forgotten at the end of the 1983 season, the year the Hurricanes defeated the Nebraska Cornhuskers for an unlikely national championship. After writing her story that night at the Orange Bowl, Brennan stopped by the Hurricanes' postgame party to congratulate Schnellenberger on his team's accomplishments. As she approached him, Brennan extended her arm for an handshake. Schnellenberger would have none of that.

"Christine Brennan," he bellowed, "I'm going to give you a kiss."

And he did. Big, gruff Howard Schnellenberger, giddy with victory, smooched the embarrassed Brennan right there in front of God and everybody.

9

Deadlines: God's Curse

Stop me if I'm overdramatizing here, but I'd rather listen to an entire collection of Mitch Miller albums than write on deadline. I'd rather watch Geraldo. I'd rather lose my wallet. I'd rather have Reggie over for dinner. Speak to the Kiwanis Club. View soccer. Attend Shakespeare in the park. I'd rather do absolutely anything than hear the ticking of that omnipresent clock, the one that marks time in gulps, not seconds, the one that tells me—no, screams at me—that my story is due. Now. Right this moment. Get it in, or else.

Deadline makes you this way. It turns grown sportswriters into sniveling, wimpering geeks or snarling, ultra-aggressive typists hell-bent on beating the second hand in a race of time. It causes heart rates to dart up and down like hummingbirds. Dead-line: The word itself makes me nervous.

As far as I'm concerned, sportswriting would be a lot more fun if you could simply file your story at your convenience rather than at the newspaper's. Deadline, schmeadline. The readers would understand. Simply explain that you felt you could do without the added stress and you'll make it up to them at a later date. Perfectly reasonable.

Well, sort of.

Among the many things they don't teach you in journalism school is how to cope with the utter horror of having to write coherent, informed prose while someone is holding a clock to your head. I mean, they do, but they don't. Miss a deadline in Journalism 101 and you get a C. Miss it enough times in real life and you get a PS, as in pink slip. Editors will tolerate just about anything except the sportswriter who doesn't know the difference between the big hand and the little hand on a wristwatch.

A confession: While covering the Gator Bowl one year for the *Dallas Morning News,* I somehow confused time zones. Don't ask how. Instead of 11:00 P.M., I thought it was only 10:00 P.M., which meant I had all sorts of extra time to conduct postgame interviews and write my story.

Oklahoma State was playing in that year's Gator Bowl and the Cowboys' sports information office had gone to extraordinary lengths to arrange for my press pass, hotel room and even transportation to the game. To them, it was worth it. Dallas was prime recruiting territory for the OSU program, so any stories, especially bowl stories, were valuable. Image, and all that.

I'm sorry to report that not a single word about Oklahoma State's play in the prestigious Gator Bowl appeared in the *Morning News* the following day. And they can blame me.

I suppose I should have sensed something was wrong when I was the only one left in the locker room after the game. I glanced at my watch—plenty of time left I thought—and found another player to interview. From there, I walked casually up the stairs and into the press box, where everyone was busily typing away.

Bud Shaw, then with the *Atlanta Journal-Constitution,* glanced up from his computer screen.

"Shouldn't you be writing?" he asked.

"I suppose," I said confidently. "I've still got almost an hour."

"Lucky you."

So I wrote. Carefully. Happily. These poor saps were pounding their brains out on their keyboards. Meanwhile, I could cruise from start to finish.

Halfway through the story, Shaw approached. He was finished with his story and was getting ready to catch a cab back to his hotel.

"Let me ask you something," he said.

I paused. I still had a half hour or so.

"Since when do you have 1:00 A.M. deadlines?"

"Midnight, Bud. We have midnight deadlines."

"Well, then you're screwed. It's 12:35 Dallas time."

Ever just want to barf? Ever get that sick, empty feeling in the pit of your stomach, the one most associated with ulcers? I did.

I sent my story five minutes later and then called the office. No answer. At last, the *Morning News* operator clicked in.

"Yes," I said, "I need someone in sports."

"I'm sorry, they've all left for the evening."

Uh, oh.

Julie Cart of the *Los Angeles Times* missed deadline at the 1984 Summer Games in L.A. and then missed it again several days later when her watch mysteriously stopped ticking. She called her boss the following morning to explain.

"I know this sounds pretty lame, but the reason I missed deadline was that my watch stopped," she said.

"That's OK," said the boss. "But you might want to get it fixed. You want to be on time for your job interviews."

Cart didn't miss any more deadlines.

Perhaps she could have saved herself some grief by following the Jack Sheppard method of deadline writing. Sheppard, now an editor with the *St. Petersburg Times,* used to cover high-school football games way back when. Almost all sportswriters begin their careers covering preps. In fact, it should be required.

Anyway, after each game, Sheppard would rush to a nearby 7-Eleven store and dictate his story by the light of the parking lot sign. And even though he had until 11:30 P.M. to finish his assignment, Sheppard was always done a half hour before the deadline. And with good reason, too. That was the time the store manager clicked off the parking lot sign.

While under the influence of deadline, I've written and witnessed some remarkable things. I've written sentences that were so cliché-ridden my computer begged for mercy. So bad were some stories that I felt as if I should stick a disclaimer at the bottom, an idea first proposed by *Sports Illustrated*'s Leigh Montville.

According to Montville's plan, a sportswriter could include an explanation of just why that particular story stank so much. For instance, *"The writer apologizes for this story. He only had about twenty minutes to finish it because the game ran long and then went into overtime when that son of a bitch Bird sank a three-pointer at the buzzer. The elevator, the one that takes the writers down to the locker rooms, didn't work, either. Then, when he got back to his seat on press row, some idiot accidentally spilled a soft drink all over him. And did he mention anything about the pep band that was playing directly behind him? Anyway, he did the best job he could under the circumstances."*

Baseball games are the worst. They take forever to be played. You could learn to split atoms in the time it takes to play some American League contests.

Naturally, this causes a teensy-weensy bit of tension in press boxes everywhere. The nervous system begins to shovel anxiety to the rest of the body. Before long, you have a sportswriter taut with mental anguish.

The first three innings go well enough. Writers chat. Pleasantries are exchanged. Then you move into your middle innings. Time for "running," a term given to the part of the game story that describes how a team scored. Running is a sportswriter's best friend on deadline. Without it, you'd have a lot of three-paragraph game stories the next day.

Now on to the most trying part of the game, the late innings. Deadline is fast approaching. Unfortunately, the game's end is not. Tick, tick, tick.

One of the friendliest people I've ever met is Mike Terry, who covers the California Angels for the *San Bernardino County Sun.* Terry is a rather large person who has biceps as thick as mallet heads. Terry is not a person you would like to enrage unless, of course, you were carrying a reliable firearm.

The 1986 season was Terry's first as a baseball writer. He was relatively new to sportswriting, he hated flying, he had yet to be fully exposed to the peculiar wit of ballplayers and he had to deal with nightly deadlines. Not exactly your mixture for success.

But Terry survived quite nicely until one evening at Chicago's Comiskey Park, site of an Angels–White Sox game. It was then, in full view of a semipacked press box, that Terry, as have sportswriters before him, temporarily lost touch with reality. The pressure of deadline can break a man.

Not only did Terry have to write a game story that night, but he also had to write a feature story on Angels pitcher Don Sutton, who was nearing the three-hundred-victory mark. As the game dragged on, it became obvious that Terry was not to be approached. He had that look of fixation, of total concentration that comes with knowing you have no alternative but to be done writing by a certain time.

At last, the game inched toward its conclusion. The seventh inning became the eighth and the eighth inning dissolved into the ninth and final inning. Terry looked like he just might make it.

That was when Carlton Fisk, the White Sox's Hall-of-Fame-catcher-to-be, rose from his squat behind home plate and walked ever so slowly toward the mound for what had to be his tenth visit of the game. Terry couldn't believe his eyes.

The White Sox were well on their way to an easy victory, and yet here was Fisk drawing out every moment as if it were the seventh game of the World Series.

Terry stood up and, much to the shock of everyone else in the open-air press box that night, began yelling at Fisk.

"What the fuck is wrong with you, Pudge!" he screamed. "Get the game going!"

Realize that ballplayers hear voices from the stands all the time. But not even Fisk, a veteran of more than fifteen major league seasons, ever had heard anything like this. Fisk turned and squinted upward. If he looked hard enough, he probably saw a defiant, frustrated Terry staring down at and through him.

Peter Schmuck, then of the *Orange County Register* and now with the *Baltimore Morning Sun,* tried to restore calm.

"Mike, sit down. You don't do that here," he said.

"There ain't no man big enough to make me sit down," Terry said.

Good point.

Terry has since learned. In 1987, he found himself with only a few minutes to spare before a game story was due. Rushing down to the Angels clubhouse for statements, he spied manager Gene Mauch in his office.

"What do you want?" asked Mauch, smiling, as Terry came dashing into the room.

"I need something."

"What do you need?"

"Talk about the game. I'm on deadline."

Mauch, as he was prone to do, considered the request for a moment and said, "You know, there are two things in the world I don't care about: tits on a man and your deadline."

Terry froze. Then he saw the grin on Mauch's face. A few minutes later, his notepad partially filled with Mauch's reflections on the game, Terry ran back upstairs to the press box.

You can always tell which writers are facing impending deadlines. They're the ones who groan with every walked batter, every pitching change, every pinch-hitter, every seventh-inning stretch. At game's end, they stand outside the locked clubhouse, staring at their watches, shuffling about as if they need to use the restroom. I know; I've shuffled with the best of them.

Once, while covering those same White Sox and Angels, this time at Anaheim Stadium, I happened to glance down at my scorebook and noticed that Chicago starter Joe Cowley—and this was unbelievable—had a no-hitter through seven innings.

You could understand my surprise. Cowley had walked something like seven Angels, including three straight in the sixth inning. A run scored when Reggie Jackson hit a sacrifice fly. Cowley was pitching so erratically that White Sox manager Jim Fregosi almost pulled him from the game—with a no-hitter intact!

I called the office to alert my editors. They said they would immediately send somebody out to the stadium.

They sent somebody, all right. His name was Rick Jaffe (now with the *National*), and he arrived after the game was finished. He wasn't even a writer, but another editor who had been paged at a nearby restaurant. He had never used a portable computer. Hell, he hadn't even seen a single pitch. In fact, it was miracle he even made it to the press box in the first place.

Jaffe had to borrow a car to get to the stadium. As he drove at speeds exceeding all those mandated by federal law, Jaffe turned on the car radio. "He's got the no-hitter!" the announcer breathlessly said for listeners everywhere, including Jaffe, who was about a mile away when the last pitch was thrown by Cowley.

Imagine a single car trying to enter Anaheim Stadium as thousands of other vehicles are trying to leave the complex. Jaffe weaved in and out of traffic. He violated more traffic codes than you would have thought possible. He endured finger gestures from outraged pedestrians. Once parked, Jaffe ran to the White Sox clubhouse, found Cowley and pretended he had seen the whole thing.

"Hey, I've already answered all these questions," said Cowley, who had showered, shaved and was fully dressed.

"Pleeeeeeaaaaaaaaassssssssseeeeeee," said Jaffe.

Cowley recounted the game quickly and then said he had to leave. Jaffe rushed upstairs, plugged in his computer, turned to me and said, "How do you work this thing?"

So there we were, on deadline, with less than thirty minutes to describe one of the most improbable no-hitters of all time. I spent ten of those precious minutes giving Jaffe a quick primer on basic computer operation. We then spent the remainder of our time writing two of the worst stories ever published in a metropolitan newspaper. What I wouldn't have given for one of Montville's disclaimers that night.

John McGrath, then with the *Denver Post* and now with the *National,* was covering the 1988 World Series at Dodger Stadium. Because of press box constraints, McGrath was seated in the auxiliary facility, which wasn't anything more than a place in the stands.

As McGrath plopped his computer onto his lap, several Dodgers fans began yelling at him and several other reporters. Unbeknownst to the sportswriters, season ticket holders had had to move to accommodate the press seating. Needless to say, the fans weren't crazy about the arrangement.

"Hey, I'm just trying to work," McGrath said.

Entering the bottom of the ninth inning, things looked bleak for the Dodgers, which was good for McGrath, who was facing deadline. Doing his best to balance the computer on his lap, McGrath began typing. He heard the announcement that Kirk Gibson had entered the game as a pinch-hitter, but didn't think much of it. After all, Gibson had been hurt. Also, Gibson would have to face Oakland Athletics reliever Dennis Eckersley, the best in the business.

"Just don't hit a home run," thought McGrath, as Gibson stepped to the plate.

Gibson hit a home run. Not just any homer, but one for the ages. The kind that made your neck hairs stand at attention.

Dodger Stadium rocked as if it were set on a gelatin foundation. Sitting glumly amidst the celebration was McGrath, who did what he could to protect his computer from the debris. A hot dog zinged by. Someone nearly spilled a beer on him. Peanut shells rained down on him like rice at a wedding. And deadline awaited.

While covering the Quad Cities Open one year, *Chicago Tribune* reporter Mike Conklin returned to the press tent shortly after a rain delay and found it completely deserted, except for a lone security man. Worse yet, darkness had fallen and there wasn't a light to be found in the makeshift facility.

So Conklin, his family in tow, pulled his car near the entrance of the tent. Leaving the engine running and the headlights on, Conklin took a seat in front of the car, propped up his computer screen so that the beams would hit it just so, and wrote his story as his deadline fast approached. He made it, too.

You are at your technology's mercy on deadline. If some cathode ray circuitry decides to fizzle out minutes before you have to file, you're dead. If the phone you're using to send your story suddenly develops a mind of its own, begin praying.

And then there are the acts of God that test every sportswriter's stockpile of swear words, acts so unfathomable that you are left stunned by their impact. I refer to the 1987 Fiesta Bowl, which featured the University of Miami versus Penn State for the national championship. Mike LoPresti of the Gannett News Service was there in the stadium press box that night. He took notes. He gathered statistics. He made observations that would later find their way into his story.

Immediately after the game, LoPresti began writing. Above him on the next level was a stadium maintenance worker. Somehow the worker pressed down on a metal roofing panel, which allowed a small body of water that had gathered there to fall directly on LoPresti and his machine.

His computer ruined, his story lost in circuitry heaven, LoPresti had to hurriedly dictate his thoughts to an angry editor.

Mike Penner of the *Los Angeles Times* was in the middle of a story when someone spilled an iced tea onto his computer. Poof went the story.

Same thing happened to Tracy Ringolsby of the *Dallas Morning News*. One moment a game story existed. The next moment, after someone had knocked a beer onto his machine, the game story ceased to exist.

Dale Robertson of the *Houston Post* watched in horror as a worker at Atlanta's Fulton County Stadium dropped a plumber's wrench on top of his computer, rendering the keys useless. Roberston was supposed to catch a flight to New York to cover the U.S. Open at Flushing Meadow. By the time he finished dictating his revised story, Robertson had missed three flights. He arrived in New York at 4:00 A.M.

Robertson never did enjoy much success with his company-issue laptop computers. In 1987, while covering a Houston Rockets game in Seattle, Robertson was forced to sit through two overtime periods. Because of the time change (a two-hour difference), Robertson was constantly changing and updating his lead to reflect the score.

At about 2:15 Houston time, just barely in time to make some of the editions, Robertson sent his story, which had been written and rewritten at least five times as the game came to a conclusion.

"Yeah, this is Robertson," he said, as someone back at the *Post* picked up the phone. "The game story should be there."

There was a long, painful pause.

"Uh, we can't get any of your stuff. One of the guys on the desk just accidentally killed all of the computer commands."

If Robertson was smart, he searched immediately for an open bar—and drank to forget.

And let's not ignore the X factor in the search for the perfect deadline nightmare: phones.

Without a working phone, a sportswriter is useless (of course, there are those who say a sportswriter is useless no matter the occasion). Phones are their lifeline. Without them, no story.

In 1989, at Buffalo's Rich Stadium, the Los Angeles Rams were playing the Bills. Because of a telephone strike, there were only two, count 'em, two, phones for about thirty or forty reporters. Because it was a Monday night game (meaning tighter deadlines), everyone would be battling for use of the phones.

It rained that night. Shortly after the rain stopped, the temperature began to drop. Inside the press box, all was quite comfortable until, without any warning, one of the huge plate-glass windows groaned and then shattered. Through the middle of the window was what looked like a bullet hole.

Said Matt Jocks, a sportswriter for the *Riverside* (California) *Press-Enterprise:* "Now we have half as many bullet holes as we do phones."

Security people were summoned, but they found no evidence of foul play. Or of any spare phones.

Peter King, now with *Sports Illustrated,* was in Chicago in 1982 to cover a basketball game at Loyola University. The game was played in an ancient gym that featured a tiny press box located in the balcony. There were no phones, a distressing fact that King discovered when it came time to send his story that night.

In fact, there wasn't a sports information director, either. He had left at game's end, stranding King in a darkened gym. At 11:30, King had to file his story. All the offices in the building were closed, as was the Loyola switchboard. Left with no alternative, King lugged his computer into the wickedly cold January air, found a pay phone in the shadows of the noisy El tracks and tried transmitting his story. Trains rumbled past. Those famous Chicago winds numbed his face. But it made it.

Phones have it in for King. On one occasion he tried sending a story, but the phone wouldn't work. Again and again he pressed the proper keys, entered the right program codes and nothing. Zilch. Faced with missing a flight, King loaded up his things and decided he would dictate his story from one of those plane phones, the ones that cost about thirty dollars a nanosecond.

King placed his credit card in the phone slot, dialed his office and began dictating. But because of nasty weather in the vicinity, King's dictation didn't exactly reach his office in the same shape in which it was sent. There was static on the line, and there were long delays between transmissions. Words were misunderstood, whole sentences were ignored.

Later, when he saw the paper, King could find little resemblance between the story he had dictated and the one that appeared in print.

If he said, "Phil Simms passed fifteen yards to Joe Morris for a crucial first down," it came out, "Phil Villapiano passed everyone, including Joe Morris, while returning a crucial interception."

King should have asked for a refund on his Visa card.

Sportswriters aren't what you'd call a handy bunch when it comes to tinkering with modern technology. They can turn a computer on and off, adjust the brightness of the screen, replace the batteries. That about does it for technical wizardry.

Still, there are those who persist. Tom Zucco of the *St. Petersburg Times* was covering his very first assignment (Florida versus Georgia in Jacksonville's Gator Bowl) when his computer refused to accept any more information. In the vernacular, it froze up.

Zucco didn't know what to do. He checked the plug. He pressed a few keys, hoping for some sort of computer miracle. Then he made a huge mistake: He asked a colleague for help.

The fellow sportswriter gazed at the offending machine and confidently announced, "Oh, I know how to fix that."

And with that, he picked up Zucco's machine, held it over his head and dropped it. The screen went blank, as did Zucco's face.

A few minutes later, Zucco was on the phone dictating his story to his office.

The most obvious case of computer abuse came in 1987, when John Feinstein, now with the *National,* was covering Wimbledon. Feinstein was a bit on the edgy side to begin with. It happens at Wimbledon, where your workday begins at 10:00 A.M. and ends at 11:00 that evening . . . for a fortnight.

Anyway, Feinstein had had trouble sending his stories back to the States all week along. On this particular day, he was doing a story on Jimmy Connors's remarkable victory over Mikael Pernfors of Sweden. It was a five-set victory, one which the venerable *Times* of London later reported in its early editions (no doubt because of deadlines) that Pernfors had won.

Feinstein's sports editor instructed the writer to do a separate story on the *Times*'s error, an idea that Feinstein resisted. "It could happen to anyone," he said.

"Do it," he was told.

Feinstein sent his story on the Connors match and later attempted to send his short story on the *Times*'s gaffe. As the computer was hooked up to the phone lines, his computer screen went blank. Tired, irritable, angry with the idea of having to poke fun at another newspaper, Feinstein looked at the empty screen and sent his fist through the machine. He then proceeded to call the desk.

"I'm dictating," he said.

The next day Feinstein took his machine to the London bureau of the *Washington Post* (he was working for the *Post* at the time) and picked up a new computer. And no, he didn't explain the damage.

Wimbledon was the site of one other deadline debacle. It involved Dave Kindred, then of the *Washington Post,* Hubert Mizell of the *St. Petersburg Times* and Barry Lorge of the *San Diego Union.*

Lorge isn't known as the swiftest of deadline writers. According to Mizell, Lorge once missed deadline from Moscow, and that was with the benefit of an eleven-hour time difference. At Wimbledon, he had eight hours to write a story.

Mizell, Kindred and Lorge were covering the 1982 men's final, which traditionally takes place on a Sunday afternoon. The next morning, Mizell and Kindred were scheduled to catch a plane to Barcelona, Spain, where a World Cup soccer game was to be played.

Mizell and Kindred wrote their Wimbledon stories, and said good-bye to Lorge and took a cab back to their hotel. They ate dinner and retired to their respective rooms for a good night's rest. The next morning, they met in the lobby to catch a taxi to the airport.

As they prepared to leave, they saw Lorge walk into the hotel. He was carrying his computer. He had just finished his story. It had only taken him forever to finish.

The threat of missing deadline can make you do things you never thought possible. You tend to suspend the notion of common sense when attempting to deliver a story to your employer on time. You take chances. You flirt with danger.

Karen Rosen of the *Atlanta Journal-Constitution* was supposed to write a general story about a bicycle race up Mount Mitchell in western North Carolina. The mountain, at 6,684 feet, is the highest peak east of the Mississippi River.

Rosen's day began at 5:15 A.M. She met a *Journal-Constitution* photographer at the top of the peak, parked her car and caught a ride down the mountain. Rosen talked to several competitors while the photographer took several rolls of film. Once at the bottom, the photographer informed Rosen that she had to immediately return to Atlanta to develop and print the film.

"But you can probably catch a ride up the mountain," the photographer said.

Rosen eventually did get back to the top and finished her story as the sun set. Now she needed to send the story, which would have been easy had there been a phone nearby. There wasn't, so back down the mountain she went, this time with nothing to guide her but a weak pair of headlights from her rental car.

Tires squealed, brakes whined as she wove her way down the road in the darkness. It seemed that it took hours before Rosen found a tiny campground and country store off the Blue Ridge Parkway. Outside the store was a lone pay phone.

It takes a while to send a computer story over the phone lines. You have to use these awkward rubber couplers that look like little suction cups. The phone fits inside the couplers, creating, so they say, a semisoundproof environment for the laptop to send its signal to the big computer at the newspaper. Of course, there are no instructions regarding what to do when several motorcyclists, the kind wearing near–life size tattoos on their forearms, rumble up to the phone and request its use.

Rosen did what any person in the middle of nowhere would do: She panicked.

First, she unhooked the couplers and let the bikers use the phone. The story could wait, she decided. As soon as they finished their call, Rosen sent the second half of her story. Just as she was ready to call her office, someone else arrived and needed to use the phone right that moment. He had to call his wife. Rosen handed the receiver over.

Eventually, she discovered the second half of the story hadn't made it. So she sent it again. That was when another biker arrived, demanding in no uncertain terms to use the phone.

This whole communications free-for-all came to an abrupt end when the plug was pulled from the soft drink machine adjacent to the pay phone. Gone was the only source of light outside the country store. By then, two more bikers had come and gone, as had a police car.

Rosen happily packed up her belongings and tried to find another pay phone, this time to see if her story had actually arrived at the Atlanta offices. At about 10:30 P.M., she found one in Asheville, North Carolina, but the mouthpiece was broken. A little while later, she spotted another phone, this one with all parts working. Never was she more happy to hear an editor's confirmation than that night in Asheville.

It should come as no surprise that Rosen hasn't volunteered for any more road races or rural assignments since the assault on Mount Mitchell.

At the 1986 Orange Bowl, Joan Ryan of the *San Francisco Examiner* decided that she didn't need directions back to her Miami hotel. It was late at night, but she had been to Miami before and, anyway, how hard could it be to find the hotel, which wasn't located too far from the stadium?

You can guess what happened. Ryan became lost in the maze that is the south Florida freeway system. She took a wrong turn here and a wrong turn there and before long Ryan didn't know where she was.

Ryan, who works for an afternoon paper, was supposed to have her two stories written and sent by 6:00 A.M. But at 1:00 A.M. she was still driving helplessly around the city, with no clue as to how to get back. At about 2:00 A.M., the worst happened: She ran out of gas.

Stuck in a residential neighborhood, Ryan searched for a pay phone to call a cab. At last she found one at a recreation center. Only one problem: Ryan had no way of telling the taxi dispatcher where she was located. Ryan looked for street sign and read off the names. There was desperation in her voice, but not enough to fully convince the dispatcher that the whole thing wasn't a hoax.

At 3:00 A.M., with only a few hours to go before her stories were due, Ryan sat on a street curb near her car and began typing on her computer. Tears ran down her face as she considered her fate: She was lost, out of gas, tired and without a ride back to her hotel. Worst of all, she could miss deadline, and wouldn't that take some explaining, what with about six hours to write her pair of stories.

Shortly after three, a cab found Ryan. Don't ask how; even Ryan can't explain her good fortune. She finished her stories back at the hotel, sent them to the *Examiner* offices, called the AAA Club about her car, showered and went to the Miami Dolphins practice facilities to interview several players for an upcoming AFC playoff story. This time she got directions.

There are but a handful of sportswriters I know who appear immune to the demands of deadline. They never break a sweat. They look as if they're composing a grocery list instead of a story. They really tick me off.

Mark Whicker of the *Orange County Register* can write a deadline column seemingly in minutes. Do you know how depressing it is to listen to somebody typing quickly on the keyboard as you sit nearby in shock? Sometimes, just so the other sportswriters don't think I'm dying on deadline, I start typing real fast on my computer. Yeah, ol' Geno's got it going now.

Except that the paragraph begins:

"Tlkjiwe;lkj;l asf;lkjisfpij likwelkjlsdf slijd0ewkjsdf;k . . ."

Pathetic, isn't it?

To show to what lengths sportswriters will go to avoid the dreaded deadline, may I present the case of Woody Paige of the *Denver Post.* Paige and about five other writers were in Seattle to cover a Seahawks-Broncos game. Afterward, they retired to a local pub and had enough drinks to render them above the legal limit.

After taking a cab back to the hotel, Paige and the writers were standing near the elevators when two comely prostitutes approached the group. One of them put her arms around

Paige and cooed, "For one hundred dollars, I'll come up to your room and do anything."

Paige struggled to keep his composure.

"Let me get this straight," he said. "You'll do *anything?*"

"Anything," she said.

"Well, you're on," said Paige, pulling out a crisp C-note. "I want you to go up to my room and write a game story and a sidebar."

And have it done before deadline.

10

And Now, Your Official Sportswriter Starter Kit

And in summary, twenty-three sportswriting do's and dont's:

1. When granted a twenty-minute interview session with a famous female tennis star, *never* begin the conversation with idle small talk.

John Feinstein, then with the *Washington Post,* was covering his first French Open in 1985 when he arranged a one-on-one interview with rising star Gabriela Sabatini of Argentina. This was a bit of a coup considering that Sabatini was fast becoming one of the players to watch on the women's tour.

Only a year earlier, Sabatini, then fourteen, had appeared at the U.S. Open and won a small amount of prize money, about fourteen hundred dollars. Feinstein was there, of course, and he remembered Sabatini's response when she was asked how she would spend her U.S. Open check.

"I have this little dog at home," she said sweetly, "and I'm going to buy it a present."

How nice, everyone thought.

On the day of his exclusive interview with Sabatini in Paris,

Feinstein decided that he would make brownie points by mentioning her young pup.

"So," said Feinstein happily, "how is your little dog at home doing?"

Sabatini's face turned ashen.

"She got run over last week," she managed, before bursting into tears.

For fourteen of the next twenty precious minutes, Sabatini cried like a newborn. During the final six minutes of the interview, Sabatini answered just two questions, which almost caused Feinstein to weep.

2. *Always* wear a handkerchief in your ear when addressing former San Diego Chargers quarterback Jim McMahon.

Midway through the 1989 season, McMahon decided he would no longer make himself available to the San Diego media after games. This didn't sit well with the local reporters, who, if anything, had gone out of their way to give the former Bears star every benefit of the doubt.

On the Monday following the seventh game of the season, several of the San Diego writers, including T. J. Simers of the *Union,* approached McMahon's locker. McMahon ignored them.

At last, one of the reporters asked a question, to which McMahon muttered, "I don't know."

Then another one tried. This time McMahon didn't even bother muttering.

Finally, Simers ventured a question.

"What about the problems the team's been having in its two-minute offense?" Simers said.

McMahon turned his back to the reporters.

"I'm sorry," said Simers, "you probably didn't hear the question. I said, what about the problems the team's been having in its two-minute offense?"

McMahon didn't budge.

"I'm sorry," said Simers, "I didn't hear your answer."

With that, McMahon turned around, looked straight at Simers and walked to the side of the reporter. McMahon pressed one of his nostrils closed and proceeded to blow bits of a loogie right on Simers's shoulder. Then he walked away.

McMahon would later explain that it was either that "or beat the shit out of him.

"You can't get sued for sneezing," he said.

Meanwhile, the Chargers were kind enough never to issue an apology on behalf of McMahon. Did this upset the beat reporters? Of course not. Shortly after the incident, one of the San Diego writers said that McMahon should immediately be elected to the Hall of Phlegm.

Countered another writer: "S'not true."

No one has ever mistaken McMahon's social graces for those of Amy Vanderbilt. While playing in a charity golf event in 1989, McMahon was put in a group that included Mike Ditka, Wayne Gretzky and Michael Jordan, among others. Each player was outfitted with a wireless microphone so that the gallery of 1,500 to 2,000 fans could hear his remarks over speakers stationed about the course. The players, of course, were told to click their microphones on or off at their discretion.

Following the group that day were *Chicago Tribune* columnists Bob Verdi and Mike Conklin. They watched as McMahon, an unorthodox (he likes to play barefooted) but talented amateur golfer, struck a tree with his drive. Later, as the group made its way to the green, McMahon, who had been drinking a beverage or two during the day, disappeared from sight.

As the golfers lined up their putts, a voice was heard over the loudspeaker system. It was McMahon. He had left his wireless microphone on, which wouldn't have been so terrible except that he was in a restroom at the time.

"Yeah, did you see me hit that ball," McMahon was saying. "Son of a bitch, I hit that tree."

Minutes later, McMahon returned to the green. After putting, Verdi and Conklin approached and informed him that the crowd had heard everything.

"Yeah, well, good thing I wasn't taking a shit," McMahon said simply.

3. *Always* examine your disability coverage before accepting any story assignments involving boxers.

You remember Tex Cobb, the former heavyweight who was as funny as he was tough? In 1989, Richard Hoffer, then with the *Los Angeles Times,* interviewed Cobb at the boxer's home in Nashville. Cobb and his wife were songwriters and songpluggers. In the music business, a songplugger is someone who goes to a publishing or recording company and tries to convince the person in charge to listen to his or her songs. It's a tough way to make a living, but no tougher than boxing, Cobb explained.

In fact, said Cobb, as he warmed up to the subject, boxing was one of the toughest professions around. People had no idea, he said, what it was like to be hit by, say, the powerful Ernie Shavers, another heavyweight of some renown. So agitated did Cobb become that he gestured toward Hoffer.

"Stand up, I want to show you something," he said, and then disappeared into another room.

Hoffer is tall but thin and he wears glasses. And while he is quite easily one of the best boxing writers ever to tap on a keyboard, Hoffer wouldn't be your first choice in a barroom brawl. Actually, he would be the guy you'd send to call the cops.

Cobb eventually emerged from a room carrying a Nashville phone book. He gave it to Hoffer and told him to hold it on his chest. Hoffer turned to Cobb's wife for help, but all she did was shake her head and say, "Stand him in front of the couch, honey."

Hoffer doesn't remember much after that. Cobb unleashed a short right that caused the air to leave Hoffer's lungs. On the tape recorder that Hoffer had somehow left on during this exhibition, you could hear Cobb's fist smack against the phone book, followed by an "ummmph" as the sportswriter was transported over the sofa.

"Geez, Tex," said Hoffer, as he struggled to his feet.

The rest of the interview didn't go especially well. Cobb was fine, but Hoffer couldn't seem to concentrate. All he could think about was whether the punch had damaged the inner lining of his heart.

4. *Always* say a little prayer for Paul Hoynes, who covers the Indians for the *Plain Dealer* of Cleveland.

Hoynes is a fine, dedicated beat reporter who just happens to be a bit absent-minded on occasion. Here is a partial list of Hoynes classics:

- Showed up at the ballpark during spring training wearing two belts.
- Was interviewing slugger Joe Carter when Carter suggested Hoynes might want to pull up his zipper. This happened in full view of the local school kid who was following Hoynes around that night to see how a "professional" journalist did his job.
- Once borrowed a pen from a kid in the stands to interview Indians outfielder Mel Hall.
- Once asked innocently, "Weren't there a lot of black catchers in the Negro leagues?"
- After being told that Ramón Romero had been shot four times in the head and thrown off a building, Hoynes asked, "Did he die?"
- Once wrote, "Swindell threw twenty-five pitches off the mound in the Indians dugout."
- Once asked, "What state is Oklahoma City in?"
- Once wrote: "Red Sox will get a shot in the arm when Burks and Ellis return." He was, of course, referring to Ellis Burks.
- Once locked his keys in his car at the stadium and had a maintenance man open the door with a broom handle.

Like I said, a great guy, but just a teensy-weensy bit
forgetful.

5. *Never* expect famous Eastern European female tennis
players to speak perfect English.

In 1980, Czechoslovakian tennis star Hana Mandlikova
raced up the computer rankings, from the mid-fifties to a top
ten placement. It was a stunning achievement and one that
Lesley Visser, then with the *Boston Globe,* was interested in.

Visser requested an interview with Mandlikova and was
told to meet the Czech star at 8:00 A.M. at an exclusive
restaurant. On the appropriate morning, Visser stumbled out
of bed and made her way to the restaurant for the early-bird
appointment. Half-awake, Visser lobbed an easy question
Mandlikova's way as they sipped tea and munched on rolls.

"So, Hana, to what do you attribute your remarkable move
up the rankings ladder?"

"Vell," said Mandlikova in a thick Czech accent, "I vould
have to say my new couch."

Visser, who had been jotting down notes, paused in disbelief.

"I'm sorry," said Visser politely, "your couch? What, do
you have some new furniture or something?"

Time stood still as Mandlikova stared coldly at the reporter.

"No, stupid," Mandlikova said, "Betty Stove—my couch,
my couch."

"Oh, your *coach*," Visser said.

6. When addressing a professional boxer, *always* begin all
sentences with the word "sir."

Tom Callahan, the gifted sportswriter for *Newsweek* magazine, was just twenty-two years old when he first encountered the
late great Sonny Liston. Callahan was working in Baltimore at the
time and among his responsibilities was the local boxing scene.

About 1969, Callahan was contacted by a promoter named
Eli Hanover. Said Hanover: "Kid, you're getting killed on

this boxing beat. Al Goldstein [the boxing writer for the competing newspaper] is kicking the shit out of you on this beat. I'm starting to worry about your job.

"Tell you what I'm gonna do. I'm gonna give you a scoop. Sonny Liston is going to have a big fight. He's going to fight at the [Baltimore] Civic Center. He's coming in tonight and I'll help you get an interview."

Callahan couldn't believe his good fortune and quickly said yes.

That night, Hanover picked up Callahan, as well as Liston's trainer. They drove out to Dulles Airport to pick up the former heavyweight champion, who was accompanied by his wife, Geraldine.

It wasn't difficult to pick out Liston from the crowd: He was the one with the hate-filled eyes and a scowl that could melt sheet metal. If he wasn't the meanest-looking man Callahan had ever seen in person, he was close. Liston refused to shake hands with anyone and didn't say a word as the small entourage climbed into the car.

Callahan sat in the front seat and Liston sat brooding in the back. At one point, Callahan turned around and asked two questions, both of which Liston ignored.

"Please, Sonny, please," pleaded Hanover.

After arriving at the Baltimore Hilton, Hanover pulled Liston aside and begged him to agree to an interview with Callahan. After thinking about it for a few moments, Liston grunted his approval.

The interview took place in Liston's hotel suite. As Callahan entered Liston's room, Hanover handed him a biography of the former champion. Nervous and intimidated, Callahan stuck it under his notepad and took the plunge.

Sitting on Liston's bed, Callahan asked a question and was met with silence. He asked another question and again received no reply. Desperate with fear, Callahan pulled out the biography and noticed Liston's age.

"Is that right, that you're only thirty-six years old?" he asked meekly.

Liston's eyes flared and he leaped off the small desk he had been straddling. He grabbed a terrified Callahan by the shirt and pressed his nose against his.

"Anybody who says I'm not thirty-six years old is calling my mother a liar," Liston said.

With that, Liston tried heaving Callahan on the bed. Instead, they both fell in a heap, rolled off the bed and smacked against a plaster wall, which gave with the impact. Lamps fell, cabinets lurched, tables moved as Liston and Callahan wrestled on the floor. During this whole time, neither boxer nor sportswriter said a word.

Finally, Liston's trainer, who had been listening to the skirmish in the other room, yelled, "What are you guys doing in there, dancing?"

Liston stopped and, for a moment, the hint of a smile touched his face. "Yeah . . . yeah, dancing," he said. And then he let Callahan go.

7. *Always* be aware of all local shower customs.

Edwin Pope of the *Miami Herald* was covering the 1984 Winter Olympics in Sarajevo, Yugoslavia, when he came upon a strange shower nozzle in his hotel room. For reasons unknown, the nozzle was located perhaps four or five feet above the shower floor. Pope isn't an especially tall man, but even he was forced to contort his body to all shapes to squeeze himself under the stream of water each morning.

This had gone on for almost the entire length of the Games when he happened to mention the odd nozzle to a fellow journalist. "See?" said Pope. "The thing's so low you've got to bend in two just to get wet."

Pope's friend reached inside the shower, unclipped what was actually a portable nozzle from the wall, and held it up for Pope to see.

Pope left quietly and humbly.

8. *Never* anger a pro wrestler.

While doing research for a long story on professional wrestling, Barry Horn of the *Dallas Morning News* decided to talk with the legendary King Kong Bundy, a four-hundred-plus-pound mountain of a man. Horn met Bundy at the local arena one day and they had a pleasant and engaging talk about the sport of wrestling.

Bundy told Horn about his childhood in New Jersey, which was curious, since promoters billed him as being from Alaska. Bundy described how he became a pro wrestler and detailed the demands of the job.

Soon thereafter, Horn wrote his story. In it, Horn said that Bundy wasn't such a bad guy after all, that he was the kind of guy you wouldn't mind leaving your kids with. All in all, it was a very positive story.

About three weeks later, Horn was attending a wrestling event at Texas Stadium when he saw Bundy in the parking lot. Worse yet, Bundy saw Horn.

"You son of a bitch, you tried to ruin my career!" he said, as he started to chase Horn.

"What?"

"You know what I'm talking about. You tried to ruin me. Why did you have to write that I'm a nice guy? I should break your neck."

Horn, without knowing it, had committed a wrestling mortal sin. He had humanized a bad guy.

"I'll never talk to you again!" Bundy yelled.

To help save his image, promoters decided to shave Bundy's head and make him even meaner in the ring. Luckily for Horn, it worked.

9. *Always* be prepared to be blamed for anything.

Tracy Ringolsby was covering the Seattle Mariners in 1981 when the team was sold to California multimillionaire George Argyros. A press conference was held to announce the sale and among those attending was Mariners manager Maury Wills. Ringolsby approached him.

"Maury, who's going to play center for you this year?"

"Well, there's a guy in the organization who's not real graceful, but he has a lot of determination and he covers a lot of ground out there. I wouldn't be surprised if he wins the center-field job," Wills announced.

"Oh, yeah," said Ringolsby, "who's that?"

"Leon Roberts."

"Uh, Maury, Roberts was part of the eleven-player deal to Texas a few weeks ago."

"Oh, sure, trying to show me up again."

10. When in Outer Mongolia, *never* do as the Mongolians do.

Back in 1987, the United States sent a national boxing team to the Soviet Union for two matches, one scheduled in Moscow and the other in Alma-Ata. The Moscow bouts went as planned, but shortly before the Alma-Ata trip, there was a political uprising in the area. In fact, someone was stabbed in the lobby of the same hotel that the American delegation, including sportswriter Sharon Robb of the *Fort Lauderdale News/Sun-Sentinel,* was supposed to stay in.

United States organizers suggested that perhaps it might be in the best interests of everyone involved if the second set of bouts were held in another location, preferably as far away from Alma-Ata, the capital of the Kazakh S.S.R., as possible.

Soviet officials did just that, which explains why Fort Lauderdale readers opened their papers one day and discovered an *Outer Mongolia* dateline on Robb's stories.

This was some place, this Mongolia. Dinners consisted of horsemeat, and no liquid, coffee included, was allowed to go without a shot or two of vodka.

The oddest sight, however, was to be seen at the nearby skating rink, where locals darted around the ice wearing shorts and no shirts. One day, Robb inquired about the daily temperature.

"Oh, subfreezing," she was told.

11. *Never* play in media-alumni basketball games.

I did, a mistake if there ever was one.

It was supposed to be a friendly, low-key affair: a mixture of media types and former University of California–Irvine players. That was before Wayne Engelstad showed up.

Engelstad, a power forward, had been cut a day or two earlier by the Denver Nuggets. Friendliness, it seemed, was out of the question.

On my first drive toward the basket, a pathetic attempt, at best, Engelstad knocked my shot (and me) into another area code. I bounced against the hardwood and vaguely remember Engelstad muttering, "Stay out of my kitchen."

Later in the game, I ventured inside the paint again, this time trying to wrest an errant shot from the air. Bad move. One of Engelstad's beefy forearms knocked me to the ground again. This time I heard him loud and clear as we jogged upcourt: "Stay out of my kitchen," he growled.

Stay out of his kitchen? From that point on, I didn't even get near his breakfast nook.

The game ended without further incident and ever since then, I've always wanted to ask him a single question: "What's life in the Continental Basketball Association really like?"

12. *Never,* ever, try to mix media.

There exists in the sportswriting business a small, brave collection of reporters who dabble in the world of television. I salute them. I envy them. Anyone who can appear natural when eleven thousand watts of light is shining in your face has my respect any day. I was on a game show once, though I can't actually remember answering a single question. I ended up losing to some lady who owned a boutique and was studying to be an actress.

You think the weirdest thoughts when a camera is aimed your way: Is my tie crooked? . . . What happens if my voice changes in midsentence? . . . Are there any prominent nasal hairs easily seen?

As for coherent thoughts, forget it. I could barely spit out my name.

But there are those who court that little red light as if it were the prettiest person in class. To them, the camera is their friend.

Howard Balzer of *The Sporting News* was one such person. Balzer covers the NFL and, at one time, contributed to ESPN's annual coverage of the league's college draft. Then he discovered the dangers of live television and, well, Balzer hasn't been seen since.

It wasn't really his fault. Stationed at the Los Angeles Rams practice facility for the 1988 draft proceedings (the Rams had all sorts of picks because of the Eric Dickerson trade), Balzer was supposed to provide occasional updates of rumors and what not. But while testing his equipment that morning, he discovered that his earpiece didn't work properly. Every time he spoke into his microphone, he'd hear his own voice come booming through the earpiece.

"If that happens when you're on the air," said the producer, "just pull it out of your ear or turn down the volume control."

"Good idea," said Balzer.

It is one thing to discuss alternative plans when the camera isn't on, and quite another when your face is being beamed across a nation's cable airwaves.

Balzer's worst fears came true. As a country watched, Balzer found himself betrayed by a piece of audio equipment. Every word he said traveled directly back to his earpiece.

Inside the nearby press headquarters that day was a big-screen television. Print reporters watched with fascination and pity as Balzer struggled to retain any sort of dignity.

At first, it looked as if a wasp had flown into his ear. One moment he was talking calmly to a television audience; the next he was flailing away at the side of his head. Rather than use his left hand to pull out the offending earpiece, Balzer reached over with his right hand in an unsuccessful attempt to pry the thing out. If you didn't know any better, you would have sworn the wasp had made its way down Balzer's ear canal.

Inside the production truck, technicians quickly turned the earpiece switch off, so Balzer would no longer hear the echo. Too late. So unnerved was Balzer that he forgot to mention several juicy tidbits regarding possible Rams selections. Truth be told, Balzer was going to predict that the Rams would take UCLA running back Gaston Green instead of Pitt's Craig "Ironhead" Heyward.

He was right, but nobody ever knew—until now.

13. *Never* underestimate the worth of a good interpreter.

The 1989 PGA Championship was a water-soaked affair at Kemper Lakes Golf Club in Hawthorn Woods, Illinois. On the third day of the tournament, thunderstorms descended upon the fairways and greens, leaving the course unplayable.

Somehow, Japan's Isao Aoki and a handful of other golfers managed to finish their rounds before play was suspended and later canceled. Aoki shot a sixty-five, which was good enough to inch him up in the standings. At least now, he was in view of the leader board.

Desperate for a story on a day when the weather kept many of the big names off the course, reporters huddled around Aoki when he entered the press tent. Because of the vicious storms, electricity had been lost in both the clubhouse and press work area. Candles were found and lit.

There in the relative darkness, a strange press conference was conducted with the bemused Japanese golfer. Serving as Aoki's interpreter was a member of the Japanese press corps, of which there were many.

A question was asked and after a brief conversation between Aoki and his new friend, an answer was given.

And so it went until finally a reporter asked, "Isao, what
do you think it would take for you to win this tournament
tomorrow?"

The question was translated and immediately Aoki launched
into a gesture-filled response that lasted for almost a full
thirty seconds. Whatever Aoki was saying, he was certainly
passionate about it.

At last, he quit speaking. It was at this point that the
interpreter turned to the hushed crowd and provided them
with Aoki's answer.

"He said, 'Fifty.' "

After a short pause, everyone, including Aoki, roared with
laughter.

14.   When covering your first yacht race, *always* pack some
Dramamine.

Richard Hoffer didn't know the difference between star-
board and starry-eyed when his editors assigned him the
yachting competition at the 1988 Summer Olympics.

He still doesn't.

Hoffer reported to Pusan, where the races would take
place, and asked what might be the best way to cover such an
event.

"The boat," he was told.

Even Hoffer, not exactly a seafaring man, knew this wasn't
altogether a good idea. Only a day earlier, the high seas had
swept several competitors overboard. Hoffer was in no hurry
to make the plunge.

"But isn't it a little rough out there?" Hoffer asked.

"We are going to have races anyway," the official said.
"The worst that could happen is you could get seasick."

So Hoffer boarded the press boat, which was packed to the
gills, mostly with Japanese photographers, all of them toting
expensive cameras and box lunches.

A half-hour later, the boat several miles from shore, Hoffer became queasy as the rough waters tossed the vessel up and down . . . up and down. Making matters worse were the photographers, who happily dug into their sushi lunches and noodles. Hoffer could take no more.

As Hoffer struggled, a young South Korean press liaison stepped forward.

"Let me help you," he said as he assisted Hoffer below the deck. Once Hoffer was seated below, the press liaison gave Hoffer some tea and provided him with several motion sickness pills. Still, nothing worked.

"If you are really sick," said the liaison, "and you want to go back, we'll take you back. It is a half-hour away, but we will do it."

"Yes," groaned Hoffer, "take me back."

The liaison seemed shocked.

"We can't do that!" he said.

"But you just said . . ."

"Sorry. We can't do that."

And they didn't. The boat bobbed in the ocean until competition's end and Hoffer, sick as could be, bobbed with it. He somehow wrote a story, which was remarkable, since he didn't see a single yacht.

15. *Always* think twice before allowing another woman (who isn't your wife) to share your hotel room.

Shelby Strother of the *Detroit News* was covering the Sugar Bowl in New Orleans once when a fellow sportswriter asked a favor. Would Strother mind if the sportswriter and his girlfriend stayed in Strother's room? All the suitable lodging had been reserved and, well, they were desperate.

Strother said they could. He would have a folding bed sent up to the room and they could sleep on that.

That night, Strother, the sportswriter and his girlfriend visited several bars on Bourbon Street. They stumbled back to the hotel in the wee hours and were still sleeping when the phone rang that morning. Out of reflex, the girlfriend answered the call.

"Hello," she mumbled.

"Uh . . . is Shelby there?" the voice asked hesitatingly.

"Just a moment, I'll wake him."

It was Strother's wife on the line.

This would take some explaining, and did. In the end, Strother had the fellow sportswriter and his girlfriend take turns detailing just how innocent the arrangement was.

16. *Never* assume anyone in the fast-food business has a sense of humor.

Shortly after filing his story one night in 1985, Mark Kiszla of the *Denver Post* decided he was hungry. He had just covered a Denver Nuggets–San Antonio Spurs playoff game in San Antonio and now he could hear his stomach churning. It needed food.

Kiszla's hotel was only a short distance from a fast-food restaurant. Rather than take his rental car, Kiszla and another sportswriter chose to walk. Bad move.

Once there, they realized the doors had been locked and only the drive-through window was open.

"Let's go back," said Kiszla's friend.

"No let's try the drive-through."

Another bad move.

Kiszla and the other sportswriter took their places in line, between a jacked-up Camaro and a noisy Volkswagen. Since they didn't weigh enough to trigger the microphone, Kiszla had the Camaro back up over the cord.

"Welcome, may I take your order?" asked a voice.

"You certainly can," said Kiszla, who then placed the two orders.

"Your total is $7.65, drive through, please."

Kiszla and the other sportswriter walked forward. When they reached the window, the cashier didn't know what to do.

"Where's your car?"

"I don't have a car," Kiszla said.

"I can't give you the food unless you have a car."

By now, cars were honking their disapproval as the cashier and Kiszla continued to argue.

"Is the food already made?" Kiszla said.

"Yes."

"Well, then, here's $7.65, now give me the food."

"I'm sorry, it's against regulations." And with that, the cashier closed the window.

Kiszla started pounding against the glass. "Give me my food!" he yelled. "Give me my food!"

The cashier did nothing. Meanwhile, the honking grew louder.

"C'mon, let's try another place," said the other sportswriter.

"No, I'm not going to get beat that easily. We'll go back to the parking garage, get my car and come back here."

So they did. Kiszla repeated his order and when he arrived at the window, he said, "Will this car do?"

"Yeah, that's fine," said the cashier, not too happily.

A few moments later, the cashier handed over the food. Kiszla checked the contents.

"Hey, you forgot my Coke."

"Oh, I'm sorry," said the cashier, who took the soft drink and Kiszla's change and purposely dropped them on the concrete.

"Kind of clumsy, aren't you," said the cashier, smiling.

Kiszla went crazy. He started honking his horn. He yelled at the cashier to give him another Coke.

"Hey, if you don't leave now, I'm gonna call the cops," said the cashier.

"Go ahead, I'd like to tell them what you did."

Much to Kiszla's amazement, the cashier called the police. It wasn't long before the sound of sirens could be heard in the distance.

"Uh, we better go," Kiszla said.

As they left, a patrol car screeched into the restaurant

parking lot. After conferring with the night manager, the police returned to their car and began chasing Kiszla. It wasn't much of a chase, really. The cops caught up with Kiszla about the third level of the parking garage.

To make matters worse, Kiszla got out of the car and tried to shake hands with one of the officers. Another bad move. The cop grabbed Kiszla's hand, twisted it behind his back and threw him face down on the hood of the car. Handcuffs were used shortly thereafter.

Three other patrol cars appeared several minutes later.

Kiszla didn't know what to do. One of the police had his palm pressing down on the back of Kiszla's neck. He could barely move, much less talk. For the next hour, the cops kept him there.

"What are you guys, out of *I Love Lucy?*" said one of the officers.

"You touristas come to our city and behave this way," said another. "Maybe a night in jail is what you need."

Kiszla tried speaking, but his lips wouldn't move against the hood. Thank goodness for the other sportswriter, David Hutchinson of the *Boulder Daily Camera*. Hutchinson calmly explained what had happened back at the restaurant. He apologized for any trouble caused and promised no other incidents. Convinced of his sincerity, the police released Kiszla.

Hutchinson, by the way, has quit the sportswriting business and is now studying to be a lawyer.

17. *Always* remember the power of gold.

If ever there was an easy column to write, it was shortly before the 1984 Winter Olympics in Sarajevo, Yugoslavia, when United States skier Phil Mahre said, in no particular order, that he didn't want to be in Sarajevo; he didn't care if he won a gold medal; he already was financially secure; the Olympics were simply another ski event.

Mahre finished poorly in the giant slalom event, prompting Steve Kelley of the *Seattle Times* to write that if Mahre didn't like the Olympics, maybe he should go home. Surely there was somebody back in the States who would appreciate being at the Games more than Mahre. There certainly had to be somebody back home who could finish higher in the standings.

Two days after Kelley's column ran back in Seattle, Mahre won the gold medal in the slalom competition. Television crews rushed to the Mahre home in nearby Yakima, Washington, for reaction. They got it all right, as Mahre's wife tearfully recounted the pain she felt after reading Kelley's column.

Suddenly, the entire Great Northwest was out to get Kelley, which was strange, since Kelley figured nobody liked a whiner. If anything, Kelley thought he would receive all sorts of letters applauding him for making such a heartfelt stand.

Kelley received some letters, but they usually began with a four-letter word. One was addressed, "Steve Canker Sore Kelley."

Several weeks later, while attending a Seattle SuperSonics basketball game, Kelley happened to open some of the mail he had brought with him from the office. Began one memorable piece of correspondence: "I'd like to know your address so I can fire bomb your house." Incredibly enough, it was signed.

Kelley was a bit unnerved. It's not every day that your life is threatened. Kelley took the letter and envelope to a nearby Seattle police officer, who was stationed near courtside.

"See this?" asked Kelley.

The cop read the note and then turned to Kelley. "I'd like to sign that letter," said the cop. He wasn't smiling.

18. *Always* pack a pair of wire cutters.

Sportswriters get locked in stadiums. A lot. I had a rat run across my foot at Cincinnati's Riverfront Stadium once as I searched for an exit in the postgame darkness. It could have been worse. I could have been Steve Kelley (yes, the same

Kelley) when he used to work for the Eugene, Oregon, *Oregonian*.

Kelley had worked at just about every small paper in the region when he was hired finally by the *Oregonian*. Presented with a weekly salary of one hundred dollars, Kelley thought he had landed a position on the *New York Times*. He couldn't believe his luck.

One of his first assignments was to cover a state Single-A high-school football championship at nearby Autzen Stadium. To Kelley, this was a huge responsibility. He wanted to write the perfect story.

Kelley tried. Long after everyone else had left the press box, Kelley was still there pounding away on his typewriter keyboard. Done at last, Kelley discovered that all the stadium lights had been turned off, the gates had been locked and the temperature was dropping into the low teens.

It was about then that Kelley determined that maybe he wasn't at the *New York Times* just yet.

After checking each gate to see if a lock had been missed, Kelley slid his typewriter under the fence and began climbing. Near the top of the fence, Kelley sheared away a piece of his pants leg on the barbed wire. To continue might mean severing a limb on the razor-sharp wire. To give up might mean freezing to death.

Kelley decided to continue his climb. As he reached the top, he tore the entire rear section of his pants. Then he jumped into the darkness. Kelley slammed against the concrete but was unhurt, except for those pants and his pride. It was about then that Steve realized that perhaps sportswriting isn't as glamorous a profession as it's cracked up to be.

19. When compiling a list of truly nice guys, *always* include the late Dick Howser.

Maybe there is a sweeter person in sports. If so, I'd like to meet him.

Howser, who died of cancer in 1987, was a sportswriter's best friend: accessible, patient and refreshingly sincere. He had time for any question, however silly.

One of Howser's finest managing efforts came during the 1984 season, the year his Kansas City Royals won the AL West title. This was the same season that Willie Wilson missed spring training and the first six weeks of the schedule because of a drug suspension. Hal McRae drove in fewer than fifty runs and George Brett hit .284 in 104 games. Dennis Leonard didn't pitch a single inning.

And still the Royals won, mostly because Howser made some bold decisions. He inserted rookies Bret Saberhagen and Mark Gubicza in the starting rotation. He switched shortstops and took a chance by placing Darryl Motley in left field. He put Steve Balboni in the lineup.

At season's end, the Royals had won eighty-four games and a division title. It couldn't have happened to a nicer guy.

The Royals won the division in Oakland on a Friday evening. Tracy Ringolsby was there that night. His follow-up story wouldn't run until Sunday, so he had plenty of time to wait for Howser to finish his many interviews with assorted print and electronic media types.

By the time Howser was through, it was close to midnight. A celebration had begun at the team hotel and Howser was late. Ringolsby figured he'd ask a couple of questions and then let Howser get back to the hotel.

That's when one of the clubhouse guys brought some Mexican food into the office. Beers were popped and soon it was 3:30 A.M. and Howser was asking the clubhouse guy about his struggle to find work and become successful in the United States. Typical Howser.

Meanwhile, the hotel party raged on. Like I said, a terrific guy who's sorely missed.

20.   *Never* entirely trust your editors.

Dave George of the *Palm Beach* (Florida) *Post* did once and look what happened to him.

George was covering a local PGA tournament when he wrote that Greg Norman, who was having an awful time converting short putts, had a case of "lipersy," which was a clever way of saying the ball kept hitting the lip of the cup but never went in.

George sent the story to his editors. The next day he opened up his sports section only to find that some dunderhead copy desk person had changed "lipersy" to "leprosy." The story now read, in essence, that Norman, one of the world's most renowned golfers, was complaining of a chronic infectious disease caused by a bacterium that attacks the skin and nerves.

Do you think the newspaper ran a correction the next day?

21.   *Always* treasure those rare moments when you outfox the geniuses.

Gary Myers, then with the *Dallas Morning News,* was covering the 1984 NFL owners meeting in Hawaii when word leaked that the Dallas Cowboys had been sold. Myers's job was to find out who had purchased the team.

After making several calls, he learned that team president Tex Schramm, personnel director Gil Brandt and the new owner could arrive only on one of two American Airlines flights that day from Dallas. So Myers drove to the Honolulu airport and staked out the gates.

Later, he learned that one of the flights had been delayed. Rather than sit there the entire afternoon hoping that the early flight was the one taken by Schramm, Brandt and the new owner, Myers called the airline again.

"Yes, ma'am, I was supposed to meet my father here today, but I don't know the flight number and I can't afford to spend the whole day waiting here," said Myers. "Can you help me?"

"Well, we're not allowed to give the names of passengers."

"But it's my father."

"What's your father's name?"

"My father is Tex Schramm."

A few moments later, Myers had his information. When the plane arrived, Myers was waiting at the gate, which was almost entirely enclosed by glass partitions. There was only one way out for the departing passengers.

You can imagine the surprise as Brandt, who was one of the first people off the plane, saw Myers, arms folded in triumph, standing at the gate. The identity of the new Cowboys owner was supposed to be one of the best-kept secrets in the league.

Brandt turned around and re-entered the plane, presumably to tell Schramm of Myers's presence. Several minutes later, Brandt, Schramm and the new owner emerged.

"This is a very smart move on your part," said Schramm. "I'll let you ask anything you want, but you can't talk to Bum [Bright, the new owner]."

"But I really need to talk to him," Myers said. He still needed confirmation that it was indeed Bright who had agreed to buy the team.

"No way," said Schramm, as they walked to the baggage claim area.

"How about this, Tex—would you at least introduce me to him?"

"That's all, just introduce you to him? Nothing more?"

"Nothing more," said Myers.

So Schramm took Myers over to Bright. Handshakes were exchanged. Then Myers sprang into action.

"Mr. Bright, I understand congratulations are in order."

"Why, yes, thank you," said Bright, "I'm very excited about it."

Myers had his confirmation and his story. He rushed to a
pay phone and dictated his scoop.

22. Remember *always* that nothing could have been worse
than covering the Texas Rangers one frightful week in 1977.

The Rangers were preparing to make a two-week road trip
to Minnesota, Anaheim, Oakland and Toronto when word
came that manager Frank Lucchesi's job was in jeopardy.
Naturally, Paul Hagen, who was covering the team for the
Dallas Times Herald, followed up the rumor.

On Monday, the team left for Minneapolis. On Wednesday, Lucchesi was fired. Eddie Stanky was named the new
manager.

That night, before the Wednesday evening game at old
Metropolitan Stadium, Stanky delivered a fire-and-brimstone
speech that shook the clubhouse walls. The Rangers proceeded to fall behind early, but staged a late-inning comeback
against the Twins and somehow won the game. Stanky was
so happy that he could barely contain himself.

Hagen wrote five stories that night and was feeling pretty
good about his efforts when he boarded the Rangers team
bus. Stanky was sitting up front and still appeared excited
about the come-from-behind victory. He talked with his coaches
and later, as the bus arrived at the hotel, told them, "Meet
you at six o'clock for breakfast. We've got a lot of things to
talk about."

The next morning Hagen received a phone call from Burt
Hawkins, the team's traveling secretary. "Be in Eddie Robinson's suite at 10:00 A.M.," said Hawkins. Robinson was the
team's general manager.

At ten, Hagen and the other beat reporters were told the
news: Stanky had resigned. He had called Robinson and said,
"Eddie, I can't do it."

"Can't do what?" Robinson said.

"I can't manage your team."

"Why don't we talk about it."

Stanky declined and flew home. Robinson decided to name Connie Ryan interim manager.

The Rangers played an afternoon game that day. It ran long, almost causing the team to miss its commercial flight to Anaheim. The reporters and players boarded with only three minutes to spare. The plane then taxied toward the runway, where it sat for three hours because of mechanical difficulties.

When the plane did finally land, the Rangers discovered that the buses sent there to take them to their hotel had long since left. Everyone had to take cabs from Los Angeles to Anaheim, at least an hour's drive.

The team began to arrive at the hotel at about midnight. Tempers were short and nerves frayed. It was no different with the beat reporters, who had been working nonstop as they tried to make sense of the week's events. To soothe their tension, the reporters and Hawkins met in the hotel bar for a few drinks.

As Hawkins sipped on a scotch and water, pitcher Dock Ellis walked up to the table. He spoke with Hawkins, whose job, among others, was to arrange all rooming assignments, and then left in a huff.

"Well, Burt, what did Dock want?" asked Hagen.

"Mr. Ellis has requested a room away from all the other players," said Hawkins. "He is distressed to find that his room is next door to 'motherfucking' Nellie Briles. I informed Mr. Ellis that, to my knowledge, Mr. Briles was not a motherfucker."

And then Hawkins resumed sipping on his drink. It had been a hell of a day for him, too.

The next day, rumor had it that Harmon Killibrew would be named the next Rangers manager. After calling several sources, Hagen learned that the rumor probably was true— that is, it was until Killibrew reportedly called owner Brad Corbett and said he was having second thoughts about accepting the position.

The Rangers finished their series with the Angels and moved on to Oakland. It was there that Corbett hired Billy Hunter to manage the team. Exhausted, Hagen finished another series of stories about another new manager.

Four managers in one week. Until proven otherwise, a modern-day record.

23. Remember, *never* take this sportswriting stuff too seriously.

Sportswriting is an inexact profession practiced mostly by cynics who were once fans. But we mean well.

Anyway, sportswriting isn't always about sports. It's about detailing human frailties and strengths. It's about understanding the differences between winning and losing, a common thread in the lives of all of us, athlete or otherwise. And when you reduce the job to its barest form, it's about describing moments of innocence—a touchdown run, a slam dunk, a double to the gap.

Tom Callahan, then with the *Cincinnati Enquirer,* once took a year off from sportswriting and joined the general news department of the newspaper. It was the same year a plane carrying the Evansville University basketball team crashed.

Callahan was sent to cover the tragedy. He was joined by other *Enquirer* reporters, including some from the city-side section and others from the sports section. It was a curious case study of priorities.

The city-side reporters huddled around the Federal Aviation authorities. Meanwhile, the sportswriters visited the local chapel and talked with the friends and families of the victims. And when the media were loaded onto a railroad car and taken to the scene of the wreckage, the city-side reporters first examined the equipment. The sportswriters took note of the Aqua Velva bottle that didn't break.

Both sets of reporters were doing their jobs, just in different ways.

Sportswriters aren't sports experts. At least, most of us aren't. My wife won a hotly contested NCAA basketball pool last year. I finished next to last. As for a baseball rotisserie league team I co-own, we've never finished higher than eighteenth.

We are observers, middlemen for a reading public. And whenever I think we're anything more than simple interpreters of sports, I remember a story involving Mark Bradley, a columnist for the *Atlanta Journal-Constitution.*

Bradley was interviewing a high-school basketball player when the player interrupted the conversation.

"Can I ask you a question about your job?" she asked.

"Of course you can," Bradley said. "What would you like to know?"

"How do y'all type so small?"

Like I said, nobody knows what we do or how we do it. Maybe it's better that way.

Index